P9-DMD-234

THE WRITER
AND
HUMAN RIGHTS

With the assistance of Audrey Campbell, Genevieve Cowgill, Connie Guberman, Daniel Schwartz, and Ira Vine. Much of the material in this book was transcribed from audio tape by Kate Hamilton (Fax writers' services), Donald Bruce, and Lorne Macdonald.

The following contributions were submitted in written form: Thomas Hammarberg, "Writers and Prison"; Nadine Gordimer, "Apprentices of Freedom"; Leon Whiteson, "The Word as a Blunt Instrument"; Romesh Thapar, "The Dilemma in Asia"; Yotaro Konaka, "That Which Korean Poets Teach Us"; Fawaz Turki, "A People's Militant"; George Woodcock, "The Future We Envisage"; Josef Škvorecký, "A Revolution Is Usually the Worst Solution"; Margaret Atwood, "A Disneyland of the Soul"; Naim Kattan, "The Market of Anonymity"; Michel Tournier, "The Writer and Political Power"; Sergio Marras, "The Writer in Chile"; Nadine Gordimer, "Censorship in South Africa"; Stanislaw Baranczak, "Poland: Literature and Censorship"; Chuong Tang Nguyen, "The Re-education of a Vietnamese Writer"; Joy Kogawa, "The Enemy Within"; Robert Zend, "Labels"; Daniel Viglietti, "On the Outside"; Per Wästberg, "Moral Authority"; Alan Sillitoe, "Against Ideology."

THE WRITER
AND
HUMAN RIGHTS

Edited by the Toronto Arts Group
for Human Rights

ANCHOR PRESS/DOUBLEDAY
GARDEN CITY, NEW YORK
1983

Library of Congress Cataloging in Publication Data
Main entry under title:
The writer and human rights.
Includes index.
1. Authorship—Political aspects—Congresses.
2. Politics and literature—Congresses.
3. Censorship—Congresses.
4. Civil rights—Congresses.
PN131.W74 1983   323.44'5
ISBN 0-385-18932-X
ISBN 0-385-18931-1 (pbk.)
Library of Congress Catalog Card Number 83-45023
Copyright © 1983 Toronto Arts Group for Human Rights
Copyright for the individual works is, unless otherwise specified,
retained by the respective writers
Published in Canada by Lester & Orpen Dennys Ltd.
All Rights Reserved
All material by Susan Sontag: copyright © 1983 by
Susan Sontag. Published by permission of the author.
Printed in the United States of America
First Edition

FOREWORD

Everyone who has worked in the struggle for human rights knows that the real enemy is silence. Political repression uses a climate of secrecy and deliberate obfuscation to instigate its terrors. Our first responsibility, then, is to speak out. Yet a recording of atrocities is not enough: we know from experience that we are easily inured to tragic litanies. In a world that has shrunk, where there are no boundaries or sidelines, where a shock to one part is almost instantaneously transmitted to others, and we recognize the network of complicity that implicates us all in any single crisis, the only solution can be a concerted effort to unite in protest.

For these reasons, seventy writers gathered together in Toronto during October of 1981 for a congress called "The Writer and Human Rights." The ambition of the congress was to give an international community of writers the opportunity to reach across geographical and ideological differences in their demand for universal respect for human rights. Writers, because of their cultural prominence, may become the first to feel the edge of violence when it is wielded by the state—their distinction is to find words for reality in all its dimensions. We thought to call on these skills in an international forum, in the name of those victims of political brutality who no longer have voices.

In the early stages of organizing this congress, we—the Toronto Arts Group for Human Rights, a small group of volunteers who share an interest in literature and a commitment to human values—wrote to Amnesty International about the project, offering to donate the funds raised by the congress to that organization. Amnesty is widely respected for its attempts to unite people of widely differing political persuasions in the pragmatic struggle for human rights. And the writers whom we approached agreed readily to our suggestion because of the high regard in which the organization is held. Amnesty was moved by their gesture of support, although it was always clear that the writers would advance political positions at the congress that would go well beyond Amnesty's mandate and perhaps contradict it.

Writers from countries as various as Chile and West Germany, Czechoslovakia and South Africa, India and England (over thirty nationalities in all) came to the University of Toronto, where the congress took place. Many of them had been victims of exile, censorship, and imprisonment. Others who had lived secure from these forms of repression offered their voices to the demand for human rights. This range of experience and testimony gave the week of symposia, panel discussions, and public readings its complex texture.

We wanted the congress to move beyond discussion to immediate action. From a list sent to us by Amnesty International, we therefore selected the names of seven writers whose situations were representative of different kinds of intimidation: censorship, exile, torture, imprisonment, disappearance. This book is dedicated to these writers, themselves symbols of countless others who have been similarly silenced. We have added to the seven the name of Alaida Foppa of Guatemala, who disappeared in December 1980.

We structured the congress to meet the questions we felt the writers would want to address; the book follows this structure. The congress began with a consideration of the contexts in which writers may be led to political action ("The Writer and Community"), and moved to a discussion of the kinds of action open to writers as writers ("Writing and Action"), and concluded with the ways in which governments may respond to these kinds of action ("Forms of Oppressions") with a final look at the role of the writer today. Disagreements arose in many of the sessions and were often left unresolved: the book reflects these tensions. The writers differed widely in their analyses of the politics of repression, in their definitions of the role of the writer, and in their strategies for action. There was no attempt to submerge their profound ideological differences. But the writers united where one would expect—in the truth of their writing. This was most apparent in a public reading attended by seventeen hundred people. Eduardo Galeano recreated the ancient myths of Latin America, showing that literature transmits condensed and irrefutable human experience from generation to generation and is the living memory of a people. Nadine Gordimer presented the brute reality of apartheid and forced her audience to see the far-off despair of an alien world as real and implicating them. Josef Brodsky brought the pain of exile to life through incantations that transcended barriers of language. Wole Soyinka arrived late because, as he said, one of his colleagues had just been killed by a "cooperative mob." Jacobo Timerman apologized for having written only one book and gave the audience a vision of simple courage. Through these voices was heard the power of literature as "a denunciation and a hope," affirming that the human consciousness must be preserved in its "thousand possible projections."

In editing this book, the proceeds of which will also be donated to Amnesty International, we had to make a selection of the speeches delivered at the congress. We have used about one third of the contributions. Some of the speeches simply did not translate into print: they depended for their impact, even for their meaning, on the speakers' presence. The speeches we have included represent the geographical and political balance of the congress. In some cases we give questions from the floor where we think these extend the discussions. We have also included short excerpts from the works of the seven silenced writers. There is more in this book than anyone attending the congress would have been able to hear, but it is not a complete and literal record of its proceedings. We hope it is something better: an expression of its spirit.

For:

Haroldo Conti
  (*disappeared, May 5, 1976; death acknowledged December 1981*)
Alaida Foppa de Solorzano
  (*disappeared December 19, 1980*)
Ahmed Fouad Negm
  (*arrested April 29, 1981; imprisoned*)
Vaclav Havel
  (*arrested May 29, 1979; imprisoned*)
Don Mattera
  (*banned November 20, 1973; ban lifted May 1982*)
Jorge Mario Soza Egana
  (*arrested May 20, 1980; tortured; exiled*)
Vasyl Stus
  (*arrested May, 1980; in labor camp*)
Yang Ch'ing-ch'u
  (*arrested December 10, 1979; imprisoned*)

CONTENTS

PART FOUR

FORMS OF OPPRESSION

REPRESSIVE TOLERANCE

CENSORSHIP AND SELF-CENSORSHIP

LIST OF CONTRIBUTORS

IAN ADAMS, Canadian novelist and journalist; editor of *This Magazine;* author of *The Real Poverty Report, End Game in Paris,* and *S, Portrait of a Spy.*

MARGARET ATWOOD, Canadian poet, novelist, and critic; author of *True Stories, Murder in the Dark, Bodily Harm,* and *Second Words.*

STANISLAW BARANCZAK, Polish poet and underground publisher, now living in exile in the United States.

MONGO BETI (Alexandre Bujidi), Cameroonian novelist, now living in France; author of *Le pauvre Christ de Bomba* and *Mission terminée.*

MARIE-CLAIRE BLAIS, Canadian novelist; author of *A Season in the Life of Emmanuel, The Manuscripts of Pauline Archange, Nights in the Underground,* and *Deaf to the City.*

HANS CHRISTOPH BUCH, West German critic and fiction writer; author of *Aus der Neuen Welt, Tatanka Yotanka,* and *Zumwalds Beschwerden.*

HANS MAGNUS ENZENSBERGER, West German poet, essayist, and translator; author of *Sinking of the Titanic* and *Critical Essays.*

TIMOTHY FINDLEY, Canadian novelist and playwright; author of *The Wars* and *Famous Last Words.*

CAROLYN FORCHÉ, American poet and journalist; author of *Gathering the Tribes* and *The Country Between Us.*

JOHN FRASER, Canadian journalist; national editor of the *Globe and Mail;* author of *The Chinese: Portrait of a People.*

EDUARDO GALEANO, Uruguayan novelist, journalist, and historian, now living in exile in Spain; author of *Guatemala: Occupied Country, Open Veins of Latin America,* and *Days and Nights of Love and War.*

ALLEN GINSBERG, American poet; author of *Howl, Kaddish,* and *The Fall of America.*

NATALYA GORBANEVSKAYA, Russian poet, now living in exile in France; first editor of the *samizdat* journal *A Chronicle of Current Events;* author of *Red Square at Noon;* twice confined in mental hospitals for political activity.

NADINE GORDIMER, South African novelist; author of *A Guest of Honour, The Late Bourgeois World, Burger's Daughter,* and *July's People.*

THOMAS HAMMARBERG, Swedish journalist; secretary-general of Amnesty International.

NAIM KATTAN, Canadian novelist and critic; author of *Paris Interlude* and *Farewell, Babylon.*

JOY KOGAWA, Canadian poet and novelist; author of *Jericho Road* and *Obasan.*

YOTARO KONAKA, Japanese novelist, essayist, and translator; author of *Tenchugumi Report* and *Rethinking Literature.*

SERGIO MARRAS, Chilean journalist.

GASTON MIRON, Canadian poet; author of *The Agonized Life, L'Homme rapaillé,* and *Courtepointes.*

CHUONG TANG NGUYEN, Vietnamese journalist, now living in exile in Canada.

RICK SALUTIN, Canadian playwright, journalist, and biographer; editor of *This Magazine;* author of *1837: The Farmers' Revolt, The False Messiah,* and *Les Canadiens.*

ALAN SILLITOE, English novelist; author of *Saturday Night and Sunday Morning, The Loneliness of the Long-Distance Runner, Travels in Nihilon,* and *Her Victory.*

JOSEF ŠKVORECKÝ, Czech-Canadian novelist and filmmaker; author of *The Cowards, Miss Silver's Past, The Bass Saxophone,* and *The Swell Season.*

SUSAN SONTAG, American critic and novelist; author of *Against Interpretation, On Photography, I, Etcetera,* and *Under the Sign of Saturn.*

MÜMTAZ SOYSAL, Turkish jurist, academic, and columnist; former member of the International Executive Committee of Amnesty

International; imprisoned for mentioning Marx in a law text-book. Since attending the congress, Soysal has been sentenced to death.

ROMESH THAPAR, Indian essayist and journalist; editor of *Seminar;* author of *Change and Conflict in India.*

JACOBO TIMERMAN, Argentine journalist and publisher of *La Opinión;* imprisoned by the military government; now living in exile in Israel; author of *Prisoner Without a Name, Cell Without a Number,* and *The Longest War.*

JULIUS TOMIN, Czech philosopher, now living in exile in England.

ZDENA TOMIN, Czech playwright and translator, now living in exile in England; former leader of Charter 77; author of *Enemies of the State.*

MICHEL TOURNIER, French novelist; author of *Friday, The Ogre, Gemini,* and *The Fourth Wise Man.*

FAWAZ TURKI, Palestinian writer and poet, now living in the United States; author of *The Disinherited, Poems from Exile,* and *Beggar from the Killing Zone.*

DANIEL VIGLIETTI, Uruguayan singer and songwriter; imprisoned by the military government; now living in exile in France; recordings include *Trópicos* and *Daniel Viglietti en vivo.*

PER WÄSTBERG, Swedish novelist and journalist; president of International PEN; editor of *Dagens Nyheter;* author of *Love's Gravity;* and editor of *The Writer in Modern Africa.*

LEON WHITESON, Canadian novelist, born in Zimbabwe; author of *White Snake* and *The Liveable City.*

GEORGE WOODCOCK, Canadian critic, biographer, historian, and poet; founding editor of *Canadian Literature;* author of *Anarchism, The Crystal Spirit,* and *Gabriel Dumont.*

ROBERT ZEND, Hungarian-Canadian poet and broadcaster; author of *From Zero to One* and *Labels.*

DANIEL MDLULI ZWELONKE, South African novelist, living in exile in Canada; author of *Robben Island,* a novel about his experiences as a political prisoner.

PART ONE

OPENING STATEMENT

WRITERS AND PRISON

THOMAS HAMMARBERG

SECRETARY-GENERAL OF AMNESTY INTERNATIONAL

WHEN he visited Stockholm in 1957, Albert Camus spoke about the role of the writer in the twentieth century. "We must realize," he said, "that we cannot escape the common lot of pain, and that our only justification, if one there be, is to speak insofar as we can on behalf of those who cannot."

He was speaking some years before the idea of Amnesty International was born, and he spoke only of the responsibility of the writer. His words, however, were printed for many years on Amnesty International leaflets. They expressed a fundamental thought of our movement.

Twenty years ago Amnesty International was launched to bring forgotten prisoners out of the dungeons. It began with a newspaper article calling on people in all walks of life to begin working impartially and peacefully for the release of the thousands of men and women imprisoned throughout the world for their political and religious beliefs. These we called "prisoners of conscience."

Our idea was to bring together people with widely differing views, but all willing to work against the imprisonment of people anywhere for the expression of their beliefs. In a sense, it would put into practice the famous saying attributed to Voltaire:

I detest your ideas, but I am ready to die for your right to express them.

Over the years, Amnesty International's mandate has developed. We work for three things. First, we seek the immediate and unconditional release of all prisoners of conscience. Second, we try to ensure fair and prompt trials for all political prisoners. Third, we oppose torture and executions in all cases.

In working for these objectives, we respect certain principles. One is that human rights are *universal*. They are an inalienable part of our birthright as human beings and transcend the boundaries of nation, race, and belief.

Responsibility for the protection of these rights is also universal. Their defense cannot be left to diplomats and bureaucrats; it rests with each of us.

Another such principle is *impartiality*. Amnesty International protests human rights violations irrespective of the color of the responsible government: military or civilian; socialist or capitalist; Islamic, Christian, or nonreligious. That "color blindness" may sometimes seem naïve, but it is deliberate. Different standards for different regimes would compromise the very foundation of our work: that *all* human beings are entitled to the same freedoms and rights. This means we would also be concerned if opposition groups or other nongovernmental entities violate these rights.

The principles of universality and impartiality, however abstract they may sound, do not imply indifference, insensitivity, or neutrality. The fight for human rights demands personal commitment and, often, great personal sacrifice.

The obstacles are enormous. Human rights face a crucial test in the 1980s, with the right to dissent under attack in country after country. Torture and murder, abduction and imprisonment—often sanctioned at the highest levels of government—are systematic practices in nations of widely differing ideologies.

Thousands have been liquidated by agents acting under official orders or abducted by security forces and never seen again. Elsewhere, special courts have ordered wholesale political executions. The victims have been shot or hanged after summary hearings, often without any right of judicial appeal. Deaths in prison or military or police custody are reported regularly, often as a direct result of torture.

In many countries, imprisonment on racial, religious, or political grounds is being prolonged indefinitely. In the words of a former victim, now free, the prisoners' cells have become "tombs for the living." Some prisoners of conscience have now been incarcerated for decades, many without charge or trial.

The taking of hostages, the use of torture, and the execution of political opponents have also been carried out by nongovernmental groups in the name of various causes. Such acts are no more acceptable than repression by governments.

Faced with the extent of the attack on human rights, many ask if the battle for those rights can be won. This conference asks what role *writers* can play.

The very fact that this conference has been organized and that you have come here is an indication that writers have a specific role in the defense of human rights and are willing to undertake that responsibility, to "speak on behalf of those who cannot."

The oppressors are relying on *ignorance* and *indifference*—among both the citizens in their country and public opinion abroad. Therefore, *information* and *education* about human rights violations are of greater importance than perhaps ever before. One single poem, one article or book, could open eyes closed by millions of propaganda dollars.

Because the present human rights battle is partly a defense against systematic propaganda warfare, today many governments are concerned about their image and are disturbed about torture reports. The South African Government took over newspapers at home and abroad, bribed politicians, and published a book slandering Amnesty International, entitled *Amnesty for Terrorism.*

We know also that other governments are investing money in correcting their international reputation. We have well-known world markets in which governments trade principles for nuclear power plants, arms, wheat, or oil.

The more that cynicism develops, the more important is the role of writers and journalists. It is not by chance that so many of the prisoners of conscience for whom Amnesty International works are writers, journalists, or artists.

Some of them are imprisoned because they tried to publish their words independently, defying state censorship. Some are in jail for manuscripts that were confiscated and that remain unpublished. Some have become victims because they tried to tell others of their prison experiences.

Other writers have joined the human rights struggle in their country and been arrested for that. Others have written about the fundamental social and political problems their nations face and been convicted of conducting propaganda against the state. Some have joined opposition political parties or banned organizations. Some have been in the forefront of the resistance to repression, continuing their struggle under successive regimes, and have finally paid for their convictions with their lives.

The purpose of shackling the writer is to create silence. But words can be stronger than chains. When the Indonesian novelist, Pramoedya Ananta Tur, was sent to the isolated island of Buru in the late 1960s, he was at first denied pen and paper. By the time he was eventually released in 1979, some twelve years later, he had begun compiling the stories he had composed and related to his fellow prisoners in the evenings. Two volumes of these stories have now been published, but in May this year (1981) Indonesia's attorney-general banned further circulation of them.

When the Venezuelan poet, Ali Lameda, was released in 1974 after six years' imprisonment in North Korea, he told a journalist, "They killed everything except my memory." By this he meant the four hundred poems and more than three hundred sonnets he had composed mentally—without pen or paper. It was extraordinary, described by a Latin American critic as "a gigantic creative effort in a world of horror and misery."

These images of the poet in prison call to mind the words of the Russian imagist poet Akhmatova, describing the seventeen months she spent in the prison lines in Leningrad under Stalin:

> Once someone, somehow recognized me. Then a woman standing behind me, her lips blue with cold . . . woke from the stupor that enveloped us, and asked me whispering in my ear (for we spoke only in whispers): "Could you describe this?" I said, "I can." Then something like a smile glided over what was once her face.

We deal with that world of whispers, desperate messages, where names and snatches of verse are scratched on prison walls, where lives are risked to pass on news to the outside world.

Out of Libertad Prison in Uruguay some time ago came a tiny collection of poems smuggled out on cigarette papers. Among them, this one:

> *You should see*
> *the contradictions*
> *in the army.*

You should have heard
the arguments between
the sub-lieutenant and the captain
while they were torturing me.

There were no names, no signatures on the poems. In a real sense, these were *prison poems*.

When we were approached by the organizers of this conference, we were asked if we could supply a list of all known writers in prison throughout the world. We couldn't. Secrecy and censorship make any complete tally impossible. We did compile a small selection of cases that could stand as symbols for all others, both the known and the unknown. The range, even in this handful of examples, illustrates that we are dealing with an issue that crosses the demarcations of ideology and government.

Ahmed Fouad Negm, of Egypt, well known throughout the Arab world for his colloquial poetry, is currently serving a sentence of one year's imprisonment in Cairo. His poems frequently describe social or political injustice, and many have been set to music and sung by the blind musician Sheikh Imam. Both have been imprisoned several times for their songs.

Jorge Mario Soza Egana, a fifty-five-year-old Chilean poet and short story writer, was sentenced in August 1980 to four years' internal exile in Freirina, a small town in the semidesert region of northern Chile. He is unable to find work there and has had to build himself a small shack to live in. He is reported to have been tortured after his arrest in May 1980 and was charged under a law prohibiting "Marxist" organizations.

Vaclav Havel, the Czech playwright, is serving a four-and-a-half-year prison sentence imposed on him in October 1979. He was one of a group of people belonging to the Committee for the Defense of the Unjustly Persecuted—known as VONS—who had been arrested in May that year for preparing and circulating information about people they considered to be unjustly persecuted.

Yang Ch'ing-ch'u, a writer from the Republic of China (Taiwan), is serving a prison sentence of four years and two months, imposed after he had taken part in a demonstration in December 1979 to mark the anniversary of the Universal Declaration of Human Rights. At the time, he was on the editorial committee of the opposition magazine *Formosa.*

Haroldo Conti, the Argentinian novelist and short story writer, was dragged out of his home by a group of armed men on May 5, 1976 and then "disappeared." Although his detention was never officially acknowledged, a released prisoner testified to having seen him in a secret detention center in Argentina.

Vasyl Stus, of the USSR, is a leading Ukrainian poet and human rights activist who is serving a fifteen-year sentence of imprisonment and internal exile for his activities as a member of the Ukrainian Helsinki monitoring group. He was convicted of "anti-Soviet agitation and propaganda" in 1980.

Don Mattera, the South African poet, is currently restricted under a second five-year banning order.

These sentences, like those imposed on all prisoners of conscience, violate agreed international standards. The Universal Declaration states: "Everyone has the right to freedom of opinion and expression. This right includes the freedom to hold opinions without interference and to seek, receive and impart information and ideas through any media and regardless of frontiers."

The same right is spelled out in Article 19:2 of the International Covenant on Civil and Political Rights.

Thus, the right to freedom of expression is part of international law. But this has not prevented governments from arresting writers who have done nothing more than speak up, or even from introducing laws which in themselves make a mockery of the right of expression. Criticism is branded as "subversion" or "antistate propaganda"; sympathy for a minority group as an "attempt to divide the nation," and so forth.

The sense of urgency that has brought you together is undoubtedly far greater than the differences that are likely to emerge. The forces that threaten to stifle creativity and freedom of expression are real and are claiming their victims. We must have the courage to work through our differences and manifest our solidarity with those who are being silenced.

PART TWO

THE WRITER
AND COMMUNITY

Isolation and Commitment

FOR HAROLDO CONTI

EDUARDO GALEANO

I'VE TRIED to say something about the subject of this congress. What is the writer's role? I'm afraid that my ideas may not be too practical. They are perhaps more related to the writer's role than to this congress's role. But I hope that they may be useful for further discussion. Because it is quite a question. I think we may try, up to a certain point, to answer it and even go beyond the question of the function of the writer at this congress to that of writing itself: is it worth it? What is the writer's role? This is a question for long, sleepless nights and days of depression. It is like a fly that buzzes and buzzes around my head, and around the heads of a lot of other writers.

I would like to begin by saying that I speak as a Latin-American writer. We come from a tormented part of the globe, and we are living in an historical period that hits us quite hard. And why? Because, basically, the contradictions of class society are much fiercer in our so-called Third World than in the rich countries. Mass poverty is the price paid by a lot of poor countries so that 6 per cent of the world's population may consume unmolested half of the world's wealth. And this is strictly and intimately related to literature. Because many of the hundreds of thousands of words that have been pronounced, and are being pronounced here, are about the forms of direct censorship: censorship of inconvenient or dangerous books or periodicals, the exile, or imprisonment, or even death that reached out to some writers and journalists. But there are a lot of countries in the world where what I would call structural censorship is much more important, even if it is not so visible. Because this structural censorship is what really defines most deeply the oppressive and prohibitory nature of a system, a worldwide system under which the majority of our countries suffer.

And what does this structural censorship consist of? It means that the ship cannot sail because there is no water in the sea. If only 5 per cent of the population of Latin America can buy a refrigerator, what percentage can buy books? What percentage can read them? Feel the need for them? Receive their influence?

I read a recent report from the International Labor Organization which indicated that at least 110 million people in Latin America live in conditions of severe poverty. So a structural censorship is being applied day by day to an immense multitude, prohibiting access to books and journals, even though these may circulate freely. There is also another problem: how can this multitude read if they don't know how? The rate of illiteracy in Latin America and the Third World is, as you know, quite high.

This is a kind of structural censorship about which I very rarely hear anything. It seems to be a forbidden subject, to which nobody pays the attention it deserves. It is exactly the censorship that restricts the right of expression and of creation to a privileged minority in our societies, this minority of which we are a part, which we come from, to which our articles and books are going.

In recent years in Latin America, there has been a very accelerated process of militarization of power. And this has meant an increased militarization of culture. In this reality some writers, artists, and scientists share the plight of the vast majority. They, too, become the victims not of the dictators themselves—General Furlano, General Mengano—but of the systems that make the dictators necessary to prevent the explosion of political and social tensions and contradictions.

There are other intellectuals who bless the executioners and who maintain a shameful silence. These are perhaps the ones who dream of a "free art" even though their society may be imprisoned. These are writers and artists who demand the privilege of irresponsibility, as if the function of culture could be separated from history and from social struggle. As if books and paintings happened through this elite, this chosen elite, whispered into their ear by fairies, or demons, or private visions; these artists are supposed to have been born with a seal of impunity.

I do not share the view of those who claim for the writer a kind of privileged freedom, a sort of sacred status in society, unconnected with the freedom of other workers. I think major changes of structure must occur in our countries so that writers may reach beyond the closed citadels of the elites and express themselves without being visibly or invisibly gagged. And I think within an imprisoned society literature can exist only as denunciation or as hope.

But there is no degree zero in culture, nor is there a degree zero in history. If we recognize a certain continuity between the stage of domination and the stage of liberation in any social-historical process, then why deny the importance of literature in its possible revolutionary functions of exploring, rebelling, and disseminating our true identity or its thousand possible projections?

The oppressor wants the mirror to give back to the oppressed just a blank reflection, and certainly no process of social change can urge forward a people who don't know who they are or where they come from. For if they don't know who they are, they cannot know who they deserve to be. Literature may help directly or indirectly in this revelation.

So I do not share the view of writers who ascribe to themselves divine privileges not granted to ordinary mortals. Nor of those who beat their breasts and tear their clothing, asking for public dispensation, apologizing in order to live in the service of a useless vocation.

We writers are neither gods nor insects. The consciousness of our limitations is not a consciousness of impotence, but a consciousness of reality. Literature is a form of action. It has no supernatural powers, but the writer perhaps may carry out his social function if what he writes is not written with impunity, if it changes or stimulates the reader in some way. Then the writer can lay claim to his part in the process of change—even in the narrow field in which he may work—without pride or false humility, but knowing himself to be part of something much vaster than himself.

In Latin America there is slowly gaining strength a literature that continues and enriches a very powerful tradition of fighting words. As I believe it is better to live in hope than with nostalgia, perhaps this national literature may be worthy of the beauty of the social forces that will sooner or later radically change the course of our history. Perhaps this literature may help to preserve for the years to come that which the poet originally wished: the true name of his theme.

You know that Haroldo Conti—one of the seven symbolic names chosen by this congress—Haroldo Conti, who might be sitting there in one of those empty chairs on the stage, officially disappeared in Argentina.

He spent his last years in Buenos Aires tormented by the suspicion that his literature was politically useless. He was a man of revolutionary political ideas. And a very close friend of mine. He always felt that he was writing politically innocuous stories and novels, because he was not using explicit denunciation in his literature. We talked about this a thousand times, during long nights on an island in the River Paraná. Long, long nights with wine and cigarettes, and I never knew how to tell him that his work as a writer had a deeply vital sense, both renewing and liberating. He was—perhaps is, because we are not absolutely sure that he is dead—a humble magician who was able to tell stories of great beauty. His stories talked about life, made life happen. And for a brief time when I read stories by Haroldo, I feel that he tears me away from time and returns me to the present. He is telling me what I am, and in that way is helping me to be. Because if I become a protagonist of history, making history instead of suffering it, I cannot ignore my own identity—and this I think is true for both individual and collective realities.

At the end of April 1976, Haroldo was kidnapped by the state terrorists in Argentina. Later, someone saw him briefly in the military barracks, after he had collapsed from long sessions of torture. He was never seen again. Like many thousands of Argentinians, Chileans, Salvadorans, Guatemalans, Uruguayans, the earth swallowed him. The Argentine media did not publish one line, not one single line about the disappearance of one of the country's best writers. I was there when it happened, and I know the circumstances very well.

And I know quite well, also, that Haroldo Conti had an inquiring mind, an anguished soul, and that he was always tormented by the idea that his literary work did not reflect his political will and was not useful. In feeling that, he got lost in the terror and the fog. Haroldo was a victim of a common dogma, which on the one hand praises literature as the craft of gods and on the other hand despises it as a harmless amusement.

I searched for the words, but I did not find them. I wanted to help him believe in what he was doing, and I did not succeed. I wanted to tell him that in lighting the little fires of identity, memory, and hope, literary pieces like his are part of the forces of change in a system organized to wipe us off the face of this earth, to disintegrate our souls, and to empty us of memory, and that therefore his words were giving shelter to many naked people left outside in intemperate weather. I tried to help him . . . and I could not. And that is why I am now saying these words like an expiation, and as a conviction.

—Translated by Mariana Valverde,
Audrey Campbell,
and Patricia Veras

APPRENTICES OF FREEDOM: RELEVANCE AND COMMITMENT IN SOUTH AFRICAN ARTS

NADINE GORDIMER

THE NATURE of art in South Africa today is primarily determined by the conflict of material interests in South African society. Make no mistake about it, when South African writers and artists gather, they do so rent by that conflict.

Equal economic opportunity, along with civil and parliamentary rights, for all 26 million South Africans, is rightly and inevitably the basis for any consideration of the future of the arts. Man has no control over the measure in which talent is given to this one and withheld from that; but man, through the state, controls the circumstances in which the artist develops. Innate creativity can be falsified, trivialized, deflected, conditioned, stifled, deformed, and even destroyed by the state and the condition of society it decrees.

"Courage in his life and talent in his work" is the artist's text, according to one of the greatest of them, Albert Camus. Certainly, every artist, wherever he lives, however circumstances use him, in any society, has to struggle through what Pablo Neruda calls the "labyrinths" of his chosen medium of expression. That is a condition of the artist's being.

As to the artist's place in the outer world, I doubt if any artist ever finds himself in the ideal condition of Hegel's "individual consciousness in wholly harmonious relationship to the external power of society." That's a Utopia where we should simply run to fat. But there can have been few if any examples in human history of the degree, variety, and intensity of conflict that exists between the South African artist and the external power of society. That external power is at its most obvious in the censorship laws, running amok through literature and every now and then lunging out at the other arts.

Yet it is at the widest level of the formation of our society itself, and not at any specific professional level, that the external power of society enters the breast and brain of the artist and determines the nature and state of art. It is from the daily life of South Africa that there have come the conditions of profound alienation which prevail among South African artists. I would go so far as to say the sum of various states of alienation *is* the nature of art in South Africa at present.

I am not invoking the concept of alienation in the purely Marxist sense, as the consequence of man's relation to the means of production, although that undoubtedly is apposite in the industrialization of millions of blacks under apartheid and therefore our society as a whole. There are many other ways in which man becomes divided from others and distanced from himself. Alienation as such is a condition of rejecting and/or being rejected. The black artist lives in a society that rejected his culture for hundreds of years. He has turned his alienation in the face of those who rejected him, and made of his false consciousness the inevitable point of departure toward his true selfhood. The white artist belongs to the white culture that rejected black culture, and is now itself in turn rejected by black culture. The white born in and nurtured by South Africa is the *non-European* whose society nevertheless refused to acknowledge and take root with an indigenous culture. He is also the *nonblack,* whom blacks see as set apart from indigenous culture. And the question that lowers over him is that he does not know as yet whether this position is a dead end or can be made a new beginning.

Any homogeneity in the nature of the work produced by these artists, white and black, is brought about by what shackles them together rather than by what they share. South African artists belong to the Dionysiac "disintegrated consciousness" that Hegel defines by its antagonism to the external power of society. If by nothing else, they seem to be united in the wish to be free of imposed social circumstances, although they would define these in accordance with a widely differing experience of circumstantial reality. From a disintegrated consciousness, black and white seek wholeness in themselves and a reconnection with the voltage of social dynamism.

Opposition to an existing society implies a hunger to create and identify with another and better one. The abjuration of a set of values implies an intention to create and relate to another set. For the artist, these general implications become part of the transformations of reality that are his work.

"Relevance" and "commitment" are conceptualizations of this movement. They become the text claimed by artists who, individually, understand different things by them, but they also become the demands made upon the artist by his people. Relevance and commitment pulse back and forth between the artist and society. In a time and place like South Africa in the last quarter of the twentieth century, relevance and commitment have become, in the words of Lionel Trilling, "the criteria of art and the qualities of personal life of men that may be enhanced or diminished by art."

"Relevance" and "commitment." How close are these terms that question the existence of the writer in South Africa today? In fact, they are juxtaposed as much as cognate. And in this, again, they signify the tension between the artist and his society, in which his creativity is generated. For relevance has to do with outside events; while commitment comes from within.

For the black artist at this stage in his development, relevance is the supreme criterion. It is that by which his work will be judged *by his own people,* and *they* are the supreme authority, since it is only through them that he can break his alienation. This is the cultural credo of the Black Consciousness movement. The Black Consciousness thinker Bennie Khoapa states that the black artist's only option is personal transformation; he must be ready to phase himself out of the role of being carrier to what the black poet, Mafika Pascal Gwala, calls white, official "swimming pool and caravan culture" in South Africa. The external reality to which relevance paces out the measure of the black artist's work is not a step away from him: another black writer, Njabulo Ndebele, says "blacks are operating" from within "a crushing intellectual and educational environment." And from the perspective of Europe, Sartre's philosophical dictum sums up: "The exploited experience exploitation *as their reality.*" Therefore the black artist has only to do what every artist must in order to become an artist: face his own reality, and as a black, he will also have internalized the standard of relevance set up outside. Then, theoretically, he has solved the aesthetic and social problem; he has put himself in a meaningful relationship to his society.

But relevance, in the context of the absolutes placed upon the black artist by the new society to which he is dedicated, has another demand. Struggle is the state of the black collective consciousness, and art is its weapon; the black artist accepts this as the imperative of his time. Now, weapons are inevitably expected to be used within an orthodoxy prescribed for the handling of such things. There is a kit of reliable emotive phrases for black writers, a ready-made aesthetic for black painters and sculptors, an unwritten index of subjects for black playwrights, and a list of approved images for black photographers. *Agitprop,* as it does always, everywhere, binds the artist with the means by which it aims to free the minds of the people. It licenses a phony subart. Yet the black artist is aware that he is committed, not only as a conscious, voluntary act, but in the survival of his own being and personality, to black liberation. It is at this point, as an artist, that commitment takes over, and the black artist has to assert the right to search out his own demotic artistic vocabulary with which to breathe new life and courage into his people. His commitment is the point at which inner and outer worlds fuse; his purpose to master his art and his purpose to change the nature of art, create new forms and norms out of and for a people recreating themselves, become one aim.

For the black artist, the tendentiousness of the nature of art goes without question. He cannot choose the terms of his relevance or his commitment, because in no other community but the predicated one which blacks have set up inside themselves are his values the norm. Anywhere else—which is to say, in a society ordered and dominated by whites—he is not in possession of selfhood.

The white artist is not quite in the reverse position; that would be too neat for the psychological complexity of South Africa's curious cultural norms. He can, if he wishes, find his work's referent in an aesthetic or ontological movement within the value system traditional to whites. White South African culture will not repudiate him if he does. Even if he were to decide to be relevant to and find commitment only to himself, or (if a writer) to dedicate himself to Anthony Burgess's definition of literature purely as "the aesthetic exploitation of the word," he could still find some kind of artistic validity so long as he were content to stay within the kind of freedom offered by that closed, white value system. Yet the generally tendentious nature of art—overwhelmingly tendentious in writing if less consciously so in painting and the plastic arts—in South Africa shows that few white artists take up these options. One could reverse the proposition and say they don't "opt out," if it were not for the fact that the rejection of whites-only values by no means implies a concomitant "opting in" to black culture. The white artist who sees or feels instinctively that exclusively white-based values are in an unrecognized state of alienation, knows that he will not be accepted, cannot be accepted by black culture that is seeking to define itself *without the reference* to those values that his very presence among blacks represents.

If the white artist is to break out of his double alienation, now, he too has to recognize a false consciousness within himself; he too has to discard a white-based value system which, it is fashionable to say, "no longer" corresponds to the real entities of South African life, but which, in fact, never did. But unlike the black, he does not have a direct, natural, congenital attachment to these entities. We are speaking here not of artistic modes and forms but of the substance of living from which the artist draws his vision. Exploitation by whites, which blacks *experience as their reality,* is something the white artist repudiates, refuses to be the agent of. It is outside himself; he experiences it as surrogate victim through a moral attitude or rational empathy. Thus, the black creation of new selfhood is based on a reality which he, as a white, cannot claim and that could not serve him if he did, since it is not his order of experience.

If the white is to find his true consciousness, express in his work the realities of his place and time, if he is to reach the stage where commitment rises within him to a new set of values based on those realities, he has to admit openly that the order of his experience as a white differs completely from the order of black experience. He has to see the concomitant necessity to find a different way from that open to the black artist, to reconnect his art through his life to the total reality of the disintegrating present, and to attempt, by rethinking his own attitudes and conceptions, the same position the black artist aims for: to be seen as relevant by, and become committed to, commonly understood, commonly created cultural entities corresponding to a common reality—which is to say, an indigenous culture.

SENSIBILITY AND RESPONSIBILITY

CAROLYN FORCHÉ

CONSIDER these two statements: *"Me obligación es esa, ser transparente,"* which translates as, "My obligation is this, to be transparent"—Pablo Neruda; and, "The poem expresses, in an exemplary way, the fact that it is not at the disposal of politics. This *is* its political content. Its political mission is to refuse any political mission"— Hans Magnus Enzensberger. Both statements are from committed poets convinced of the social function of their poetry, but they represent opposite poles of the theory of commitment. Neruda defines his poetic task as an *"obligación,"* a duty, a commitment, a service, a point of honor; and his poetic aspiration as *"ser transparente,"* to be transparent, to choose only those forms which allow the explicit content to shine through. For Enzensberger, to admit explicit political commitment into a poem is to destroy it. The poet's only obligation is to *refuse* to be reduced to the political. Poetry is social, certainly, but as language, not as message.

Both these poets assume that poetry will, or even should, fall foul of the authorities. For Enzensberger, reflecting the experience of Eastern Europe, poetry is subversive precisely because it *is* irreducible, opaque; intolerable because not at authority's disposal; subversive in its very existence. For Neruda, and for Latin America in general, the poet is attacked not *qua* writer but *qua* revolutionary. Poetry is regarded as subversive because it is at the disposal of social conscience and political opposition.

We can resolve this polarity by invoking the absolute duality of the literary text. It is always art; and it is always interpretation. As language and as vision, it speaks about the world; as art, it says nothing. It is both transitive and intransitive, transparent and opaque. Though a poem may be composed of denunciations, exposés, and exhortations, it is not any of these, nor any other kind of speech act; it is only a poem. The conscious, committed poet recognizes that literature may challenge and discredit existing reality, but may never change it alone. However musical, poetry will resist becoming instrumental. But it will equally refuse to disappear into pure music. Poetry is irreducible to mere content, but it is equally irreducible to mere form. Social reality is there, whether the poet intends it or not. The very creed of aesthetic detachment—silence, exile, and cunning—only makes sense as detachment *from* something, exile *from* something. The real polarity is not between Neruda and Enzensberger, each equally committed within the terms of his own culture, but between the unconscious vision which thinks we have to choose between form and content, or between commitment and detachment, and the conscious vision, which recognizes their dialectic. The simple either/or model leads on the one hand toward jejune, fragmented poetry of the aestheticized private life, and on the other hand to Stalinist hackwork. What we require, as Sartre says, is an absolute commitment both to literature and to engagement—to the fullest vision of the material and social world. I suggest that the writer's duty is to pursue both these commitments as far as possible, toward the point where they merge, combine, and drop away.

Here is another paradox: I recognize, as a critic, that creative freedom for the writer is inseparable from a sense of social responsibility, that freedom is choice; yet, in the act of writing, I often feel that I have no freedom of this kind, that the poem is already complete and alive within me. I know, as a critic, that I choose my subject, and that every revision of a line is a weighing of alternatives. Yet it feels not like a choice, but rather like a search for the inevitable, the pre-existent. At the heart of this experience, there is no such thing as a choice between commitment and disengagement.

This is what I mean by transcendence of the polarity. The poet begins with a talent as seemingly inborn as a child's gift for drawing or ear for music; this ability is then nurtured and developed, but alone it will produce only virtuoso juvenilia. To mature, to signify in the world, a poet must also develop a sensibility. By this I mean not merely a local sensibility, but a whole quality of engagement with the world. Sensibility determines what you see when you enter a new room, or a new country: the pattern of selective obsessions, the network of inner necessities, which shapes your response to the human condition. Such development may be conscious to a degree, but never self-conscious. The mistake is to write *about* one's sensibility, rather than with it.

All language, in my view, is political. Vision is always ideologically charged; perceptions are shaped *a priori* by our assumptions, and sensibility is formed by a consciousness at once social, historical, and aesthetic. There is no such thing as nonpolitical poetry. The time, however, to determine what those politics will be is not the moment of taking pen to paper, but during the whole of one's life. We are responsible for the quality of our vision; we have a say in the shaping of our sensibility. In the many thousand daily choices we make, we create ourselves and the voice with which we speak and work.

For example, when I made the decision to work as a human rights investigator and journalist in El Salvador, I was not thinking of the poetry that might result. Indeed, I regarded these areas of my life as separate. It was not—as friends and other poets tried to warn me— that poetry and politics was a deadly mixture, and that I could preserve my "artistic integrity" only by keeping them apart. Nor was I naïve enough to think that the revolution would somehow automatically become my muse. Poetry simply did not come into it. Looking back, I realize that my work in El Salvador made the profoundest difference in my poetry, precisely because it was not poetic. It did not confirm my preconceptions. The transformation occurred in my sensibility; it was my life that was changed, and hence my poetry. This is what I understand by commitment. To locate a poem in an area associated with political turmoil does not in itself render the poem in the narrow sense political. In the larger sense, to write at all in the face of atrocity is in itself a political act.

THE TWO VOICES: A DISCUSSION

SUSAN SONTAG AND CAROLYN FORCHÉ

SUSAN SONTAG: I've spent the last two weeks, along with Nadine Gordimer and Per Wästberg, at the PEN Conference in Lyon, talking with other writers about the situation of writers in prison, of writers who are censored and persecuted. And after this spell of intensive thinking about these problems—although there is not a day of my life when I *don't* think about them—I'm impressed by the fact that there are very different ways of describing our subject. Let me give you one example. When we talk about protecting the writer's *freedom,* about his or her right to speak the truth, we often think in conflicting ways about the source of that moral authority.

We talk about the writer as representing a larger collectivity which is being oppressed or restricted by the state: the writer who speaks for a group. Sometimes it's called a minority; often, as with certain races and with women, these minorities are in fact majorities. The claim of the writer, then, is to speak for a collective voice that is being repressed or inhibited.

But then there is what seems to be a quite contradictory defense being made of the writer's liberty, which conceives of the writer as the unauthorized voice, the private view. And what we are defending is precisely the right to have an intensely private view of public matters.

There is a strong difference of approach here. We all agree that the liberties of writers should be defended, that freedom of conscience, whether or not the bearer of this conscience is a professional writer, is a sacred value. I imagine that there is no one here who doesn't assent to that principle, but there's much disagreement about how writers best serve conscience. If I had to choose between the two approaches, I would be for the second.

Let me give you an example of the problem. We have not only the writer as spokesperson for opposition to a repressive power, we have orthodoxies and repressive forces within the opposition. We have writers who silence themselves: opposition writers, unauthorized writers, dissenting writers (these terms also have to be properly distinguished), who exercise self-censorship, because they feel that their writing must contribute to the good cause which they are pledged to serve. They cannot speak in a private way without letting down their comrades and colleagues who are persecuted, censored, or repressed. We know this phenomenon already among black writers in North America; we see it among women writers in North America, some of whom are under attack for not being sufficiently militant as feminists. Pressure has been put on women writers to devote more or all of their activity as writers to promoting the cause of women. I don't want to see writing become the socialist realism of the virtuous, as opposed to the socialist realism of the tyrants.

Another example, which is more painful to me: there is some reluctance to draw attention to the condition of writers and of people of conscience who are imprisoned in communist countries, particularly in Cuba. It is felt that in this part of the world the principal culprit is American imperialism, which has caused tremendous suffering in Central America and South America; that Cuba is a besieged country; that the weight of the United States is overwhelming; and that to denounce the Cuban regime is simply serving the cause of Reagan. Think of the attitude of Garcia Marquez. But to me it's scandalous that a writer of such enormous talent should be a spokesperson for a government which has put more people in jail (proportionally to its population) than any other government in the world. Like many Western intellectuals, I was once convinced of the justice of operating a double standard in certain circumstances—for example, Cuba. For about ten years, since the Padilla case, I have thought differently.

Whatever our criticism of American imperialism and whatever dangers the American military machine poses to the world, we must operate the same kind of judgment everywhere. And by those standards, the situation in communist countries is appalling—much worse, in fact, than many of us were willing to admit. Worse, even, than under most countries called fascist. This is a tremendous revelation, which has been brought to us in the last decade by the force of testimony from Czechoslovakia, from Poland, from the Soviet Union, from Hungary, from Yugoslavia, from Cuba. It cannot be denied, it cannot be refuted, and I think it strengthens us: we are now on the right track; we're not applying a double standard anymore. Our commitment is to the truth. Our commitment is to the defense of prisoners of conscience, of people speaking for the truth, wherever they are.

But there is not only the Republic of Letters—there is also the Aristocracy of Letters. These notions are not mutually exclusive, but they are different approaches to what a writer is and what the authority of a writer is.

There are some real divisions that we try to ignore. Let me cite the word "elitist," for instance, which covers a multitude of moral horrors. It is a term often used by the enemies of the writer's freedom, in order to persecute unauthorized private voices, though it is sometimes used with the best of intentions. We hear over and over again such declarations as "We must open up writing, we must open up literature, to people who have not had a chance to write, to talk, to have access to publication"; and often the people under attack—as elitist—are simply the best writers. This invites a kind of democracy of literature that destroys literature, that destroys the very notion of literature, which has an intrinsic relationship to excellence. We know that excellence exists, that some writers are better than other writers, and that only a few writers in any time are great. And that literature has to do with participating in activities which make it possible for there to *be* great writers—and not just writers.

Great writers are not necessarily writers with just views. I think that Céline's best books are *Rigadoon, North,* and *Castle to Castle,* the books that he wrote after the Second World War. They are, certainly, fascist and anti-Semitic. Much great literature expresses hatred and contempt for women. I'm not, either as a feminist, or as a woman, or as a writer, going to say that writing is to be judged by its correct attitudes toward women. There are racist attitudes too in great literature. We can hardly ignore these things. But I can't comfort myself by saying that the greatest relationship to the medium—

which in the case of writers is the language, the collective property of the whole human race in all its different forms—is going to mean that a stupid thing, a false thing, an unjust thing, can't be said in it. That is also part of the struggle, to do what we can to find something that is truer or more just, with the full knowledge that great writers have not always spoken for truth or justice.

CAROLYN FORCHÉ: In certain works of literature by persons of, say, fascist tendencies—and it's frequently the case with myself as well—, the work is more intelligent than the writer is. There are certain circumstances in which the portrayal of the world, the creation of the world, the presentation of the world back to society, is often a more admirable thing than the writer's own conclusions about that world.

Now, as Susan Sontag pointed out, that is not the interesting question: the interesting question is when the explicit content *is* expressive of misogyny or anti-Semitism or what have you. My response is that I would question what we mean by "great literature"—what do we mean by this notion that we have of great literature? I can admire the technical facility with language, perhaps, as such, but I also have a bias to view literature in its social function. Literature also *means*, we also interpret, and so I would have to deplore certain statements and perhaps not admit them to my category of greatness.

I also do not believe that we are necessarily living at the pinnacle of our enlightenment. I should hope not. Much of our writing probably reflects attitudes that are unconscious on our parts but may in some future time be deplored. And in a sense, the literature of the past is interesting for me as the artifact of the intelligence of that past. I am interested and can learn about the attitudes prevalent in a certain period—or perhaps the origin of certain attitudes—by reading the literature, but there is an idealization of literature that I'm uncomfortable with. I would like to examine the text for what it is, and not have this category of greatness for writers, unless perhaps their work stands the scrutiny of time.

SUSAN SONTAG: I'd like to make one remark in connection with what Carolyn Forché has just said. We may not be living in the final stage of enlightenment. However, from the point of view of a writer—

and, for that matter, from the human point of view—it's always better to believe that we are living in the last stage of human history, if only because that attitude makes you scrutinize what's going on much harder, pay greater attention to every detail. Maybe the curtain won't fall tomorrow, but it's better to think it may. Then we will take better care of what's going on in front of us.

THE GRAND INQUISITOR: A DISCUSSION

QUESTION FROM THE FLOOR: I have a question for each of the participants. To my mind, one of the highest achievements in literature is the Grand Inquisitor chapter from *The Brothers Karamazov*. In some ways an index of how fine it is, is that critics continue to debate whether there is any answer to the Grand Inquisitor's argument, even though the novel was written as a refutation of it. The reason for the confusion is that in the Grand Inquisitor, Dostoevsky has created a figure of grand humanity and passion, a decent man whom Dostoevsky disagrees with entirely. How would the participants respond to the proposition that the highest achievement in literature is to express the voice and humanity of those with whom you most strongly disagree?

JULIUS TOMIN: What does it mean to express the voice of somebody with whom one strongly disagrees? For example, should I express the voice of President Husák strongly? It really is a very difficult thing for me to contemplate.

MARGARET ATWOOD: Your answer would be no?

JULIUS TOMIN: It's not so simple. I am just trying to imagine that somebody with whom I strongly disagree. I actually tried once, I remember, at the end of the police raids against my philosophy course. There were two interrogators, and they wanted to make me talk; I didn't want to talk, so they shouted at me to stand up; I didn't, so they jumped me and pushed me up against the wall; and I stood there, and the chief said, "OK—one step forward; don't dirty our wall." So I made one step forward, and he said, "OK, it wasn't that difficult." And in that moment—yes, for me it was always extremely important not to *hate* anybody—I felt in that moment, "If I keep standing, I will have to hate that man." So I went to sit in the chair again. He was very mad with me, so he jumped at me and wanted to keep me standing. It was a hard job, because I didn't cooperate. Then they decided to drop me. I lay there on the floor. They didn't like it, so they thought that I would perhaps resent it if they were to try to stand me on my head. But again I didn't resent it, and they found it quite difficult to keep me standing on my head.

Anyway, the next week—I was regularly invited to police interrogations every Wednesday—I was interrogated by a Major Fisher, a very thoughtful man. He asked me, "Mr. Tomin, why stand on your head?" And I told him that I didn't know why. And he said, "Well, Mr. Tomin, you are a very thoughtless person, incapable of thinking." Going home, I thought about it, really thought about it—this accusation that I cannot think, and that question, "Why stand on my head?" And then I figured it out. In the sixties I called myself a Marxist. Now, Marx found Hegel on his head and tried to set him on his feet. And the big trouble for Marxism was this attempt to set Hegel on his feet. So perhaps the police thought that they ought to undo this trouble, at least in my person, and put things back in their proper places, put me back on my head. I wrote this whole episode down, and I tried to be as correct to Major Fisher as I could, but I don't think he liked it that well. So it is really important to try to understand the views of those whom you oppose most. But the question is who it is, how you do it, and whether your opponent will like it. The question is how to do it in such a way that he likes it.

NADINE GORDIMER: I must say I thought the question was rather an insult to writers. To question at all whether writers deal with characters whose views are opposed to their own is amazing. It's propagandists who don't do this; it's the work of propaganda writers to represent only one side. Imaginative writers are constantly dealing with the conflict of ideas and ideals through character; it's part of the stuff and the drama of fiction.

SUSAN SONTAG: I agree entirely with what Nadine Gordimer has said.

MARGARET ATWOOD: I will add that it's amazing the extent to which readers will think that everything that anybody in any of your books says is an expression of your own opinion. Literature just doesn't work like that.

Terrorism

VICTIMS AND ACCOMPLICES

HANS CHRISTOPH BUCH

I COME from West Germany—West Berlin, more exactly—which in the past few years has been in the headlines in connection with terrorism. And I want to say a few words about that, from my personal point of view.

The word "terrorism" is somehow doubtful to me, and I use it only in quotation marks, because it's much too simple, as a notion.

Writers can be involved in terrorism in many ways. The simplest way is by being either accomplices or victims of terrorism, and the two roles are not easy to separate. For instance, during the Third Reich, many writers became accomplices of terror simply by keeping their mouths shut, by remaining silent, and others became victims, either by being killed or tortured or by being driven out of the country. This is a relatively clear case.

A more complicated case is the recent decision of the West German Government to do something against so-called sympathizers of terrorists. These legal measures affected literature a lot. One article in our law, Paragraph 88A, was passed four or five years ago and was directed against "advocating violence." This is such a large and vague notion, because advocating violence is something that Homer does as well as Shakespeare, and you could ban practically any book with this legal prescription. And in fact, some German writers did get into trouble, writers who were not at all sympathizers of terrorism but simply tried to analyze what was going on.

Other writers became accomplices of terrorism for reasons which are more difficult to explain. For instance, I took part in the '68 student revolt. It shaped my political views and was very important for me and my writing, for the rest of my life. Some of the people who later turned to terrorism were my friends at that time, or at least I knew them—Baader, for instance—although I did not share his political opinions and I was against what he did. His group, the Red Army Fraction, tried to overthrow the state by carrying on a violent struggle through military means. All the writers and intellectuals and most leftists that I knew in West Berlin and West Germany were against that, because they thought it was childish and could never succeed. However, we did not dare to say no openly, we did not dare to condemn this strategy, because of a somehow misunderstood concept of solidarity, because we did not want to ally ourselves with the state, and with sections of the press. To us Baader's Red Army Fraction were political desperadoes and were misled, but we did not want to put them outside of human society, or treat them as if they were not human beings. We felt sorry for them.

For instance, Heinrich Böll tried to intervene, to keep the Baader-Meinhof group from doing what they did, and at the same time, he tried to stop the state from persecuting them. Böll did not succeed, and they're all dead now, under circumstances which have never been clarified. So writers had a difficult role at that time, because some of them understood emotionally why people like Baader and Ulrike Meinhof turned to terrorism, but on the other hand, they did not share their opinions; maybe it was wrong that they did not say this loud enough. It was a kind of weakness, which came from this pressure for solidarity even with things you don't like.

It's a problem which is known to writers all over the world. It's an old story, this pressure on a writer, not to speak out because of a notion of solidarity. But a writer has to speak out in all cases when he feels something is going wrong. The best ideas can turn into a nightmare when they are carried out the way the Baader-Meinhof group tried to carry out their ideas. In the end, only innocent people were killed or shot at, by both the police and the group.

This kind of solidarity becomes even more questionable when it's possible for such a revolutionary group to take over the state. This has not been the case in Germany, but in many countries of the Third World, writers who have been very critical toward colonialism, toward racism, suddenly keep silent after the revolution they fought for has won. And thus they become accomplices of another kind of injustice or even terrorism. For instance, many people who like the Cuban revolution think they should not speak out, because of that, about imprisoned writers and about injustices which are being committed in Cuba, or in other Socialist countries.

However, this is only one aspect of the problem. In my view, all states, not only fascist states or totalitarian states, are terrorists, because they have the monopoly of power, an army and police, and they exert it to enforce their laws. The state by definition is a terrorist organization.

This may sound too radical. I would like to give you an example of a German writer who has become a victim of the state in this sense. His name is Peter-Paul Zahl, a famous—by now famous—young writer who was a sympathizer of the Baader-Meinhof group, but a sympathizer who was never involved in their activities. In 1971, when there was a real hunt for the Baader-Meinhof people, he was arrested and he resisted arrest. The police found a gun in his car and thought that he was part of the group. Now, the strange thing about the story is that he would have liked to be part of the group, but he wasn't. So he gave very violent, very radical statements when he was interrogated, saying he was for armed struggle, and so forth, and he was sentenced to seven years' imprisonment, practically for nothing. Well, it wasn't nothing: he had a gun and he had resisted arrest. There was an appeal, but afterwards the sentence was even more severe. He was sentenced to fifteen years' imprisonment, which is practically equal to a life imprisonment, simply because the appeal came at a time when the hysteria about terrorism in Germany was so strong that the state thought it had to defend itself with all means, and the civil liberties of this individual, Peter-Paul Zahl, were not really being taken into account.

The tragedy is that he is still in jail. He has served almost ten years now. Before coming here, I called him—now I can reach him on the phone; he has had some improvements in the conditions of his imprisonment—but he's still in jail. And I asked him, "What can I do for you at this conference?" He said, "Nothing." Because Heinrich Böll and Ernesto Cardenal and some of the most famous writers of the world have tried everything. They asked the German state to pardon him, but it was not granted. He's still in jail, and—this is a footnote, but it's important too—he's become a good writer in jail. He was a pretty poor writer before, but he has had enough time to improve his writing, and now his books are widely read. At the same time he has become a symbol of repression in Germany. In West Germany young people read him a lot.

The strange fact is that this kind of repression does exist in West Germany, while on the other hand, we do have much more freedom, of course, than people in East Germany. We have practically the same political system that you have here, and maybe if you really investigate your minds and your files, you'll find that there are similar cases in this country. Although repression exists in communist and fascist countries on a much broader level and in a much more brutal way, such things happen in our countries too, in our parliamentary democracies. That's why I say that by definition the state—I don't want to accuse any particular state—is a dangerous political animal.

THE WORD AS A BLUNT INSTRUMENT

LEON WHITESON

THE QUESTION of terrorism can be argued endlessly. Is it justified or unjustified? Is it ever legitimate as armed resistance or state suppression? How may a writer aid or resist it?

This question is urgent in many places now, in Italy and Ireland, in the Middle East and Latin America, in the Soviet Union and South Africa. In Canada it can seem remote.

But the question of terrorism is not one I want to argue here. I want to look at the word itself. As a writer, I want to attack the language. I want to say that "terrorism" is just a word.

I grew up in Rhodesia. I was born into that small minority of Europeans who believed they had a right to rule the African for his own good. The law—and its instrument, the police—was a blatant means of intimidation. Colonies often nakedly reveal the hypocrisies of the motherland's ruling class.

In Rhodesia the word "terrorist"—or "terr," in the local white slang—sprang into use as soon as the blacks mounted a coherent armed opposition to the colonial order. The African insurgents called themselves "freedom fighters" or "guerrillas," but to the whites they were simply "bloody terrs."

The word was propaganda that worked two ways. On the one hand, it legitimized a brutal military suppression, a suspension of due process of law, a dehumanizing of dissent. On the other hand, the word brutalized the minds of the whites.

The word saved whites from confronting the causes of violent protest against their precious privileges. They could carry on partying by their pools while the killing went on in the bush. "It's just a bunch of terrs," they murmured, clinking the ice in their gins. The word numbed their brains as the chilled booze numbed their bowels.

This word magic didn't work for the Rhodesians. The terrs broke through the barrier of brutalized language. Now, in Zimbabwe, the bloodiest terr of all is now their respected Prime Minister. Robert Mugabe, once a "black Marxist devil," a "beast in human form," is the hottest "white hope" in Africa! Human flexibility is a marvelous thing. . . .

Terrorism was justified in Rhodesia—if you accept the language. The Africans, confronted by stupidity and suppression, had no other means to self-government. But the trick is in the word. If I say "freedom-fightism" in place of "terrorism," my statement that violence was justified in Rhodesia lacks shock. The shock is all in the word.

Moving to Britain, where I lived for twenty years, I found another and more subtle form of state intimidation. The famous British bobby is its symbol. To the well-spoken middle and upper-class British, the bobby is an icon of decency and civil order. He is respectful, polite, and unarmed. To anyone with his own working-class accent, the same nice policeman is likely to be brutal. He knows his own sort are up to no good. How could they be, having nothing to protect?

The bobby in his pointed helmet is another kind of terrorist.

The sense is always in the word. Words are sense. This is a writer's concern. That's what our trade is all about. Language is our basic human right.

Language is the writer's concern. Words are his tools, which he must keep clean and sharp. In a time when the manipulation of language for devious purposes—from state coercion to slogan-mongering to hard-sell advertising—is rampant, the writer's job is to use words with some sense of their meaning and resonance.

The word "terrorism" has a complex origin, in etymology and politics. It derives from the Latin *terrere* (to cause to tremble). It is linked to words like "deterrent" (to frighten off) and "intimidate" (to strike fear).

Politically, the modern use of terrorism was born in the French Revolution. Before that watershed in the history of society, such a concept would have baffled most minds. In 1793 terrorism as an act of state was used openly for the first time. The naked Red Terror of the Jacobins was a shock that rang around the globe.

The shock reverberates. The anarchists Bakunin and Kropotkin embraced it with glee as a weapon *against* the state, in Russia and elsewhere. Terrorism has become a universal instrument, used alike by governments and antigovernment revolutionaries, radical or reactionary. Hitler used it as a club to beat Weimar Germany to death. The Zimbabwe insurgents used terror as a weapon to politicize their own people.

The concept may be modern, but the use of terror to coerce is not. It is as old as humanity.

The Jehovah of Exodus terrorized Pharaoh with plagues of darkness, frogs, and death into letting Israel out of Egypt. Turning on his own children, Jehovah used the threat of dire chastisement to bind his Chosen People to the rule of law.

Intimidation is intrinsic to the nature of society. All human groups use police to preserve civil order. Wherever people need to be coerced to conform to social structures, the threat to "strike fear" hovers always. It is implicit or explicit in the "rule of law."

In a social order striving for democracy, such intimidation—the threat of prosecution—is countered by "due process": the ideal that a citizen is innocent until proven guilty.

That's the ideal. In reality, in any society, the police are hired to protect the haves from the have-nots. The irony is—as with the British bobby—that these police are often drawn from the same class they're hired to keep in line. They are have-nots in uniform. They are effective precisely because they know best how to intimidate their own kind.

Every society has its classes, whether they acknowledge this structure or not. In a democracy, a necessary hypocrisy operates. There is a broad consensus of consent, a subtle tension of acceptance of social privilege, and resentment. Marx's insight that "all history is the history of class struggle" is suppressed. The word "class" is taboo.

Wherever you have classes, you have social intimidation, that is, the striking of fear, or the threat of prosecution. You have, in a word, "terrorism."

This is no specious wordplay. Rather, it is a recognition that every human relationship is, to some extent, a power struggle. We all want life on our own terms and are prepared to bully others to this end.

There is terror in families. Parents use it to keep kids in line. Husbands use it against wives, wives against husbands. Children use it against children, lovers against lovers, bosses against workers,

workers against bosses. The blunt fact is, intimidation is a glue to bind all social contracts.

All forms of intimidation are intimately linked. Private and public terrorizings are part of the same human chain. There is a spectrum that runs from emotional terrorism to street-gang terror to state terror and its twin, counterterror. The streetwise terror of alienated blacks and Latins in Harlem or Watts differs from the bombings, kidnappings, and assassinations of the Italian Red Brigade or the Irish Republican Army only in its freedom from ideology.

Every human interaction is, under the necessary polite pretense, a war to the knife.

Language is a weapon in this war. It is also a liberation. To keep our hearts strong and our minds sane, we need to know what words mean.

We are clubbed on the skull by words used as blunt instruments of obfuscation. Behind this brutal use of words lies a brutality of purpose. The writer, concerned for his tools, must reveal the intent behind this verbal assault. What must most concern us as writers is the brutalization of language.

Language is not some abstract "truth" that must be defended from the messiness of life. Language is a fact of life. Words are crucial to man's struggle to civilize his soul. "I speak, therefore I am human."

Writers must always try to clarify the confusion between what people say and what they really mean. Utterance and intent can never be the same. A certain necessary hypocrisy is vital in any social structure. But the tension between utterance and intent must be kept taut.

"Terrorism" is just a word. To argue along the lines of the word is to accept a definition that is utterly unclear. The word has many resonances, covers a cloud of meanings, gives a spuriously sharp silhouette to a dangerous confusion.

We are all terrorists, to some degree. At the same time, we are all victims of intimidation. It could be said that my job as a writer is to terrorize into truth. I will use words I believe to be true to "strike fear" into the hearts of all those people who yearn to fudge facts.

"Terrorism" is just a word. As long as we allow one bald word to stand for a vast complexity, we can be manipulated like puppets. But we invented words to speak to one another. I hope we invented them to convey meaning. I distrust anyone who sets words up as hard facts, then uses them to club our brains.

If writers won't use words properly, who will?

DEFINITIONS: A DISCUSSION

A STATEMENT FROM THE FLOOR: There seems to be confusion about the term "terrorism," and I hoped that somehow I'd come away, after listening to writers talk about it, with the term better defined. Instead, what I find is that in the same context, we're talking about the intimidation between two lovers, and we're talking about throwing a bomb in a cinema at people who happen to be watching a film. And suddenly there's no innocent, there's no guilty, there's nobody. We've just fudged the whole issue. I find myself even more confused than when I came in.

THOMAS KINSELLA: That's one of the main contributions of a writer in a democracy!

A STATEMENT FROM THE FLOOR: In that sense the panel has amply succeeded. But I would like to finish on this point: I'm not talking about armed people fighting against armed people. Everybody knows violence exists all the time on different levels. We're talking about terrorism, and a distinction can be made between acts of violence aimed at a baby carriage and acts of violence aimed at a military position or at an armed individual. If you lose the qualitative distinction between aiming at school buses for the purpose of some higher cause and aiming at military installations, as you have done here by making it all quantitative, you lose a very important element.

LEON WHITESON: Once you erect a word like "terrorism," it's a thought stopper. You're an example. You wanted a definition; we couldn't give you one. We couldn't give you a qualitative one or a quantitative one if we talked till we were blue in the face.

HANS CHRISTOPH BUCH: It may have sounded—if someone did not listen carefully—as if we were advocating terrorism. Of course, it's more complicated than that. I had a long conversation a couple of years ago with Herbert Marcuse, the philosopher, at the time when

Baader and Gudrun Ensslin died, or were killed, in jail, and we tried to define some limits in this respect. Marcuse insisted that you can't exclude violence from political struggle or from revolutionary struggle. It simply doesn't work, because there is violence every day, and the violence which is exerted by repressive states is never taken into account, only the violence which is exerted by those who defend themselves against repression.

So you can't exclude violence. But does that mean that anything which is done for a just cause is good? Of course not. Here you must try to find some definitions—and not only tactical definitions. In my view, that's one shortcoming of Marxism, which has only the tactical definitions to offer, arguing that violence should be accepted by a broad majority in order to become revolutionary. For me this is an opportunistic argument. Furthermore, Marcuse said (or we developed this idea together in our conversation) that the means, the methods you employ—which include violence, as I said at first—should have a connection with the aims. That's the difference between, say, fascist violence and progressive violence, if such a difference exists.

For instance, if you look at El Salvador, you can see that difference quite clearly. The liberation army does not torture. The liberation army does not kidnap people and kill them indiscriminately. The same applies to Nicaragua. And although I do not want to minimize the violence that is exerted by revolutionary groups, I want to draw your attention to this point, which I think marks a qualitative difference. At the same time, writers do have the duty to say no even to their political allies when they employ methods that cannot be justified by the cause. These methods betray the cause, and the cause gets lost in the struggle; only the methods remain.

THE CONTEXT OF TERROR

CAROLYN FORCHÉ

IN THE SPRING of 1980, in El Salvador, I met with six young labor leaders to hear their views on agrarian reform and their account of atrocities committed against civilians by security forces. By that time rape, mutilation, and murder were so common there were already too many corpses to bury, and some were left for days in the fields or roadsides to be picked at by dogs. They spoke of an incident the year before, when a young *campesino* active in union organizing was abducted, tortured for several days, killed, and dismembered, his body scattered in a ditch.

"We found those soldiers," one of them said quietly, "and we took them to the ditch and made them assemble our friend again on the ground like a man, and ask forgiveness of the corpse." The soldiers were then released, unharmed, because it was felt that in so doing an important lesson had been learned for both the soldiers and themselves: that such acts of forgiveness, if practiced, would continue to be possible.

Though we were in danger that night of attack by the right-wing death squads, my friends found time to ask me what I did for work in the United States, when I was not in their country documenting human rights abuses. I found myself peculiarly embarrassed to answer that I was a poet. My friends were incredulous and exhorted me never to be ashamed of that kind of work, that poetry was important to those imprisoned, fighting, or afraid, to pass the time uplifted when it is terrible to wait.

Some of these men did not yet read or write, but each had committed to memory some lines of verse, particularly those written by José Martí, and they proceeded to recite them for me. Poetry was certainly enough, they said. The world for which they might be com-

pelled to fight would certainly not be without poets. "Most of ours
are dead or in exile now," they said, "but there are young ones still
alive here." Would I like to meet them?

The poets who gathered for the meeting a week later were quite
young, perhaps none older than twenty-two, and all were or had
been students at the national university. They asked political questions first. Did I think my country would intervene militarily against
them? Would it be possible for Reagan to become elected? At what
point did I suppose the escalation of military aid would occur? Only
later, after talking about the struggle for which they were all willing
to die, did we speak about poetry. There was some language
difficulty at times, but there were smiles of recognition at the names
of poets and poems we knew in common. "The problem is, our poets
are dead or out of the country; the problem is, we have no means of
publishing our poems, no way right now of bringing them to our people." One of them jostled a cardboard box gently, where his infant
daughter slept. "This is all we have now, but after the struggle, we'll
teach poetry everywhere in the country, like Ernesto Cardenal in
Nicaragua."

During 1981 each of those young poets was killed. The security
forces of El Salvador are now seeking to exterminate every trace of
oppositional culture, every attempt to forge links between literacy,
articulacy, and social justice. The young poets were murdered not
because of their poetry, however, but because of their opposition to
the regime. The writers at highest risk in El Salvador today are those
who witness and record: the journalists, foreign and Salvadoran; the
authors of impassioned homilies in the churches, or of torture reports; the authors who simply list the dead. The simple compilation
of such statistics has come to require the utmost courage. Consider
the conditions under which such information must be gathered. The
wire services, and all telecommunications, are monitored by the military. Pseudonyms provide no security. The death squads operate with
impunity in every hotel. No one can afford to sleep in the same
house, or travel in the same vehicle by the same route: it is dangerous to become traceable. Effectiveness becomes self-limiting. Between January 1980 and May 1981 thirteen members of the press
were deported or barred from entering the country, twenty were cap-
tured and/or tortured, three disappeared, nine were wounded, and
twelve died. Radio stations, print shops, newspapers, media offices,

and press vehicles have all been dynamited. Twice last year, death lists were compiled of journalists thought to be unfriendly to the regime, both foreign and Salvadoran.

The intimidation is often far more brutal. A Salvadoran photographer, Cesar Navarro, and his *Cronica del Pueblo* editor, Jaime Suarez Quemay, were seized during a coffee break. When their mutilated bodies were found, it was evident that they had been disemboweled before death. I was once told by a U.S. embassy official that events in Central America must be viewed in a context. Regarding the meaning of human rights for the writer in El Salvador, *that* is the context.

Colonialism

THE DILEMMA IN ASIA

ROMESH THAPAR

WRITING in Asia, by its very nature, is terribly elitist. Anywhere from 60 to 80 per cent of the population is hardly touched by it—a kind of massive isolation. And yet, if writing is to be relevant, it should concern itself with the condition of those who seldom, or never, feel its touch. In other words, the writer in Asia is in a bind from which he can only free himself by a conscious sensitization to the awesome reality around him.

This is more easily said than done. Unless the writer is able to feel, to know, to experience the brutalized condition of his people, and visibly and constantly to reduce the gulf between his preaching and his practice, he soon drifts into what we call "populism," which in essence is radical rhetoric without the political and economic infrastructure to ensure social change. This sketchy description applies to most of us, whether in creative writing, in analytical journalism, or in plain reporting.

I believe that the barrenness of modern political/economic thought in Asia, the almost obsessive tendency to imitate the more dominant trends in developed lands, and the widespread servility, financial and inspirational, among those who have or who seek a place in the sun, is very much rooted in the inability of Asian writers to find that vital communion with the traumas of their people. Without this communion, we cannot articulate the answers to the problems of our age.

Asia is the home of the oldest civilizations. But the continuities of tradition which prevent isolation have been grievously disrupted by colonialism in its various guises. Indeed, it is almost possible to measure mathematically the degree of civilizational disruption by the intensity of the colonial presence. If today the quality and texture of life in South Asian lands is akin to an untidy, unplanned patchwork quilt, somewhat different from China, where the so-called "barbarian" influence was less direct, there is Japan to tell us of a more integrated and thoughtful development. It is in the context of these realities, which change from region to region in the sprawl of Asia, that modernization has to be grappled with. And it is here that the writer is tested, daily, hourly, almost minute to minute.

Let me illustrate the predicament. From a largely elitist position, often working in a language environment which is foreign and contrived, the isolated writer surveys a massive tangle of problems. A majority of his people struggle to rise from the trap of poverty to which they are condemned. They cannot be expected to attempt sophisticated and necessarily slow-moving remedies. Something must be done within a life span. The traditional self-reliance of a people, and the skills which they have inherited through centuries of triumph and despair, are then deliberately undermined by the very processes which proclaim development, growth, and enlightenment but do not produce them. The alternatives or choices are many, stretching from the amoral freewheeling of local buccaneers to the stolid regulatory systems of brutal and corrupt ideologies, but invariably encrusted with the unsolved aberrations of societies wedded to consumerism. The writer, developing his consciousness from the days when the atomic weapon was used in Asia, knows that there are no answers in these models. He has experimented with many mixes. Nothing works.

We are at this point. The democratic structures are collapsing, unable to cope with the assertive tempers of awakened peoples. In the developing anarchy, individuals, parading their charismas or using enormous funds to manipulate organizations, are tempted to build their muscle with military spending. It is the military, increasingly strengthened by arms mostly from the developed lands, that is ultimately the receiver of power over the people. The whole global system, with its annual 500-billion-dollar investment in systems of kill and overkill, of confrontation and the balance of terror, is designed to hand us over to the authoritarians of the world. Asia, together with the rest of the southern hemisphere, is the first to suffer the torment of this twisted scientific and technological advance.

The writer in Asia, if human rights mean anything to him, must create an integral model of growth and fulfillment drawn from or inspired by the catalytic thoughts of a Gandhi and a Mao and from those who claim to interpret them in real terms, the Nehrus and the

Dengists. Inevitably, the effort is distorted by the imitators, the pseudomodernizers, who see the future only in frameworks provided by a crisis-ridden, affluent world. To expose this truth of our condition, to dissolve the delusions, to crack the deceptive status quo, is the central task of the writer. It is no ordinary task, and it brings him into frontal collision with the prevailing structures of power.

An elitist approach to the explosive questions which have formed around human rights—an approach that is too easily taken in the context of free speech and censorship—can isolate the writer from the mainstream of the struggle of his people, who may see the issues in wider perspectives. Then again, these perspectives, if made paramount over those critical human rights, could drown the quest for a humane society. That is the central dilemma. Either way, bread and liberty cannot be isolated one from the other. They must go hand in hand if rights are to be human. And yet without liberty, all is lost. Liberty has to be a paramount right even in imperfection. So much of the exotic claptrap of liberation movements is a cover for the brutish ambitions of individuals or coteries. Increasingly, in the complexity of today's situation, the writer is compelled to cultivate his roots and his independence. In Asia this is the challenge—even though the present response tends to be listless, feeble.

A rooted, independent mind. What goes into the amalgam of such a mind? There can be no healthy, powerful development without this knowledge.

In Asia it is necessary that priority be given to the effort to sensitize oneself to the vibrations of one's people. This is not as simple as it sounds. For the elites, colonialism snapped the emotional and philosophic links with a living tradition in grotesque ways, producing creatures and languages, designs and textures that belonged nowhere. We are finding that these sudden ruptures in the name of so-called progress produce nothing but wastelands. Fortunately, there is still time for us in Asia to pick up the strands still alive in the people's consciousness and to weave them anew. Without this act of commitment—and let it not be viewed in any other way—there can be no defense against the quiet takeover of the writer's sensitivities and consciousness by the environment of a not so distant, affluent world. In other words, the first commitment is to a segment of humanity often very different from other segments, and this commitment must become a disciplining passion.

A parallel commitment is to the quality of humanity, a quality which must pervade all exercise of power. Here there can be no quibbling, no rationalization, no compromise. Brutality of one human being toward another has to be fought all the way. Not without reason is this the area where the greatest retreats on human rights are witnessed in every country of the world without exception. The intellectual somersaults which writers in Asia indulge in to justify the inhumanity of those who exercise power, their failures and betrayals, are an everyday happening. And there is little pressure from the people, confused by populist politics and economics, to keep them firmly committed.

In a sense, the collision of ideologies and movements heightens the disarray and provides convenient justifications for oppression. The confusion is intense. Somehow, the struggle for human rights— and as an Asian I cannot but use the phrase in its widest sense—must cut through the confusion. A commitment to the complex ramifications of one's community and culture, so long as it is rooted in humane concerns, becomes part of the global effort to purge our planet of its brutalities. It may yet yield new structures of living which release initiative and liberate the humanity of man.

I have emphasized these elements of life in Asia because it is so easy to slip unconsciously into isolated, elitist postures on human rights, seeing them only as assertions of the paramount right to free expression and assembly and not as part of a more all-embracing texture of humane existence. Certainly in Asia, a restricted understanding becomes a possible framework for self-deception. Political, economic, and social change is not a menu that can be ordered at will. I suppose we have to learn this lesson from bitter experience— and then pass it on elsewhere to those who care. There are no shortcuts out of elitism and isolation.

The crisis may well be within the mind of man itself, conditioned and confined with every leap in technology. How can we break through the limitations of our mind, probing deeper within ourselves, as we must if there is to be a surer awareness of what is human and what are rights? Perhaps that is the role of the hero of tomorrow.

THAT WHICH KOREAN POETS TEACH US

YOTARO KONAKA

THERE are two main reasons why we should be interested in and concerned about the human rights of writers in Asia: they are our responsibility and our moral example.

We feel responsibility because industrialist enterprises of Japan
are economically exploiting the people of Asia. Japan is giving aid to
dictatorial regimes in many Asian countries. Its history in Asia has
been one of military aggression.

The second reason is more positive. Many Asian people still have
a love for nature and the wisdom to live in harmony with it. In this
regard, there is much we can learn from Asian people.

I would like to talk about Japan's relations with Korea because I
feel this relationship is representative of Japan's relations with other
Asian countries. It consists of bribes and torture, and economic and
political exploitation. Yet there is strong resistance and solidarity
among those who are being oppressed.

I would like to tell you about a poet who has become a symbol of
this resistance.

I often wonder why it is that greatness of a cosmic magnitude tends
to manifest itself in a world as minute as the atom. A poet was born
in an obscure place called Korea. This poet was confined in a tiny
prison cell not fit even for an animal. Yet the emanation of his spirit
seems powerful enough to penetrate into the farthest corners of the
world. The name of the poet is Kim Chi Ha.

Some people liken Kim Chi Ha and his literary works to the
exquisitely beautiful porcelain ware for which his country is re-
nowned. But I know Kim Chi Ha would scornfully reject any attempt
to compare his work with this princely product, because he strives to
identify himself with the lowest stratum of Korean society: beggars,
lepers, shoeshine boys, trash collectors, peasants, day laborers,

whores. His language is biting, rough, sarcastic, down-to-earth, and full of humor, capable of generating tearful laughter from these downtrodden people.

Kim Chi Ha was born in February 1941, barely ten months prior to the Japanese attack on Pearl Harbor. When he was four, there came the "liberation"—which was actually a huge calamity for the Korean people. It set brothers against brothers, sons against fathers, by separating the country into two hostile camps, with the Americans on one side and the Chinese on the other. All Kim Chi Ha's thinking, all his visionary efforts to see things beyond space, beyond time, flow from these painful memories.

When a dramatic student uprising forced the dictator Syngman Rhee to succumb to the popular will and abdicate in April 1960, Kim Chi Ha was only a fledgling poet at Seoul National University. But his fellow students turned to him to lead them during this period of turmoil. The experience of mobilizing student power against a dictatorial regime prepared him for larger and more decisive roles. But then TB forced him to retreat to a sanatorium. When he returned to school in 1964, the southern half of the Korean Peninsula was again in a whirlwind of unrest and anger.

The new dictator, Park Chung Hee, formerly an officer in the Japanese Imperial Army, was about to formalize a treaty with Japan. The entire nation rose in protest, and thousands of students took to the streets, bringing the Park government to the verge of collapse. This violent popular resistance was put down only by heavily armed troops mobilized under martial law.

Kim Chi Ha was at the heart of this movement, which sent him to prison and further trained him as a fighter of "poetic violence." The treaty, nevertheless, was signed, opening the way for the unchecked penetration of Japanese neocolonialism. And in 1968 the recurrent TB again put Kim Chi Ha into a hospital bed. From there, battling for his life, he watched the May Student Revolt in Paris and the brief Prague Spring. He also read *Populorum progressio,* issued by Pope Paul VI in 1967; writings of liberation theology such as the World Council of Churches declaration of the 1968 Uppsala Convention; and *Mater et magistra* by Pope John XXIII.

His long and searching contemplation of God and the affection he felt for Bishop Chi Hak Sun of Wŏnju Diocese led him in 1971 to the Catholic faith. He says: "I became a Catholic because Catholicism conveys a universal message: not only that spiritual and material burdens could be lifted from man but also that oppression itself could be ended by the salvation of both the oppressor and the oppressed. I believe that Catholicism is capable of assimilating and synthesizing these contradictory and conflicting ideologies, theories, and value standards into a universal truth."

Inevitably, as a Catholic radical, Kim Chi Ha faced Park—a symbol of corruption and injustice—in unretractable confrontation, like David standing before Goliath. He wrote in succession two ballads in such scathing language that the Park regime consigned him twice more to prison. But the decisive confrontation came early in 1974, when Park Chung Hee, facing another student revolt, issued Presidential Decrees No. 1 and No. 4. These decrees authorized him to arrest anyone opposed to his rule and to send that person to the gallows.

Kim Chi Ha had to go into hiding, and he wrote about his experience in the following words:

> The light extinguished from your eyes
> at the announcement that afternoon on the street—
>
> Call it death.
>
> When the others had all been dragged off,
>   leaving you
> strangely alone, and you had hidden yourself
> away by the distant sea,
>
> in the dim corner of a mirror
> on some unfamiliar wine house wall,
> some wretch's fear-worn face, his back
> riven by the knife of this dark age—
> Call the lines of weariness on his face,
> call them death.
>
> After so much
> hardship, that day love began,
> that cold, windy day I first took your hand
> and for the first time overcoming my fears
> looked at your face
> directly, that day
> of parting from you
>   Call it death.

Park's police hunted him down, put him in jail, and after ritual torture and mental indignity, sentenced him to death. The sentence was later commuted to life imprisonment, and in February 1975 international protest brought him briefly out of jail. But within a month he was back in prison. During his temporary freedom he accused the government of fabricating the case against the "People's Revolutionary Party," whose members were subsequently hanged. This accusation, written in "Asceticism 1974," and various thoughts he had jotted down in four notebooks while in prison, earned him the charge of violating the "anti-Communist law" and added seven more years to his life term. The jottings were for a ballad that would deal with a fictitious Korean character, Chang Idlam, whose life, death, and resurrection would testify to the possibility of merging the Christian gospel with the Marxist vision of social change. After being imprisoned in a tiger cage in the Sudaimoon Prison of Seoul, Kim Chi Ha was put under house arrest. He still had the courage to say, "Our age demands truth and the passion to endure the suffering necessary to learn the truth."

This brief sketch of his life, however, should not categorize him as a mere political agitator. It is true he speaks of the suffering of the poor and powerless. He condemns those who hold power and use it against the people. But he does this not in the spirit of revenge but in the hope of salvation. Branding him as an agitator or a political ideologue would be as wrong as so labeling St. Luke, who speaks of exalting those who are humble and bringing down rulers from their thrones.

As was pointed out by a Korean critic in Japan, his irreconcilable zealotism (in Toynbee's sense) should not be overlooked. His similies, metaphors, and quotations are firmly rooted in traditional legends and folk arts. He seldom loses a chance to show his passionate disdain for anything foreign, particularly anything Japanese or American. All this, as the critic says, is strongly reminiscent of Judea and its people at the time recorded in the New Testament. When the Jews were exposed to the relentless encroachment of the Roman civilization—which was infinitely stronger than their own, economically and militarily—many of them became the so-called Herodites, attempting to survive by assimilating themselves. However, some remained Zealots: they refused to capitulate and stuck to their age-old local traditions. As we know, it was these unbending Zealots who fought the Romans and thereby transcended Jewish localism to produce a universal message. The zealotism of Kim Chi Ha holds extreme importance when we realize that his country may well be likened to a Judea whose survival is threatened by the modern-day Rome.

The following is a statement that Kim Chi Ha made to the judge presiding over the court that was intent on destroying him:

> I am a poet, and what is the mission of a poet? It is to throw himself among the throng of the wretched, share their pains, groan with them, say in their stead to the world what their suffering is like, and expose the root cause of all the evils that are chewing them up. He is also required to undertake the arduous climb to the mountaintop to see a blessed future that lies ahead and tell those who are in despair what he has seen.

My country, Japan, once attempted to rob the Korean people of their language and bury it in oblivion, never to be excavated. The Korean language, however, seems to have retained its innate vitality. The power of its words, as written by the hand of Kim Chi Ha, keeps pounding in the hearts of many Japanese. Japan has possibly ceased to produce poetry capable of moving the common people with humor, laughter, sorrow, and indestructible hopes expressed in subtle symbolism as well as with direct candor. The same dissipation may also be true of contemporary Western poems.

The dictator President Park Chung Hee was assassinated in November 1979, and General Chun Doo-Hwan took control of the government through a coup d'etat. South Korea experienced a short-lived "spring" in 1980, during which Kim Chi Ha was released from prison and put under house arrest but was forbidden to publish anything. Then in May 1980, the citizens of Kwangju city staged an uprising, demanding democracy. President Chun sent in paratroopers who mercilessly massacred students, women, and workers, leaving more than fifteen hundred dead. Following the uprising, President Chun had his main political opponent, Kim Dae Jung, sentenced to death; and charging that Dae Jung had ordered the poet Koh Eun to agitate the students to revolt, President Chun sentenced Koh Eun to fifteen years in prison.

Incidents such as these are happening not only in Korea but all over Asia. On the one hand, dictatorial regimes are releasing famous writers in order to improve their international image. On the other hand, they are quietly arresting other lesser known writers. This is true in Thailand, Taiwan, and Vietnam. In other countries where regimes are even more dictatorial, it is difficult to get reports concerning the suppression of the human rights of writers, but it can be said with certainty that such suppression goes on secretly.

I would like to close by reading a poem by Koh Eun:

> Even if we die
> we do not want to go to Paradise.
> If we die, if we die
> we will remain here in this country.
> When we die our bodies
> will become the earth, the water and the wind.
> That is all.
> Yet our spirit will become a
> new demon
> and we will remain here
> in the mountains and the rivers.

A PEOPLE'S MILITANT

FAWAZ TURKI

IT IS crucial that we begin with one basic premise: we cannot examine the plight of the writer in any part of the Third World—indeed in any part of the world—without a critical appraisal of the political realities in this writer's social system.

The problems of the Palestinian writer are in many ways unique, for not only does he belong to a society and a people who are threatened at their most vulnerable points of self-definition—the right to be free and the right to be the only determining force in their destiny—but he belongs to a society and a people who exist, for the most part, in isolation of their native ground. They are, because of that, a people and a society engaged in national struggle, in armed struggle, in the kind of struggle that has accompanied the transformations of peoples and societies in many parts of the Third World since the turn of the century. Paradoxically for the Palestinian writer, this is a source of both grief and joy.

To understand the problems of the Palestinian writer, it is important to examine the dialectical tension that has traditionally existed between him and his social system.

Everywhere in Palestinian society, everywhere in its poles of cognition between the inner and the outer, between the private and the public, the writer has always had a leading positional value. He is what Palestinians, in their vernacular, call *kateb el shaab,* a people's militant. His work is never created in isolation of the national struggle, but rather in cogent and manifold encounter with it. He is plunged, by choice, into the mainstream of the historical processes of his people. In effect, he does not only write about history. He writes history. Whether his work is belles lettres, poetry, drama or social commentary, it is rooted in the vivid immediacies of the national anguish, the national struggle, the national aspirations of the masses.

The work of the Palestinian writer, in other words, contains response and responsibility. Once he steps outside this particular skin of consciousness, he is no longer a *kateb el shaab*. He is no longer committed. He is no longer read.

The fact that the writer's imagination, the writer's commitments, are seen thus by Palestinian society, stems from the objective realities of that society: after more than eighty years of struggle for freedom and statehood, Palestinians have discovered in the work of the writer and the poet—especially the poet—a starting point to meaning, and to their place in that meaning. Very simply, his work is a reflection of their mythology of hope, of their subconscious formulations, of their introspections, of their metaphoric and pragmatic conjectures on national meaning.

In the dynamic of this interactive relationship, the writer, then, finds himself at the forefront of the struggle. He *is* at the forefront and as a consequence suffers. The price he pays for this role that he has chosen to play, structuring and being structured by the sensibility of struggle, is a terrible one indeed.

The Palestinian writer today finds himself located, like his own society, between the rock and the hard place, either under Israeli military occupation inside Palestine or in exile under the repressive regimes of the Arab world. In both cases, he is in confrontation with forces that, knowing of his positional value in Palestinian society, subject him to censorship, preventive detention, imprisonment, torture, and deportation.

To begin with, under Israeli military occupation writers are not allowed to organize in any fashion, under any circumstances, whether as unions, associations, congresses or even *nadis*—the clubs where writers have traditionally met to discuss their work. All literary output, from a short poem to a long fictional work, from an article to a play, must be submitted to the Israeli military governor's censors for approval. The military governor may not be gifted with literary acumen, but he is gifted with an eye for any reference—any remote reference—to the writer's political commitments, and for his particular political idiom. Any material the military governor does not like can be arbitrarily rejected for publication. If he does not like a poem, or part of a poem, or one line in a poem, he can do whatever he deems fit to that poem. Newspapers, magazines, and publishing houses can be closed down—as they have often been closed down—

for printing material that has not been submitted for censorship or that has infringed censorship laws.

Over the years, this situation has resulted in an interesting transformation in some of the literary output of many Palestinian writers. In an effort to prevent their imagination from remaining captive to the arbitrary laws of censorship imposed upon them by a foreign military occupation, Palestinian writers have resorted to the ploy of using allegorical and metaphoric references that are accessible to the cultural sensibility of the Palestinian reader but that may pass over the head of the Israeli authorities. In recent years, however, the military governor's headquarters have been getting wise to that—with the resulting increase in the instruments of censorship prevalent today. A poem dealing with the poet's undying love for a woman may not see publication because the Israeli military governor's censors would claim, often correctly, that the woman in question is Palestine. Sometimes, censorship can go to absurd or pathological extremes, as in the case of a fellow writer of mine, a poetess called Fadwa Toukane who lives on the West Bank, who had decided to call a forthcoming book of hers by a certain title followed by a question mark. The censor, in his wisdom, explained that her title—and that meant her entire book—would be approved only if the question mark was removed. It took weeks of negotiations to reach a compromise. The title would be approved if it was followed by an exclamation mark, not a question mark.

Censorship can take not only a pathological but also an ugly twist. In Palestine today, no writer is allowed to use the word "Palestine" in his writing. Indeed, a law was passed two years ago in the Israeli Knesset making it a crime, punishable by two years in jail, for a Palestinian to display, in his attire, let alone in his writing, the word "Palestine," or the Palestinian flag, or the term "Palestine Liberation Organization." Soon after the law was passed, the well-known Palestinian artist, Suleiman Mansour, had an exhibition of his work at an art gallery in the West Bank. One of his paintings was of a rose, simply a rose, whose petals were painted red, green, black, and white—the colors of the Palestinian flag. Before the day was out, Mansour's exhibition was closed down, his paintings were confiscated, and he himself was carted off to jail.

All of this is the light side of the oppression of Palestinian writers living and working under Israeli military occupation in Palestine, although Heaven knows no one should call this or any other kind of censorship of a writer's work "light." But we Palestinian writers call it light when we juxtapose it with the other kinds of oppression that we daily have to endure: harassment, imprisonment, and deportation.

The Palestinian writer is always under observation. There is a direct correlation between the degree of his activism and the kind of observation he is subjected to. The knock on the door, in the middle of the night, is all too common, and always takes place after the writer has given a reading, a lecture, or a poetry recital that the authorities did not like. Their excuse is always that he is "cooperating with terrorists." His house is searched and his manuscripts are confiscated. Virtually every major Palestinian writer in the West Bank and Gaza, as well as in pre-1948 Palestine (where the Palestinians who live there now are called Israeli citizens) has been at one time or another imprisoned. Or placed under preventive detention. Or under house arrest. Or confined to their towns. Incarceration, in this case, always implies abuse—physical abuse.

The well-known Palestinian poet, Saleh Baransi, who lives in Israel as an "Israeli citizen," is the founder of the Land Movement in Palestine. It is essentially a spiritual and literary movement that calls for an examination of the exquisite nexus binding man to his environment in a coherent biospheric relationship in Palestine. Baransi spent thirteen years in Israeli jails. And when he was released, in 1974, he spent another two years under house arrest. Sabri Jiryis and Habib el Kahwaji, two prominent Palestinian writers, allegedly Israeli citizens, were deported. Others, like the poet Mahmoud Darwish, found it so difficult to write that they left voluntarily. Others still, who have chosen to remain in their country regardless of the conditions, like Samih el Kassem, Tawfic Zayyad, Mahmoud Dassoufi, Jamal Kawar, Emile Habibi, Salem Joubran, and Abdel Latif Akel, have all been behind bars at one time or another.

That is the plight of the writer under occupation in the West Bank/Gaza and in pre-1948 Palestine.

The plight of the Palestinian writer in exile, in different parts of the Arab world, is actually identical to what every Arab writer endures. He is not, in other words. singled out because of his national identity.

As is well known, the Arab world is ruled predominantly by insecure, repressive, and violent regimes whose continued existence derives from suppression, by state power, of any kind of democratic dissent; by regimes whose survival, for the most part against the mass sentiment, is underwritten by either one of the two superpowers. Why Arab society finds itself under such conditions is not, of course, our concern here. But obviously, it has to do with the colonial experience that the Third World, of which the Arab world is a part, has had to endure for something like five hundred years, and with the fact that decolonization, when it came, was a process of continuing colonization (under a different guise) undertaken by indigenous landlords subservient to the interests of foreign powers.

Suffice it to say here that the Palestinian writer, like the Arab writer in general, must publish material that is responsive only to the political paradigm in the country where he lives. The moment he becomes, by virtue of his being both craftsman and militant, an adversarial current in his host state, he becomes the object of censorship, abuse, imprisonment, and worse.

I said at the beginning of my presentation that working under these wretched conditions can be, and often is, a source of joy as well as grief for the Palestinian writer.

The joy comes from the knowledge that, by being part of the whole landscape of awareness of his people's struggle, the writer in Palestine is pre-empting tomorrow with his dream. And he knows, as a *kateb el shaab,* a people's militant, that in the end it is the people who wake up from his dream, enriched and revitalized by it.

And in this, I believe, lies the liberating function of the creative impulse: its capacity to encapsulate within its individual consciousness the principal postures of national life.

In many drastic ways we err, therefore, in ascribing to the writer, any writer, in any part of the world, a primarily or straightforwardly traditional function—say the reflection in his work of the diverse levels of cognitive awareness in his reality. We err even more drastically when we ascribe this role to Third World writers, whether they are from Palestine or El Salvador, whose social systems are in struggle for national liberation. For at its intimate center, a society like that is in struggle for meaning. Certainly, in national struggle, where the stuff of history is every man's currency of rational exchange, a nation is being thrust beyond its fixed meaning. It is re-experiencing itself. It is transforming and revitalizing its creative centers of apprehension and query.

Surely the writer could not ask for a richer, a more vitalizing array of material to draw on for his work. And who is the writer, after all, having taken the commitments he did, that he should single himself out from all other beings in his social system and demand that his oppression be lifted? He is demanding that *all* oppression should be lifted. That is the nature of his work. And the act of writing is nothing if it is not an act of commitment. And literature is nothing if it does not outlast oppression. If it does not outlast death.

A COMMENT

JACOBO TIMERMAN: The description by my brother Palestinian—as you called me yesterday your brother Israeli—of discrimination, oppression, and censorship by the Israeli military government in the West Bank is absolutely true. There is no question about that, and there is no justification. Not even the state of war justifies the way the military government is dealing with the control of expression, and the national identity, of the Palestinian people. This description is correct. But there is something important missing in his description. And that is to stress that the people who are fighting most openly for the rights of the Palestinians are the Israeli democrats, including myself. I have read, in the Israeli press, in newspapers like the Jerusalem *Post,* much stronger statements demanding freedom of expression for the Palestinian than the statement made by our Palestinian poet here today. And I have read, in the Israeli press, better descriptions of the persecution and discrimination against the Palestinians *in the Arab countries* than I have seen from any Palestinian writer. So we must be very precise, not only in describing persecution and repression, but also in describing who is fighting against persecution and repression. Because a key to the solution of the Middle East problem, and the Palestinian problem, is to see if the people who are fighting for peace and democracy can talk to each other and produce peace and democracy in the Middle East.

A great number of Israeli writers and newspapermen are ready to proclaim a Palestinian state. They are ready to speak and deal with members of the PLO. They are ready—and they have done it—to proclaim the right of the Palestinians to have a Palestinian state. But I haven't seen, from the PLO or from any of the Palestinian writers and journalists, a readiness to recognize the right of the Israelis to exist and to have an Israeli state. We are trying in Israel to make a bridge with the Palestinian people, and we are rejected by the Palestinians. And this is very important to keep clearly in mind.

A PERVERSION OF THE MIND AND SOUL

MONGO BETI

IF WE take into account the relatively small number of inhabitants, there is no doubt that Africa is the continent where human rights are the most frequently and seriously violated.

This is essentially for two reasons. On the one hand, our countries are experiencing very rapid and profound transformations, because they are among the most underdeveloped from the point of view of economic and technical organization. Thus, it is necessary for these countries to "catch up" rapidly. As a consequence, traditional structures are being drastically modified—which means, obviously, that these structures are very fragile. Adventurers can easily seize power and retain it for many years, sometimes for a great many years, with no other method of government than violence.

On the other hand—and this reason seems to me a much more serious one—the vast majority of African republics still find themselves under the real, if not legal, domination of major foreign capitalist or communist powers. This is notably the case with central Africa, particularly Cameroon and Gabon, and France; it is the case with Zaire and the U.S.A.; it is the case with Ethiopia and the U.S.S.R.; it is the case with South Africa and all the Western powers, including West Germany. For if Africans are poor, Africa is rich.

As one might expect, the major foreign powers implanted in Africa defend their interests, and in doing so they do not hesitate to commit any crime. In particular, they help dictators to seize power and retain it by violence. And while the African dictators subject their populations to various forms of violence, the large Western multinational corporations discreetly pillage our wealth: lumber; oil, to an ever increasing extent; strategic minerals such as uranium; and many other minerals, such as gold and copper.

Now, the maintenance of order signifies an extremely cruel repression of all opponents. This ranges from arbitrary arrest to the extermination of whole categories of the population, and runs the gamut of imprisonment without trial, torture, concentration camps, and pure and simple disappearance.

In order to illustrate these statements, it is useful to cite a few names. You have undoubtedly heard of a certain Idi Amin Dada; you have also heard of a certain Emperor Bokassa; perhaps you have even heard of a man called Francis Commasios Guehma. In their day, these three individuals were stars of the Western press. However, they resemble—to use a familiar proverb—the trees which hide the forest. For we can easily name other dictators in Africa, and there are few African countries which have not been theaters of the practices that have just been mentioned. I am going to mention a few leaders who are particularly "muscle-bound" and who are not one bit less sinister than the three men just named, the difference being that they wear the mask of moderation.

We can begin with my own country, Cameroon, which has been governed for twenty years by a man named Mr. Ahmadou Ahidjo. In this country, we can cite immediately the cases of two people who have been imprisoned since 1961, without trial, without explanation, and without the slightest hope of being released. And why? Because they are *suspected* of having been militants in a clandestine party—and that suffices.

I will mention another great African leader, General Eyadéma of Togo. He is a past master of the art of kidnapping his opponents while they are abroad, particularly in France. General Eyadéma was recently involved in another exploit. A Togolese intellectual by the name of Mr. Midi Ouen was arrested in Gabon, where he was teaching, for trying to publish a satirical story about the President of Gabon. The Gabonese police put Mr. Midi Ouen on the first plane for Togo. When he arrived in Togo, General Eyadéma had him put in prison. It is not known why. When word of the incident started to go around and the press threatened to publish it, General Eyadéma deported Mr. Midi Ouen to Benin. And by decree of General Eyadéma, Mr. Midi Ouen ceased to be a citizen of Togo.

Since I have mentioned the President of Gabon, a Mr. Bongo, I would like you to note that he, too, has a specialty, namely murdering his political opponents when they are abroad.

That will do then (without speaking of other regimes) as a brief summary of the state of human rights in Africa. It was indispensable that I make these things clear at the beginning, because I would like to tell you how the African situation is experienced by an African who no longer lives in Africa, but rather in Europe.

For some time, I have been increasingly persuaded that in the unique case of Africa what must be condemned most is the perversion of the mind and soul surrounding the crimes I have enumerated rather than the crimes themselves. I would like to explain this, because it is something of a paradox.

You should be aware that abominable prejudices have weighed down on Africans for centuries. These prejudices, particularly in the West, have prepared public opinion to accept other prejudices, in a sort of vicious circle. There are crimes which are considered monstrous when they take place on other continents, but (at least in the eyes of an African intellectual who attempts to understand the actions of Westerners) it seems that nuanced and even indulgent explanations are frequently offered when it is a question of Africa. The violations of human rights in Africa resemble violations of human rights elsewhere. Yet the Westerner, the European, without going so far as to deny the African the right to have these rights, regards these violations with a certain perplexity, a certain amount of doubt. In particular, this doubt is quite widespread in France, in all the political parties, in all the social classes, without exception.

How, then, does this perversion manifest itself in France? It manifests itself in the media by a selective silence which greatly surprises the African who has just arrived in France. Newspaper readers and television viewers are carefully kept up to date about the exactions of the Argentinian generals, about the violence perpetrated by the masters of El Salvador, about the massacres of Indians in Guatemala, and about the events in Afghanistan. However, the same French newspaper reader and the same French television viewer—the situation is no different in most other Western countries—remains totally ignorant of what is happening in Gabon, for example, or in Cameroon: that is, in those African republics which are "closely tied to France," as it is discreetly said. People are very well informed in France about the sufferings of the inhabitants of violent countries, except for those countries in which France has major interests.

This perversion manifests itself also in the ideological domain.

Thus, when a scandal explodes which is too difficult to dismiss, such as the massacre of the schoolchildren in Central Africa, it is with surprise and even consternation that we hear the so-called authorized voices of the major newspapers formulate exceedingly nuanced judgments about the matter—judgments which suggest that certain peoples, such as Africans, either because they are divided into tribes, or because they are poor, or because they speak un-Christian languages, must first of all prove their aptitude for freedom, as if freedom were not inalienable.

These are arguments which reappear quite frequently. One can present Western audiences with the facts about dictatorships that are just as bloody as the one in Chile—against which the European Left has been waging a relentless campaign for years—but there will always be someone who will ask, "Yes, but aren't you talking about people who are divided into tribes?" By this is meant that a man living in a tribal framework cannot be as sensitive to the privation of freedom as someone living in a middle-class apartment in the center of a city.

This perversion manifests itself equally in the midst of organizations which are supposed to defend liberty. I will make use of the opportunity offered me here in Toronto at this congress in aid of Amnesty International to relate an anecdote which concerns me as well as Amnesty.

I must reveal to you that I am probably the only person to have been expelled from Amnesty International for his opinions. I was an active member of the French section of Amnesty International from 1976 to 1978, which was the year I was expelled for having said and written that the French section of Amnesty had shown an enormous amount of accommodation toward the francophone dictators in Africa. Abominable things could happen there—I brought a number of political trials in Cameroon to the attention of the French section, for example—without the French section taking any action at all. Therefore, I wrote in some marginal militant newspapers that the leaders of the French section of Amnesty International were far too easy on those francophone dictatorships in Africa that were linked to France.

For stating this, I was expelled from the organization, even though the facts were obvious: the woman who was president of the French section of Amnesty International was at the same time the editor of a government publication which specialized in praising African dictators. My expulsion from Amnesty International was itself rather suspect, for I had no lawyer to represent me. Indeed, I did not even know that I was to be judged. The French section of Amnesty International thus committed the crime they condemned in others: they were both judge and accuser.

I relate this anecdote in order to demonstrate how very difficult it is to defend human rights in Africa in a neocolonialist situation.

The great difficulty for us, for those writers who militate with the pen or otherwise for human rights in black Africa, lies in the general situation of francophone Africa as an area of the world which is not dominated directly but rather indirectly and skillfully: those who dominate hide behind African facades, behind African presidents. And it is quite in vain that the press in the former colonizing countries proclaim: "But these are all matters you can settle among yourselves!" They know very well that there is no truth in this.

A last word: as far as Amnesty International is concerned, the French section has begun to do some good work, perhaps as a result of my own unfortunate incident. If my trials have contributed to this in some small way, I am satisfied.

—Translated by Donald Bruce

COLONIALISM AND LANGUAGE: A DISCUSSION

LEON WHITESON: One point which seems central to the question of writers is language. Writers from ex-French colonies write in French; writers from ex-English colonies write in English. Inherent in each language are its own particular structures; it embodies certain ideas and notions about the world. The writer who writes in that language has to struggle very hard to overcome them. Often, as I think Nadine Gordimer pointed out, one of the worst effects of colonialism was that the whites accepted as a given that black culture was inferior. For example in Rhodesia where I grew up we learned English in the schools, but then we had a choice between French or Afrikaans. I grew up in an area where Ndebele, which is a Zulu language, is spoken, but they didn't teach it. It was not considered a language.

And that leads you to the audience. In Africa, which has a very high level of illiteracy because often the colonial powers weren't interested in educating Africans, the African writer is speaking, often, to a public that is semiliterate, in a language which is not their native tongue and carries a white man's view of the world. French and English organize the world in terms of concepts which are white-minded. Whether you're aware of it or not when you write, it has to be dealt with.

It's a form of profound colonization of the mind, which is very, very hard to throw off. In many countries which have become independent, an attempt is made to retrieve their own culture and throw off that sense of inferiority inherent in the European attitude. Yet when they draw from a different set of concepts, they then have to translate them into French or English, which are the two dominant languages that "took" in western Africa, and that makes for very particular difficulties. It's like using a tool that was never made for your mind, or your soul. It comes out of a different kind of soul, a different kind of mind. And that is one of the human rights: the right to write in a language which comes out of your own soul and wasn't given to you by somebody else. It is a human right that is hard to define or clarify or even fight for; it's a subtle deprivation of human rights in that respect.

A STATEMENT FROM THE FLOOR: I think that without intending to, you simplified the question. Very few African countries—in fact, none—are homogeneous as far as the vernacular languages are concerned. In India the great issue after independence was which language was to become the national language? We have seen in Canada that the existence of only two languages is deeply divisive. There are some fourteen major vernacular languages in India, and they've not resolved this question yet. The main result of the controversy in India has been the slow death of English, which was the only lingua franca—and still is the only means by which all educated Indians—and I don't simply mean anglicized—can communicate with each other. I wonder how members of the panel, like Mr. Zwelonke, for example, would solve this issue of language when considering the question of the future Azania, because, as we know, there are several major vernacular languages in the country that would be Azania. Does one ask oneself at this stage if this is not a major roadblock in the process of becoming an African country with some homogeneous character? I think it is. It's a mistake to leave a rather easy sort of equation between reviving our native language and achieving full spiritual independence; because of course the colonial grid that cut through Africa has cut right across the old (if you'll allow me to use the word) "tribal" boundaries.

DANIEL MDLULI ZWELONKE: That's true; the question of the language is a very difficult one. Up to now, the national liberation movements have tended to use English most of the time. Only when they go to the grass roots, to talk to the people, do they talk in the languages that the people understand. But we know that for the moment the oppressive regime is using these ethnic languages to divide the people: the Bantu education system is used in such a way that Zulus speaking Setswana should think themselves different from those who speak Sotho, and so on. The people there try hard to challenge this divisive method of the government. In the national liberation movement, for instance, two languages are now recognized: Zulu and Sotho. Even the national anthem is sung in these two languages. Many other dialects are appended to these, so that those whose language is akin to Zulu come to speak in that way, and others come to speak Sotho.

The trend toward language unification started with King Shaka, when the Zulu nation was forged. And simultaneously, Moshweshwe in Lesotho did the same thing by bringing together the clan groups under one language group. Now we are committed to the use of two languages, because Zulu and Sotho are quite different. It is one thing we are very careful about. When a language is imposed on a people, one group emerges dominant. Or if a government adopts one language of one group and takes it as the official language, then the government has disregarded the other languages. This is what has happened in Ethiopia, for instance, where the Amharic language has been imposed. What we would do is to educate and persuade the people to accept a growing and developing language, a future language of Azania.

As far as English is concerned, I think 90 per cent of the African people don't use it; they may not even be able to read it. So that to think of English as the language that would unite the people in Azania is false.

PART THREE

WRITING AND ACTION

Journalism and Human Rights

Journalists and Human Rights

A NEW CRIME

JACOBO TIMERMAN

THE SUBJECT of this panel is journalism and human rights. Of course, there are different aspects to this subject. I will summarize very briefly the aspects which I feel are the most important.

First, what do you do as an independent journalist in a country where there is a military dictatorship, and persecution of free expression, and the systematic violation of human rights? This was the case in Argentina, and it was not very easy—it never is—to draw a line, to understand your duty as a journalist and as a human being.

The situation in Argentina is quite horrible: a government decided to exterminate all opposition, or what they thought was the opposition, in a way that was absolutely unusual in history. They decided to create a new category of punishment: disappearance. This is a new crime, and up to now there has been no legal approach to this kind of crime. After the war, the Western countries found that the Nazis had invented the destruction of whole populations. Not knowing what to do with this kind of crime, they convened a group of lawyers that in 1948 created the notion of genocide. It was described by these lawyers as a crime against humanity. That means that nobody involved in this crime has the right to live in any country of the world and not be extradited. This was the only new crime that appeared in our century—up to the moment when the Argentine Government created a new kind of crime, the crime of disappearance. They kidnap whole families, destroy their bodies, and declare that the victims never existed—and if they never existed, there is no crime.

At the end of January of this year, we had a meeting, in the Senate of France, sponsored by the International Federation of Catholic Lawyers. We were trying to establish a legal notion of this new crime and trying to have it approved by some kind of international institution. In 1948 it was very easy to have the United Nations recognize the crime of genocide, because the United Nations was an institution built up by the Western countries who fought against Nazism. But now, if we want to have this new crime of disappearance converted into the category of a crime against humanity and recognized by the United Nations, we will find—and we did find—that it is absolutely impossible for the United Nations to approve a thing like that. From the beginning, we knew that the Soviet Union would veto any kind of condemnation of the Argentine Government, because they are allies at the moment; and that it would be impossible to get the countries of the Third World to approve anything against Argentina, because Argentina is a full member of the Conference of Non-Aligned Countries. We are still trying to have disappearance—the crime of the missing people—recognized as a crime against humanity, by all the churches, by all the religions, by all institutions, professions, and so on.

In Argentina there were probably one thousand guerrilla fighters when the armed forces took over in 1976. In five years, they killed thirty-five thousand people in their war against the subversive terrorists. The armed forces of Argentina *created* what our greatest living writer, Jorge Luis Borges, described as the terrorism of the state. There was no censorship in those years in Argentina, after the armed forces took over; but according to the Commission of Families of Missing Journalists, one hundred journalists have disappeared. So it was a kind of biological censorship. Many times, like many of my colleagues, I had to make a decision about what to do in these conditions. People who had fought against the Nazis in Germany usually said that in these conditions you could go underground or you had to go into exile. But for an independent newspaper, this is practically impossible. Many journalists who were part of a political party, or of some other kind of organization, could go underground together with their political party, or they could go into exile. But somebody who's working on a newspaper that is open to the public, legally published, has to make another kind of decision: whether he is going to accept self-censorship, to close his eyes, or whether he is going to try to do something. If he decides to do something, it is very difficult to define—every day if you have a daily newspaper—exactly what you are going to do.

Of the ten national newspapers in Argentina at that time, only two newspapers were badly persecuted, my own and the Buenos Aires *Herald,* an English newspaper—in different ways, of course. I had no ambassador who represented me, but the editors of the Buenos Aires *Herald* were British citizens; they had the British ambassador supporting them, and they could have their fight in quite a different way.

This is one decision a journalist has to make when he is independent, in a country where the violation of human rights is so horrible. History teaches us that in every country something like that has happened, in the Italy of Mussolini or the Spain of Franco or the Germany of Hitler. The majority of the population, as well as the majority of the journalists, accepted in one way or another a compromise with reality, accepted self-censorship, agreed to survive and not to know—not only not to tell, but also not to know, and sometimes, as was once said in Argentina, they even agreed not to think.

A second aspect of the fight for human rights and the role of journalism is how the international press describes a situation like that in Argentina. Very recently, at Harvard University, there was a symposium of all the Neiman fellows. The Harvard Neiman Fellowship is an institution for journalists. In a discussion of the coverage of foreign news, the question was raised, why was it only after Timerman wrote his book and it was published that so many people realized what the situation in Argentina actually was? What was happening for four years that the international press could not transmit it to large segments of populations in many countries? All the countries that excel in freedom of the press could not really express the horror that was going on in Argentina. This is a difficult question, because we know that many newspapers in the world covered the Argentinian situation; but nevertheless, they could never transmit the horrors exactly the way they were happening, because there were no official sources.

Mort Rosenbloom, a foreign correspondent who was head of the Associated Press agency in Buenos Aires and then editor of the *International Herald Tribune* in Paris, wrote a book about his experiences. In one of the chapters devoted to Argentina, he tells the story of having lunch in a fancy restaurant with one of his connections in the Argentine Army. This man told him that the day before, they had killed a man and a woman from Uruguay, and they were holding their two little children, a boy and a girl. If he—Mort Rosenbloom was married and had no children—if he wanted them, he could have them; if not, they would have to send these children to some other place. Explaining this conversation, Rosenbloom writes that being the local head of Associated Press, he could not send a telegram about it, because the head office would ask him about his source; and of course, he could not mention the source. This is another of the problems that we face in covering such horrible news.

The third aspect of this situation is what the international institutions of journalists are going to do about the missing journalists in Argentina. When there are twenty thousand people missing in Argentina, one hundred journalists is not a big number. But it is a big number when you take into account how many journalists work in Argentina. In that context, one hundred journalists missing in Argentina is the first genocide of journalists known in our century. It is only comparable with the killing of the Jewish writers by Stalin at the beginning of the fifties. During meetings with the International Federation of Newspaper Publishers in Jerusalem, with the Inter-American Press Association in San Diego, with the International Press Institute in Nairobi, in many other places, I pointed out this problem. I said that we really need an international forum to discuss it, a kind of Nuremburg trial to discuss, to *do* something about the first genocide of journalists in history. And up to now, not even we journalists have been able to come up with an answer to this problem.

So you see we have apparently three problems in connection with human rights and the role of the journalist. First, what a journalist can do in the horrible situation of a country in which human rights are violated, when he's only a newspaperman who doesn't belong to any of the powers of the country, any of the political or military powers. Second, we have the problem of whether international coverage of these horrors can ever really show the world what is going on. And third, what are we going to do about a country like Argentina, where journalists are experiencing a biological censorship—they are either just killed, or kidnapped, or they are missing—and there is no way to try to defend not only their right of expression but their right to live.

THE LOST BY-LINES

Drawn from the files of Amnesty International and the magazine *Index on Censorship,* the following list includes the names of seventy-five journalists and writers who have disappeared in Argentina, whose fate is unknown, and whose families are prepared to publicize their disappearance. The dates following the names are the dates of disappearance.

Claudio Adur. Freelance journalist. 11/11/76.
Lucina Alvarez de Barros. Editor of *Barrilete* magazine. 5/7/76.
Lidia Alvarez de Sadot. 9/29/76.
Maria Amadio. Editor of *Dimensión* magazine. 3/30/76.
Marcos Arocena. Uruguayan writer. 7/9/76.
Juan Azcone. Freelance journalist. 5/15/77.
Rolando Baradino. Television journalist. Date unknown.
Oscar Barros. Journalist on *Barrilete*. 5/7/76.
Maria Bedoian. Magazine subeditor. 6/12/77.
Horacio Bertholet. 10/1/76.
Guillermo Betianin. Journalist on *Noticias*. 5/7/76.
Victor Boichenko. Writer. 4/4/76.
Miguel Bustos. Journalist and writer. 5/30/76.
Juan Capdepont. Journalist. 6/78.
Aldo Casadidio. Political journalist. 12/7/76.
Conrado Ceretti. Freelance. 7/27/76.
Ines Cobo. Journalist. 9/1/76.
Haroldo Conti. Journalist and writer. 5/5/76.
Luis Cordoba. Journalist. 7/27/78.
Julian Delgado. Journalist on *Cronista Comercial*. 6/4/78.
Beatriz d'Elia. Writer. 3/77.
Hector Demarchi. Journalist on *Cronista Comercial*. 8/5/76.
José Espinosa. Journalist. 1/8/78.
Rodolfo Fernandez Pondal. Associate editor of *Ultima Clave*. 8/5/77.
Jorge Foulkes. Journalist. 4/24/78.
Marcelo Gelman. Journalist on *Gente* and *Noticias*. 8/24/76.
Raymundo Gleyzer. Journalist and filmmaker. 5/25/76.
Cecilia Gomez. Agency journalist. 12/31/78.
Alberto Gorrini. Photographer and journalist. 6/3/77.
Claudio Grandi. Writer. 6/22/76.
Felix Granovsky. Journalist. 11/19/76.
Luis Guagnini. Correspondent for foreign papers. 12/21/77.
Diana Guerrero. Editor of *Difusión*. 7/27/76.

Mario Hernandez. Editor of *El Decamisado*. 5/12/76.
Mario Herrera. Subeditor on *Confirmado*. 11/76.
Juan Higa. Correspondent for Japanese paper. 5/7/77.
Hugo Idelman. Journalist. 9/29/76.
Mario Ikonicoff. Freelance subeditor. 6/12/77.
Santiago Illa. Journalist. 6/12/76.
Juan Jordan. Bolivian student journalist. 1/17/78.
Wilson Kehoe. Journalist. 6/13/77.
Carlos Lagorio. Journalist. 1/27/77.
Miguel Lizazo. Journalist on *La Causa Peronista*. 4/76.
Susan Lugones. Freelance journalist. 12/24/77.
Hector Marghetich. Student journalist. 8/19/76.
Eduardo Marin. Journalist on *La Nación*. 5/14/77.
Elsa Martinez. Journalist. 5/31/78.
Mario Martinez. Freelance journalist. 1/23/77.
Susana Medina de Bertholet. Freelance journalist. 10/1/76.
Luis Monaco. Freelance journalist. 1/11/78.
Liliana Montelli. Graduate of journalism school. 6/20/76.
Cristina Morandini Huespe. Student journalist. 9/18/77.
Daniel Moyano Vega. Journalist on *Los Andes*. 5/12/76.
Juan Nazar. Journalist. 3/21/77.
Hector Oesterheld. Television scriptwriter. 6/77.
Carlos Perez. Journalist and editor. 4/76.
Marta Perez. Journalist on *La Razón*. 4/76.
Rafael Perrota. Director of *Cronista Comercial*. 6/77.
Enrique Piera. Editor of *El País* of Montevideo, Uruguay. 7/13/76.
Luis Piris. Journalist and psychologist. 7/76.
Enrique Raab. Journalist on *La Opinión* and *Primera Plana*. 4/16/77.
José Ramos. Newspaper and television journalist. 11/1/76.
Alcira Rios De Cordoba. Journalist. 7/27/78.
Edgardo Sajón. Journalist on *La Opinión*. 4/1/77.
Maria San Martin de Valetti. Writer. 7/1/77.
Roberto Santoro. Founder of *Barrilete*. 6/1/77.
Juan Satragno. Journalist on *La Nación*. 2/26/78.
Victor Seib. Journalist. 7/30/76.
Angel Stival. Journalist. 8/7/76.
Eduardo Suarez. Freelance journalist. 8/12/76.

Virginia Suarez. Student journalist. 5/13/76.
Patricia Villa. Agency journalist. 8/14/76.
Enrique Walker. Freelance journalist. 7/17/76.
Rodolfo Walsh. Freelance journalist. 3/25/77.
Tilo Wenner. Director of *El Actuál*. 3/26/76.

JOURNALISM IN CHINA

JOHN FRASER

I WANT to sketch briefly some problems of journalism in China, which next to Canada is the country I know most about.

First, there's the official Chinese press. It's too simplistic to dismiss it as an arm of the government. It is that, but because of the remarkable factional and ideological warfare that has gone on in the thirty years since Mao Zedong took over, there has been a great deal of repression *on the official level.* Many of the journalists who were working on official newspapers and also semiofficial newspapers which didn't feel the weight of government control so heavily up to the beginning of the Cultural Revolution, became notable victims in the Cultural Revolution itself. Those who survived are now back in power, and those who were notable journalists during the Cultural Revolution are now themselves notable victims. That in itself is a fascinating twist on the problem of being a journalist in China. It is the one thing I got out of my time there: no one seems to learn what the repression of each other does.

With that overview of the official press, it was very intriguing that the major form of protest to emerge after the Cultural Revolution and after the death of Chairman Mao should be the so-called unofficial journals and wall posters—and wall posters are simply newspapers put up on a wall. Quite often, the unofficial journals would first have their articles put up, on large pieces of cardboard, on the walls of various cities. They're printed rather crudely on the most primitive kind of copying machines, usually in someone's basement or apartment.

The protesters are called dissidents now, although I think that's a wrong phrase because it brings to mind a Western concept of the dissident, like Solzhenitsyn—a lone individual standing up against the might of the state. Most of the Chinese activists I saw weren't like that. They were more in the Chinese tradition of protest, trying to work to correct the system from within the system, either having allies within the leadership or making the kind of statements that they hoped would somehow be within the bounds of permissible debate. Repeatedly, throughout Chinese history, they've discovered there is no safe quarter, but nevertheless that's what they were trying to do.

It started in Peking in 1978 and was allowed to go on unfettered for about four months. And then although the young journalists, the unofficial journalists, were deemed a tiny minority, the full weight of state oppression came down on them nevertheless. No one understands better than the Chinese Communist party the power of a small group of committed idealists. That was, in fact, what they were once, and I think that's one of the reasons why you find them coming down so hard on any sign of a protest movement arising in China.

The interesting thing about writers during the Xidan Democracy Wall period—and that includes writers in all the major cities in China—was that their age ranged from twenty-four or twenty-five to thirty-five. That meant they'd all been activists during the Cultural Revolution; in a number of cases, they'd been rather ferocious Red Guards. Wei Jingsheng, probably the most notable of the activists, told me once that what he had done to some of his teachers was something he could never forgive himself or forget for the rest of his life. He understood fully the politics of the day and how he and many other young people had been manipulated and betrayed, and his campaign was to try and make other Chinese people understand this. He saw himself as a journalist, because he saw journalism as the most effective means to communicate the problems in Chinese society. He engaged the government—or tried to engage the government—in a debate. He started off by looking at the ferocious campaign going on then in China to criticize the Gang of Four and Lin Biao (who was the former Defense Minister, and rose to great heights, supposedly to be Mao's chosen successor until he fell from grace after a factional fight: he was supposed to have died in an airplane accident). Wei Jingsheng asked, how can you isolate the criticism, how can you look simply at Lin Biao, who held sway from 1966 to 1971, and the Gang of Four, who held sway from 1971 to 1976, without examining the system that allowed them to gain such power and to hold on to it for so long? But that's what you're not allowed to do: if you're making

criticism, you must confine it to specific things. He couldn't understand how these monsters (as many Chinese people would call
them), who gained control for nearly half the period the Chinese
communists have been in power, could be considered an aberration.
Weren't they simply a natural product? By the time his arguments
were starting to build a following, the government came down
heavily on him and his supporters. He was made an example of.

Before I stop, I want to put in a bit about the role of Western
journalists in China. Most of us, no matter how much we tried to
study the circumstances people live under in China, came to that
country rather ignorant, and certainly ignorant of the potential of
people there to speak out. When I first arrived, it was considered a
practical impossibility for anyone even to think of criticizing the record of Chairman Mao or the present government, and by the time I
left it was patently clear that there were many people who were
willing to do so. The irony of it was that of the forty-five to fifty
accredited foreign journalists during my time there, from 1977 to
1979, only six maintained any kind of contact with these people—
even after it was possible. All you had to do, at least in Peking, was
to go down to the Democracy Wall, in the beginning of the movement, and at the very least you'd find some English-language students wanting to practice their English who would translate the wall
posters, and it was also a chance to meet many of the activists. But
most Western journalists, for a variety of reasons, found this a very
threatening experience. I don't really understand all the reasons for
this. I know some of them: part of it is that Western journalists are
united with academics and theologians in having a horror of being
found inconsistent. A lot of the things that we were finding out about
Chinese people were diametrically opposed to what we'd been led to
believe. And that wasn't very comfortable, because one had to go
back on much of what one had written.

Another reason was simple fear, and self-censorship. I went over
there succeeding a journalist who had been thrown out—Ross Munro,
the seventh correspondent for the *Globe and Mail*—and I went over
cocky as hell. I was going to prove to them that nothing was going to
frighten me, and nothing did—until my wife and I started getting Chinese friends. I realized too slowly that the government was aware of
most of the people I was in contact with, and that anything I wrote
that obviously came from Chinese sources might be traced. So one

has on one's conscience the possibility that one can do people a lot of harm. You have to take a whole bunch of things that you get trained to do in the West—aggressively going after a story, and bravely putting forth all the facts—and try to consider what in fact your bravery and your aggressiveness are going to do to a number of real people. That confronts you, head on, with self-censorship in a very real way. I don't know the answer to that one. In any authoritarian or totalitarian country, this problem is faced by any Western journalist with a conscience.

OUTLINE OF UN-AMERICAN ACTIVITIES:
A PEN AMERICAN CENTER REPORT

ALLEN GINSBERG

WHAT I am here for is to discuss the harassment and sabotage of the underground press in the United States during the years 1968 to 1972, and up to the present, by the FBI, the CIA, the army intelligence, Narcotics Bureau agents, the state police and local police, local red squads. Around 1968 there was a large movement of underground intellectuality, and there was an enormous press: 400 to 500 newspapers scattered all over the country from Florida to San Francisco to New York, and in Canada also. You had some really great newspapers, the *Georgia Strait,* and in Montreal *Logos,* which was one of the most beautifully printed. It was obvious to anybody who was involved with the underground press that there was also a large-scale campaign of harassment, a government conspiracy to suppress the alternative media. And so as a member of the New York chapter of PEN—I was a member of the Freedom to Write Committee from the mid-sixties and still am—I asked for authority to begin assembling information on the harassment of the underground press by the FBI and other agencies.

I began collecting newspaper clippings, anecdotes, copies of the underground press that were busted, larger-scale surveys from the University of Missouri journalism school. I interviewed a lot of people and circulated an open letter asking for information to be sent to the PEN club through the Coordinating Council of Literary Magazines. So actually there was a network to receive information, and one central place to get it. This book, called *Un-American Activities: PEN American Center Report: Campaign Against the Underground Press,* is primarily a sort of white paper by the PEN club; it has that weight and authority.

The reason PEN was interested was that the underground press, of course, is writing, but the underground media in America serve as a vehicle for avant-garde literature as well. Amiri Baraka published a great deal, and was also under attack by the FBI, both in his print and in his person. Charles Bukowski first published in the underground press; he is not perhaps so well known here, but is a giant literary hero in Italy and in Germany. William S. Burroughs was first interviewed extensively in the New York *Rat* by Jeff Shero (later known as Jeff Nightbyrd) who, having been driven out of New York by the FBI, went and founded the Austin *Rag*. Gregory Corso published in the underground press, I published extensively, both poems and prose, Norman Mailer published in the alternative media. And Ed Sanders, who had earlier had the rock-and-roll group The Fugs, edited and published in the underground press. So actually, there was a large-scale literary movement representing subculture, or what was called "alternative culture."

What we found when we actually surveyed the field and took individual case histories and compiled and compared them was that there *was* a systematic campaign of harassment, though it needed very little encouragement, because J. Edgar Hoover (FBI Chief) already was willing to use force and violence and subterfuge and illegality to stamp out what he thought were un-American opinions.

The methods were as follows.

First, there was harassment of distributors. The distributor for the New York *Rat* was called into the FBI and told it was a subversive newspaper and that he would be in trouble if he kept distributing. So distribution was curtailed. That was one example; it happened all over the country.

There was harassment of printers. A fellow in Milwaukee who printed underground newspapers for the entire Midwest was constantly harassed by the FBI. They would also call up his aboveground clients and send anonymous letters to them, forcing him to move from city to city to continue printing. He held out, and finally, years later, there was a long exposé in a bunch of magazines, because his case was so singular and the harassment had been so official and so blatant.

There was harassment of vendors in almost every city. While regular newsboys were selling newspapers on the street corners, stands where the underground newspapers were distributed were seized.

Vendors were arrested on charges of distributing obscenity or vending without a license or blocking traffic. In no case were any of these vendors ever convicted of anything, but it was a harassment by constant arrests.

Then there was harassment of publishers. Older people in the community who were publishing the newspapers would be the subject of anonymous letters written to fellow businessmen, chambers of commerce, university trustees, parents, city councils. Usually they were signed "An Outraged Taxpayer" or "An Outraged Citizen" or "An Outraged Alumnus" or whatever. And these outraged alumni, citizens, taxpayers, were a stereotype for a sneaky FBI agent, on government time, with government money, writing poison-pen letters.

Harassment of advertisers was another technique—poison-pen letters written by an annoyed or "anguished citizen," or "outraged taxpayer," to advertisers to discourage them from contributing to the underground press coffers. Or FBI agents would simply visit an advertiser and say that it was acting un-American by supporting the Milwaukee *Sentinel,* or the Atlanta underground newspaper, which had the most brilliant title of all: *Great Speckled Bird.*

There were FBI conversations with trustees and presidents of colleges, urging the college to ban the distribution of such smut and un-American matter as was supposed to pervade the underground newspaper. So there was a constant battle, especially in Austin, Texas, to get student rights to read the newspapers and have them circulated along with *Playboy* and the *National Enquirer,* which were left alone.

Then there were constant prosecutions by local prosecutors, very often instigated by the FBI, for obscenity. Since there was a breakdown of old-fashioned obscenity laws to admit the literature of Jean Genet, William Burroughs, myself, Henry Miller, Lord Rochester, D. H. Lawrence, and other authors, by the late sixties, porn satire had become a funny kind of underground joke and language. Samples of that were constantly seized and the newspapers were prosecuted, including a lot of Canadian underground newspapers, specifically *Georgia Strait,* which went through *enormous* problems with that kind of censorship. Once some copies of *Logos* from Montreal had been sent to me in New York. I was so pleased with them, I brought them when I was supposed to come up here, and they were seized by Canadian customs for obscenity. That was one of the major ways of persecuting the underground press. Very few convictions resulted—I don't know of any long-term convictions that held—it was just a method of harassment and also of draining the finances of the newspapers, because they were shoestring enterprises in any case. An obscenity accusation could involve getting lawyers, getting involved with litigation, with evidence, having to look up all the old obscenity laws, maybe even printing long articles about it in the newspaper, which then would be busted again as a sort of feedback.

A major way of harassing the underground newspapers was on drug charges. Very often the Narcotics Bureau would send an agent provocateur to hang around and inveigle everybody into giving him pot or smoking his pot or buying pot from him or selling him pot. If they couldn't, they would hide pot in a typewriter drawer, and then that night raid the office, seize all the files, destroy all the machinery, take everybody down to jail, and ultimately the government would lose their case, because it was generally a setup.

There was sabotage of the large-scale news services—Liberation News Service and the United Press Syndicate (the UPI and AP—of the underground network) in the late sixties and early seventies. They would be raided for either drugs or obscenity or conspiracy, and files would be taken, machines would be destroyed, legal papers taken. The late Tom Fourcade of the United Press Syndicate told me that back in '69 in the Midwest, where UPS had its office at the time, they were raided by the local police and the files they had kept on the harassment of the underground press were seized. So a huge body of evidence on harassment of the underground press from 1965 to 1969 was destroyed by the police. He said that there were about four hundred underground newspapers, and that 60 per cent of them had been sabotaged or harassed or busted illegally or framed, or the vendors intimidated or publishers intimidated or printers intimidated or distributors intimidated. Or *landlords* intimidated. That was another way of dealing with the underground press: the FBI would visit the landlord and say, "You got a subversive newspaper here, and you'd better make them move, or *raise their rent.*" That happened in a number of cases—San Diego, Ann Arbor, New York, and Austin, Texas.

A major way of harassment was, as I mentioned, the use of spies. Their role would be to incite violence, to write excessively nutty, violent copy so that everybody was offended, to delay business and editorial conferences with all sorts of left-wing harangues—"Bring the

War Home," "anybody who isn't as revolutionary as we are is a petit bourgeois white honky creep"—or just to act stupid and clog the pipelines of intelligence, so that a lot of editorial meetings were hung up for hours on minor ideological debates instigated by FBI agents chosen for their familiarity with left-wing competitions and animosities, and encouraged to escalate animosities between left groups as much as possible. That was one of the major techniques: to take advantage of the already existing arguments and escalate them to a point where nobody would be talking to each other.

There was *dis*information spread by the FBI. An underground newspaper would be called and told that a march called for noon was really scheduled in a different place at 5 P.M.

There were midnight raids, both by the FBI and local police, *and* by vigilante groups ostensibly unconnected with the government but secretly paid, or armed, or working in close cooperation with FBI or local red squads. That involved bombings—fire bombings as well as auto bombings. It involved destruction of machinery—typewriters, typesetting machinery—desks, lists of subscribers, lists of contributors, thefts of lists or burning of lists of all kinds.

One constant practice was the theft of legal papers, as with the United Press Syndicate. During the Chicago Seven Trial, both newspaper and lawyers' offices were burgled by vigilante groups actually working with Chicago police. Legal papers pertaining to the trial were stolen by the vigilante groups, passed on to army intelligence, and then to the local D.A.s in Chicago.

There were wiretaps, that was customary; there was harassment of subscribers, that was customary; there were threats of bombs when there were no actual bombs. There were conspiracy charges formulated and brought into court. One group, the Juche Cooperative which worked a great deal with Denise Levertov, the poet, in Cambridge, was actually set up on a charge of armed conspiracy to start a revolution because they found guns in the house. The case was ultimately dismissed because there was a license for the guns, which had been purchased by the Juche people to defend themselves against vigilante and Nazi threats that had been pouring into the office with the collaboration of the local cops. There were physical assaults: cop cars pulling up to a vendor or a reporter and cops threatening to beat him up or actually beating him up. There were insults, which may be ultimately the most mentally violent form of harassment: the distribution of obnoxious photographs and satirical cartoons by the FBI, making fun, satirizing the people involved with the alternative media.

Those are the generalizations. To back them up, what I'd like to do is 1) read one FBI directive, which will give you the whole master plan by the FBI against the entire underground movement of newspapers, and 2) tell you a few anecdotes about situations where I was involved.

The twelve-point master plan was issued July 5, 1968, just before Nixon was elected, or around the time of the Chicago Convention and the mass protest there. It was from the director of the FBI; this copy to the FBI office in Albany, New York, with a footnote: "This to all field officers," which means all the officers all over the country.

Counterintelligence Program Internal Security
Disruption of the New Left

Bulletin of May 10/68 requested suggestions for counterintelligence action against the New Left. The replies to the Bureau's request have been analyzed and it is felt that the following suggestions for counterintelligence action can be utilized by all offices.

1. Preparation of a leaflet designed to counteract the impression that Students for a Democratic Society and other minority groups speak for the majority of the students at universities. The leaflet should contain photographs of New Left leadership at the respective university. Naturally, the most obnoxious pictures should be used.

2. The instigating of or the taking advantage of personal conflicts or animosities existing between New Left leaders.

3. The creating of impressions that certain New Left leaders are *informants for the Bureau* or other law enforcement agencies.

4. The use of articles from student newspapers and/or the "underground press" to show the depravity of New Left leaders and members. In this connection, articles showing advocation of the use of narcotics and free sex are ideal to send to university officials, wealthy donors, members of the legislature and *parents* of students who are active in New Left matters. (*So this is not only interfering with free speech, but interposing government obnoxiousness between father and son, mother and daughter. Actually interfering with family life.*)

5. Since the use of marijuana and other narcotics is widespread among members of the New Left, you should be alert to opportunities to have them arrested by local authorities on drug charges. Any information concerning the fact that individuals have marijuana or are en-

gaging in a narcotics party should be immediately furnished to the local authorities and they should be encouraged to take action.

6. The drawing up of anonymous letters regarding individuals active in the New Left. These letters should set out their activities and should be sent to their parents, neighbors, *and* the parents' employers. This could have the effect of forcing the parents to take action. (*Heartless, I'd say, that one.*)

7. Anonymous letters or leaflets describing faculty members and graduate assistants in the various institutions of higher learning who are active in New Left matters. The activities and associations of the individual should be set out. Anonymous mailings should be made to university officials, members of the state legislature, Board of Regents, and to the press. Such letters could be signed "A Concerned Alumnus," or "A Concerned Taxpayer."

8. Whenever New Left groups engage in disruptive activities on college campuses, *cooperative press contacts* should be encouraged to emphasize that the disruptive elements constitute a minority of the students and do not represent the conviction of the majority. The press should demand an immediate student referendum on the issue in question. . . .

9. There is definite hostility among SDS and other New Left groups towards the Socialist Workers Party (SWP), Young Socialist Alliance (YSA), and the Progressive Labor Party (PLP). This hostility should be exploited whenever possible.

10. The field was previously advised that New Left groups are attempting to open coffeehouses near military bases in order to influence members of the Armed Forces. Wherever these coffeehouses are, *friendly news media* should be alerted to them and their purpose. In addition, various drugs, such as marijuana, will probably be utilized by individuals running the coffeehouses or frequenting them. Local law enforcement authorities should be promptly advised whenever you receive an indication that this is being done.

(*And this is the one that I think was actually the most effective, in terms of intellectual or emotional or* propagandiste *counterattack—this next point is what has settled in on the somewhat traumatized college era of the seventies and driven them a little bit off any participation in political activity.*)

11. Consider the use of cartoons, photographs, and anonymous letters which will have the effect of ridiculing the New Left. Ridicule is one of the most potent weapons which we can use against it. (*Very intelligent. And it's also a method used in Germany on the Jews and used in communist countries on dissidents.*)

12. Be alert for opportunities to confuse and disrupt New Left activities by misinformation. For example, when events are planned, notification that the event has been cancelled or postponed could be sent to various individuals. (*The final comment:*) You are reminded that no counterintelligence action is to be taken without Bureau approval. Ensure (*and William Burroughs liked these next sentences as being inspired Burroughsian, Swiftian comment*) ensure that this program is assigned to an agent with an excellent knowledge of both New Left groups and individuals. It must be approached with imagination and enthusiasm if it is to be successful.

There was also, a year before [see Appendix 1], a directive about black nationalists, which said that "the purpose of this new counterintelligence endeavour is to expose, disrupt, misdirect, discredit, or otherwise neutralize the activities of black nationalist hate-type organizations and groupings, their leadership, spokesmen, membership and supporters, and to counter their propensity for violence and civil disorder." Among the groups that they were going to expose to this treatment were the Student Non-Violent Coordinating Committee and the Southern Christian Leadership Conference. Those were groups that Martin Luther King worked with. At that time, J. Edgar Hoover was collecting as much obscene information as he could on Martin Luther King, including tapes of him making love in hotel rooms, and he tried to peddle it to UPI, the New York *Times,* the Washington *Post,* and so forth.

In Detroit there is a rock and jazz impresario named John Sinclair, who was a poet much beloved of Charles Olson. In 1965 we had a big poetry meeting in Berkeley, and Ed Sanders, Anne Waldman, and John Sinclair were invited specifically by Olson to represent the younger generation. Sinclair had an organization in Detroit called the Artists' Workshop, which published huge mimeographed volumes of local poetry, as well as pamphlets by correspondents. He put out a long anticommunist manifesto (*Prose Contribution to Cuban Revolution*) that I wrote in 1960 about the Cuban Revolution, a sort of challenge to the spiritual foundations of it saying that it was too materialist. So he wasn't exactly a riotous red. His main thing though, his main "shtick," so to speak, was uniting black and white in the otherwise tense, riot-torn areas of Detroit, through the Artists' Workshop, because there was collaboration between black jazz musicians and white jazz musicians, black writers and white writers, black poets and white poets. It was a kind of heroic effort, actually. He had a newspaper, and after a while he had a thing called the White Panther party, sort of in collaboration with the Black Panthers, or in defense of the Black Panthers, who were also being subjected to this kind of double-dealing and harassment by the government.

So the narcotics police sent in a young married couple to hang around with John Sinclair and wash his dishes and do mimeographing and distribute papers, and they were constantly harassing him: would he please give them a joint, would he give them some grass? Which he didn't do, fortunately, for a long long while. Finally, one late night, they were really on his back to give them some grass, so he gave them a stick of marijuana. He was busted several weeks later, set up for a long trial, had to pay a lot of money for that, was convicted of peddling marijuana, and sentenced to nine and a half to ten years. Of which he spent several years in the federal penitentiary in Marquette. That was an FBI attempt to silence a dissenter and a poet. In jail he wrote a really interesting poem. He said, "My books wait for me on the shelf, myself, my typewriter sits empty, urging me onward. Nine and a half to ten years is not enough!" So actually, he was a sharp poet. And a worthy citizen. He's now the chief impresario of black and white jazz in Detroit, and has rock and roll, jazz, and old blues concerts.

Yoko Ono and John Lennon, working with Jerry Rubin at that time, 1969 to 1971, decided that they would go on a tour of all the persecuted areas, the hot spots as they called them: to visit Lee Otis Johnson, who was in jail in Texas for thirty years for a joint, John Sinclair, Angela Davis, and others. So they formed a giant touring group and went to Ann Arbor, where they had a giant Free John Sinclair concert while he was still in jail. They had Phil Ochs, myself, Ed Sanders, Anne Waldman, reading poetry; they had John Lennon and the New York Street Band and Yoko Ono to sing; they had limousines—all the luxury of rock and roll turned to political agitation, propaganda, entertainment, education, illumination. They had an itinerary: they were going to wind up in 1972 at the Republican Convention in Miami. So the concert was actually a very powerful political gesture. Based on pacifism, actually, that being Lennon's and Yoko Ono's obvious bent. It might have resulted in enormous cultural changes, a sort of cultural revolutionary shot. The consequence for Lennon was that the FBI and Immigration and the Narcotics Bureau got together to try and expel him from the country. Lennon—and Yoko Ono, who was a citizen—had to drop their whole political campaign, not go to Angela Davis's trial; not go to Lee Otis Johnson's domain in Texas. As for John Sinclair—the concert was on a Friday night. By that Monday, the state legislature had altered the draconian law of "ten years for one joint," and John Sinclair was out of jail by that Monday. So it was actually an effective cultural-political instrument that they had devised. Aborted, then and there, by FBI and government conspiracy. Lennon was not, ultimately, deported, because the method for deporting him was that he had been busted in London on a pot charge, and the Sergeant Pilcher who busted him on the pot charge actually had planted the grass, and was himself later indicted for selling hashish. He was a celebrated narc in England who had busted Mick Jagger personally, as well as Lennon, as well as McCartney; he had some kind of love for the counterculture musicians and went around busting them for narcotics charges. There was actually a campaign against the Beatles in the United States, to make sure that every single one of them got busted on narcotics charges. I know, because a federal narcotics agent in New York tried to get someone to bring marijuana to my house to set me up for arrest, and this guy was asked did he know me, and did he know Ringo Starr? (Ringo Starr being the only Beatle that was never busted.)

The harassment and the busts of the Beatles and other rock-and-roll candidates for immorality is paralleled in Czechoslovakia by the harassment of the Plastic People of the Universe, the great modern/new jazz/new rock and roll/punk/new wave group, that was inspired by American contemporaries—Ed Sanders and the Fugs, and Frank Zappa and the Mothers of Invention, and Tuli Kupferberg. So on both sides of the Cold War, there seems to be a hatred of youth/music/speech.

Actually, I don't think the ruling elites hate each other as much as they hate their dissidents. They need each other in order to burgeon and prosper. When I was kicked out of Czechoslovakia in 1965, as I was on a security list, within a year there was an attempt to set me up for a marijuana bust. I went into Robert Kennedy's office, and also to my local congressman's office—Charles Jolson, from Paterson, New Jersey—and complained, and tried to put the heat back on them, and so got a little story in the New York *Times* and Washington *Post* and *Life* magazine. My congressman wrote to the Narcotics Bureau asking them what kind of hanky-panky was going on? When I got my Freedom of Information Act papers several years ago, I found that they had translated a scurrilous article from the Prague youth newspaper accusing me of being a homosexual, a narcomane, and, in addition, an alcoholic! And had sent my congressman that information! So that the police bureaucracies both inside the socialist countries and in the capitalist countries use each other's material and use each other's scripts, and have a working relationship against the dissidents of both.

There was further complication in the John Sinclair case—which is a nexus in a way, because it was in the Ann Arbor-Detroit area, which was a center of underground, alternative, counterculture activity. An agent provocateur, who was a nut employed by the FBI, came to John Sinclair saying that he wanted to blow up the CIA office in Detroit. Sinclair said, "No, for the love of God, no! Out!" So the guy went and blew it up and then accused Sinclair of encouraging him to do it. Sinclair was indicted on a conspiracy charge; the main witness was the crazed agent provocateur. Sinclair obviously won the case, because it was flimsy, but it also occupied his time and legal attention, with William Kunstler and others, for many months—about a year and a half.

A further complication relating to Sinclair and this Detroit-Ann Arbor nexus came from Washington. The antiwar Mobilization was going to have a giant national meeting in Washington in the early seventies. All the different groups under the umbrella of the War Resisters' League would be there: pacifists, Trotskyites, women's groups, gay groups. But David Dellinger and others who were organizing the Mobilization in Washington were told by the Black United Front in Washington that, although they as middle-class liberal honkies thought that it was so important for them to fan their egos by going to Washington and demonstrating, it was going to create a lot of unsettlement in Washington among the black population, and those blacks were the leaders who were going to have to clean up their turf after them with the outraged police. So if the antiwar movement wanted to have its meeting, it should give the "just" contribution of twenty-five thousand dollars to the Black United Front in Washington to feed the grass-roots war, because that was where the war really was, not in Vietnam. As it turned out later, the spokesman for the Black United Front who wanted to do this was an FBI agent trying to harass the antiwar movement. As part of his maneuver, an anonymous letter was sent to the *Michigan Daily,* the Ann Arbor student newspaper, and to Black Panther leaders in Detroit, telling them to put pressure on John Sinclair and the White Panthers to put pressure on the white liberals in Ann Arbor that they should accede to this "just and honorable demand" from the Black United Front. The commentary under this FBI directive [see Appendix 2] said: This will cause trouble between the White Panthers and the Black Panthers, as well as between the White Panthers and the liberals; will offend all the liberals; and will have the ultimate effect of putting the entire community into dispute with itself, as well as draining it financially.

Copies of these demands were sent to all radical groups and were printed in the *Michigan Daily* newspaper. Naturally, all the white liberals were either intimidated or astounded or put off; it caused a tremendous amount of controversy. And one of the centers that was used for dissemination of this kind of double-dealing was the *Michigan Daily* newspaper. In fact, the FBI directive said the *Michigan Daily* would be glad to print such a radical letter.

The result was that my dentist, a white liberal in Washington who worked with blacks, threw up his hands and said, "If the blacks in Washington are so nutty, how can we whites work with them, so I'm just dropping out of the whole problem of black-white relationships."

So, all within that one nexus of Ann Arbor you get a picture of FBI sabotage and disruption of race relations. Throughout the sixties the celebrated black-white paranoia was fanned by the FBI. And a lot of poison-pen letters were written by supposed blacks denouncing white participation in the black movement. For those of you who do remember the paranoia of the sixties between white and black, you should understand that though there may have been a seedbed for such a neurosis, its escalation into unworkable psychosis, miscommunication, and lack of direct face-to-face working it out, emotionally and intellectually, was the result of FBI manipulation. It was a large-scale thing, which still has a hangover: black and white are still afraid of each other on the political front because of that old trauma.

What was accomplished was simply a kind of discouragement, a duping, a hypnosis of a kind, of the general public, or the kids, who were told that they were "creepy jerks who couldn't get their act together." There was a kind of cultural discouragement, or a *propagandiste* discouragement. But basically, there is an alternative media now, and if Reagan has to send troops into El Salvador this winter—as was prophesied by reporters for *Newsweek,* United Press International, the Washington *Post,* and Knight-Ridder newspapers, in round-table conversation in Mexico City three weeks ago—I'm sure there'll be an underground press springing up to oppose that.

Actually, the alternate press has a great present and future, because its stylistics and its outrageousness affected the aboveground press. Many people working today in the aboveground press, and in the other media also—television, radio, public radio, private channel, cable, the New York *Times*—started with the underground press, and they have that inoculation of understanding. Its visual style affected a lot of the aboveground press. Certain big publications have survived, like *Rolling Stone,* which is relatively radical in terms of its investigative reporting, and there is the *Real Paper* in Boston. There is the *Distant Drummer* in Philadelphia; there is still your Vancouver newspaper, now called the *Sun,* edited by Dan McLeod, the same as before. There are lots of presses, and they have quite an influence.

COVERING EL SALVADOR: A DISCUSSION

A QUESTION FROM THE FLOOR: Do you think there's some sort of policy in the American State Department to keep the news from reaching us? I have the impression they don't want us to know what's happening in Central America.

CAROLYN FORCHÉ: That is quite an accurate impression. I had a very difficult time publishing material on El Salvador in the States before the deaths of the American nuns, which made the issue "hot," so to speak, in terms of the media. The directives, the suggestions that we play down El Salvador, became impossible to follow at that point. I do believe there is a concerted effort by the State Department to direct media coverage, not only of El Salvador but of American foreign policy in general. It takes the form not of official censorship but of innuendo, in briefings given to publishers and editors.

A QUESTION FROM THE FLOOR: What is the situation of foreign journalists in El Salvador? How much are they isolated from what's really going on there?

CAROLYN FORCHÉ: I have a document with me that you can refer to: it is number three of the *Index on Censorship* (1981): "How the Press is Treated in El Salvador." There were stages. First, there were no foreign journalists in El Salvador; then they arrived from all countries but the U.S., oddly enough. When I was in El Salvador, I was functioning as a freelancer, and I was pointedly asked by many journalists what I was doing there, since I was the only U.S. citizen they had seen. My reply was that I didn't work officially for anyone, so I was allowed to be there.

Then, when foreign journalists began to report, the intimidations began; journalists would receive death threats. Different journalists reacted differently. Some journalists were expelled from the country. Some felt that it was not worth the risk. Some got off the plane, stood behind the velvet rope in the airline gate, and did a stand-up routine for the cameras about what it was like to be in El Salvador, after two minutes. Some journalists risked their lives and went into the hills with guerrilla groups, documenting what it was like to live, to try to eat, to try and have medical care, and to fight, all at the same time.

The government has responded with harassment and intimidation —forbidding journalists to go into certain areas without permission, refusing to renew visas or shortening the period of their validity. They responded differently to journalists who were not in favor with the American embassy. Freelancers had the most freedom, and therefore were treated the most harshly. John Sullivan, a freelancer, and René Tamsen of WHUR radio, Washington, D.C., are still missing. Freelancers are in the greatest jeopardy because the government of El Salvador knows that the American embassy has greater difficulty with them than with those who, credentialed and officially working for the wire services or newspapers, depend on their ongoing assistance.

It's a big question, and you can read this *Index on Censorship* report, which will give you a lot of answers. In order to write the truth about what is going on in El Salvador, you have to go in, pay attention, try to stay alive, file from outside the country, and maybe not go back for a while. It's a bit difficult. It's a trick, you know: you have to balance certain things. It's very hard to stay alive there.

The other side of the question is that journalists often get discouraged when editors will not print their stories. Eventually you get printed, but it's a very tiring task to try and persuade editors of the importance of the situation. When you have photographic evidence that's very difficult to refute—piles and piles of corpses—editors don't believe their readers would be interested or prepared to endure the visual assault.

The Writer and Revolution

THE FUTURE WE ENVISAGE

GEORGE WOODCOCK

A FRIEND I have recently gained is an Iranian filmmaker who has left his country, perhaps for good. He created a splendid film about the power of superstition and the way it helped enslave his country. His film was banned by the Shah's government, because the truth he revealed was seen to be subversive. When the Shah departed, my friend imagined that his film could now be freely shown, that it would help people understand the roots of the revolution. But three weeks after Khomeini returned to Iran and took power, it was banned again. Even though the angle from which the mullahs judged it was different from the Shah's, they also saw the truth he revealed as subversive. Twice he was called to interrogations that became progressively more ominous; after the second, he wisely fled the next morning. Some of the artists he knew and admired have since been slain by the mullahs' firing squads.

My friend believed that in making his film he was contributing to the kind of change in public opinion that would bring an end to the Pahlavi tyranny. But the revolution that came was not the revolution he had foreseen.

I believe we can apply his experience to the situation of the writer and his relationship to revolutionary change. A writer can and often does help prepare the climate of opinion and feeling in which a revolution occurs. The writings of Voltaire and Beaumarchais, each in his own way, prepared the people's minds for the French Revolution. If they had not fostered in the French middle classes a mood of rejection toward the ancien régime, the Revolution of 1789 could hardly have taken place. But what happened in that Revolution—the Terror, the dictatorship of the Jacobins, the grim spectacle of the revolutionaries slaughtering each other after they had rid themselves of the aristocrats, and the eventual rise of the dictator Napoleon—neither Voltaire nor Beaumarchais ever foresaw. None of this was part of the future they envisaged. Voltaire's bones were buried with honor in the Pantheon by the revolutionaries, but if he had been alive in the 1790s, he would probably have shared Condorcet's choice of poison or the guillotine. Even Beaumarchais, master of intrigue though he was, had to flee from France and was condemned to death in absentia by the revolutionary tribunals. These are the men we often think of as the fathers of the French Revolution.

Revolutions are not realizations of the idealistic visions of writers; they are sociopolitical eruptions in which the collapse of an existing structure of power creates a vacuum into which many forces rush, seeking to take over the vacant situations of authority. The freedom that may have been the dominant desideratum in the prerevolutionary period is the first victim of the struggle for power. And writers and other artists, whatever their roles before the revolution, now appear as challengers—because they represent the free intelligence—to all those who seek to impose new forms of power. Thus artists, unless they become the lackeys of the ruling group like the painter David in the French Revolution and the novelist Sholokhov in the Russian Revolution, are among the first victims, doomed to death like André Chénier and Isaak Babel, or to exile like Beaumarchais and Evgeny Zamiatin. Revolutionary authority differs from other kinds of authority only in being more openly ruthless. The writer cannot serve it and at the same time manifest the free intelligence that is man's only hope if he is to proceed beyond the new tyranny the revolution has imposed.

REVOLUTIONARY WRITING IN NORTH AMERICA

RICK SALUTIN

I FEEL a bit unsure of my ground, perhaps because I am the only person on this panel who grew up in North America, and it seems to me that I should speak as such on the topic of the writer and revolution—as someone who writes in sympathy with and about the revolutionary tradition; and by revolution I don't mean any random, violent upheaval. I mean "revolutionary" in the modern and Marxist sense of an upheaval which is undertaken for and by the mass of working people.

It seems to me that in North America—in Canada and the United States, that is—the writer was most involved with revolution during the thirties. That was the heyday of revolutionary writing. And the manifestation of that was primarily the relationship between writers and the Communist party, in both Canada and the United States.

Since that time, or growing out of that time, one could say the main phenomenon concerning the writer and revolution in North America has been the disaffection and disillusionment of the literary community with the revolutionary cause. This was due, I'd say, primarily to two forces. One was an excessively optimistic and unrealistic enchantment with the Soviet Union, and the gradual and increasingly severe disillusionment with the upshot of Soviet-style socialism. The other factor, at least as important, was the incredibly virulent attack on the Left in all its variations in Canada and the United States in the forties and fifties—a phenomenon, by the way, that has been more thoroughly exposed with regard to the United States than to Canada.

Writers tended to abandon the revolutionary banner to which many of them, some of very high literary quality and others of lesser quality, had rallied at that time. The fifties was a particularly bleak period. During the late nineteen sixties and early nineteen seventies, there was a lot of language about revolution among writers, but it lacked the solidity of the connection in the thirties.

Today I'm always struck, in listening to writers from such countries as El Salvador, by the naturalness with which they discuss revolution in all it aspects. Here in Canada I find that one feels a certain pressure to apologize and be embarrassed at discussing topics in a revolutionary vein, and even at using the language. In polite literary company, one doesn't use the term "revolution." Similarly with terms such as "class" or "struggle." "Struggle" is a particularly hard word to get away with if you're writing for the mass media. (I hasten to add that this is largely internalized: you feel a little bit of a jerk when you start to say "struggle," and you find yourself looking for another way of putting it.)

Simultaneously, you have the problem that art is usually assumed in our society to deal primarily with personal or private issues, as though, for example, the conflict of workers with a company, or of any collective body with whoever has authority over it, is somehow not fit material for artistic treatment; that there's something impersonal about the struggles of a union or political movement, whereas the conflict over "Do I divorce?" or "Who do I sleep with?" is considered personal. In another social setting one gets the reverse. I was approached once by a Chinese visitor to Canada who had seen a contemporary play dealing with romantic and sexual conflicts and who was absolutely certain she'd misunderstood the play. I asked, "Well, what do you think you understood?" She described it, and I told her, "Yeah, that was it." And she said, "Why would anybody write a play about that?"

I believe that the problem of writing in the revolutionary vein or tradition in our society has to do with the simple fact that almost nothing around us encourages such writing. We're not surrounded by people evidently demanding revolution, demanding the kind of upheaval that would qualitatively alter their reality, or by people evidently struggling for it. There are some signs, but they don't surround us, they don't force themselves on us. In a society such as El Salvador, you simply look at the reality of your society, and you portray it. If we were surrounded by such political or revolutionary struggles, it would be self-evident and writers would portray them.

For this reason, I think there's a tendency among many of us to turn to other societies where the struggles and the contradictions and the conflicts are at a raw point, for a kind of encouragement. I found myself almost compulsively traveling to Mozambique several years ago when I learned that the majority of the people in the most important positions in the government were well-known, published poets. As it turned out, I couldn't talk to them—I stayed an extra couple of weeks to speak to them, but there were crises in agriculture, foreign relations, and finance, and all of the major poets were involved in solving them. What I'd wanted to ask them was, "Do you miss writing poetry?" A friend of mine did ask some of them, and the answer was no. Actually, the answer was that the question was out of court: it was considered an individualistic question. But I came to feel that the answer would have been and should have been no. That is, the writer's impulse to describe the world as it ought to be, out of frustration with the world as it is, can be equally fulfilled by the opportunity to engage in trying to alter that world—successfully or unsuccessfully. I think I would be just as happy not writing, if those energies could be channeled directly into something that was a genuine effort to overthrow and radically alter the structures that oppress people around us.

I should add that this kind of thing can easily lead to the danger of voyeurism on the part of Western writers, or Western socialists in general; that is, of getting off on other people's revolutions. For writers that danger is mitigated, because you can't really go and write about somebody else's revolution. You have to write about the society in which you live in the language in which you live.

If, then, one asks where the energy to write in this vein comes from, if the people and struggles around you don't constantly give it, then I would say, just in a personal way, that one source is acute embarrassment. One of my main senses of living in Canadian society, or Toronto society, is an ongoing sense of embarrassment. And it comes particularly if I imagine anybody looking from the outside (somebody, say, three hundred, or five hundred, or a thousand years from now, however long it takes to establish a society which has decent, humane, and rational arrangements for people to live amongst each other) looking back at the way this society has chosen to live. I'm just horribly embarrassed to be part of all this. A certain energy comes from that.

But the odd thing is that revolutionary commitment has very little effect on the act of writing. Somehow, that's not what you're engaged in when you're writing. The particular agencies or actions or programs that one supports, even how one chooses to vote, have very little relevance to one's actual work as a writer, when you sit, or pace, or however you write. In writing, it seems to me, one is trying primarily to tell the truth about reality, to pull back the curtain and reveal how the world functions. The political effect of such writing, or the revolutionary effect it could have, is not in recruiting people to a certain cause or point of view—to revolution—but in enabling them to see how the world around them works, instead of all the ways its workings are usually veiled from them. So that as they continue to encounter it, they may freely evaluate and choose and shape the world which has so often misshapen them.

Perhaps I could conclude with an example. I remember, while working on a play collectively with a group of actors in Newfoundland several years ago, having a great argument about how we would portray the politician who we all agreed was the villain of the piece—Joey Smallwood—in smashing a strike. They wanted to do a very Oil-Can Harry kind of *real* villain, and they said, in great irritation, "Well, you don't *disagree* with us! You just want to *soft-pedal* it so you can manipulate people more!" I had to think hard about that. And I decided that the point is not to recruit people, in a play, to your point of view. Because we were planning to tour that play, and we did tour it, and it went into the town of Badger, where the strike which we were portraying had torn the town apart. So we take our play in, with our point of view; we do a good job, and the people go out of the theater convinced that we're right and that Smallwood was wrong. Next night, along comes, let us say, a right-wing touring collective theater company with an interpretation of the event from the other side, and people go to that, and they're very impressed because these are good artists, good actors. People walk out of it convinced on the other side or, more likely, simply cynical and apathetic about figuring out the whole thing. So it seems to me that you're not trying to press a point of view. What you're trying to do is present a way of viewing reality which helps people to view reality themselves; so that never mind what they think about the last strike, the next time they're confronted with a situation that demands some sort of political view, they will have been helped to evaluate it for themselves. So that ultimately—and this is the democratic impulse that is at the core of the revolutionary impulse—they'll be able to take over and shape their own lives.

A REVOLUTION IS
USUALLY THE WORST SOLUTION

JOSEF ŠKVORECKÝ

FRANKLY, I feel frustrated whenever I have to talk about revolution for the benefit of people who have never been through one. They are —if you'll excuse the platitude—like a child who doesn't believe that a fire hurts, until he burns himself. I, my generation, my nation, have been involuntarily through two revolutions, both of them socialist: one of the Right variety, one of the Left. Together they destroyed my peripheral vision.

When I was fourteen, we were told at school that the only way to a just and happy society led through socialist revolution. Capitalism was bad, liberalism a fraud, democracy bunk, and parliamentarism decadent. Our then Minister of Culture and Education, the late Mr. Emanuel Moravec, taught us this, and then sent his son to fight for socialism with the Hermann Göring SS Division. The son was later hanged; the minister, to use proper revolutionary language, liquidated himself with the aid of a gun.

When I was twenty-one, we were told at Charles University that the only way to a just and happy society led through socialist revolution. Capitalism was bad, liberalism a fraud, democracy bunk, and parliamentarism decadent. Our then professor of philosophy, the late Mr. Arnost Kolman, taught us this, and then gave his half-Russian daughter in marriage to a Czech communist who fought for socialism with Alexander Dubček. Later he fled to Sweden. Professor Kolman, one of the very last surviving original Bolsheviks of 1917 and a close friend of Lenin, died in 1980, also in Sweden. Before his death, he returned his party card to Brezhnev and declared that the Soviet Union had betrayed the socialist revolution.

In 1981 I am told by various people who suffer from Adlerian and Rankian complexes that the only way to a just and happy society leads through socialist revolution. Capitalism is bad, liberalism a fraud, democracy bunk, and parliamentarism decadent. Dialectically, all this makes me suspect that capitalism is probably good, liberalism may be right, democracy is the closest approximation to the truth, and parliamentarism a vigorous gentleman in good health, filled with the wisdom of ripe old age.

There have been quite a few violent revolutions in our century, most of them communist, some fascist, and some nationalistic and religious. The final word on all of them comes from the pen of Joseph Conrad, who in 1911 wrote this in his novel *Under Western Eyes:*

> . . . in a real revolution—not a simple dynastic change or a mere reform of institutions—in a real revolution the best characters do not come to the front. A violent revolution falls into the hands of narrow-minded fanatics and of tyrannical hypocrites at first. Afterwards comes the turn of all the pretentious intellectual failures of the time. Such are the chiefs and the leaders. You will notice that I have left out the mere rogues. The scrupulous and the just, the noble, humane, and devoted natures; the unselfish and the intelligent may begin a movement—but it passes away from them. They are not the leaders of a revolution. They are its victims: the victims of disgust, of disenchantment—often of remorse. Hopes grotesquely betrayed, ideals caricatured—that is the definition of revolutionary success. There have been in every revolution hearts broken by such successes.

I wonder if anything can be added to this penetrating analysis? The scenario seems to fit perfectly. Just think of the Strasser brothers, those fervent German nationalists and socialists: one of them liquidated by his own workers' party, the other having to flee, first to capitalist Czechoslovakia, then to liberal England, while their movement passed into the hands of that typical "intellectual failure," the unsuccessful artist named Adolf Hitler. Think of Boris Pilnyak, liquidated while those sleek and deadly scientific bureaucrats he described so well—who were perfectly willing to liquidate others to bolster their own careers—bolstered their careers, leaving a trail of human skulls behind them. Think of Fidel Castro's involuntary volunteers dying with a look of amazement on their faces in a foreign country where they have no right to be, liquidating its black warriors who for years had been fighting the Portuguese. Think of the German communists who, after the Nazi *Machtübernahme,* fled to Moscow and then, brokenhearted, were extradited back into the hands of the Gestapo because Stalin honored his word to Hitler; the Jews among them were designated for immediate liquidation, the non-Jews were sent to Mauthausen and Ravensbrück. It is all an old, old story. The revolution—if you don't mind another cliché—is fond of devouring its own children. Or, if you do mind, let me put it this way: the revolution is cannibalistic.

It is estimated that violent communist revolutions in our century have dined on about one hundred million men, women, and children. What has been gained by this sumptuous feast? Basically two things, both predicted by the so-called classics of Marxist-Leninism: the state that withered away, and the New Socialist Man.

The state withered away all right—into a kind of Mafia, a perfect police regime. Thought-crime, which most believed to be just a morbid joke by Orwell, concocted when he was already dying of tuberculosis, has become a reality in today's "real socialism," as the stepfathers of the Czechoslovak Communist party have christened their own status quo. The material standards of living in these postrevolutionary police states are invariably lower, often much lower, than those of the developed Western democracies. But, of course, the New Socialist Man has emerged, as announced.

Not quite as announced. Who is he? He is an intelligent creature who, sometimes in the interest of bare survival, sometimes merely to maintain his material living standards, is willing to abnegate the one quality that differentiates him from other animals: his intellectual and moral awareness, his ability to think and freely express his thought. This creature has come to resemble the three little monkeys whose statuettes you see in junk shops: one covers its eyes, the other its ears, the third its mouth. The New Socialist Man has thus become a new Trinity of the postrevolutionary age.

Therefore, with Albert Camus, I suspect that in the final analysis capitalist democracy is to be preferred to regimes created by violent revolutions. I must also agree with Lenin that those who, after the various Gulags (and after the Grand Guignol spectacle of the Polish Communist party exhorting the Solidarity Union to shut up or else the Polish nation will be destroyed—and guess who will destroy it), still believe in violent revolutions are indeed "useful idiots."

In the Western world, such mentally retarded adults sometimes point out, in defense of violence, that capitalism is guilty of similar crimes. Most of these crimes, true, have occurred in the past, often in the distant past, but some are happening in our own time, especially in what is known as the Third World. But to justify crimes by arguing that others have also committed them is, to put it mildly, bad taste. To exonerate the communist inquisition by blaming the Catholic Church for having done the same thing in the Dark Ages amounts to an admission that communism represents a return to the Dark Ages. To accuse General Pinochet of torturing his political prisoners, and then barter your own political prisoners, fresh from psychiatric prison-clinics, for those of General Pinochet is—shall we say—a black joke.

Does all this mean that I reject any violent revolution anywhere, no matter what the circumstances are? I have seen too much despair in my time to be blind to despair. It's just that I do not believe in two things. First, I do not think that a violent uprising born out of "a long train of abuses and usurpations, pursuing invariably the same object" which "evinces a design to reduce" men "under absolute despotism" should be called a revolution; because when such a revolution later produces another "long chain of abuses and usurpations" and people rise against it, to be linguistically correct we would have to call such an uprising a "counterrevolution." In our society, however, this term has acquired a pejorative meaning it does not deserve.

Second, I do not believe that any violent revolution in which communists or fascists participate can be successful, except in the Conradian sense as quoted above. Because quite simply, I do not trust authoritarian ideologies. Every revolution with the participation of communists or fascists must eventually of necessity turn into a dictatorship and, more often than not, into a state nakedly ruled by the police. Neither fascists nor communists can live with democracy, because their ultimate goal, no matter whether they call it *das Führerprinzip* or the dictatorship of the proletariat, is precisely the "absolute despotism" of which Thomas Jefferson spoke. They tolerate partners in the revolutionary effort only as long as they need them to defeat the powers that be—not perhaps because all communists and fascists are radically evil but because they are disciplined adherents of ideologies which command them to do so, since that is what Hitler or Lenin advised. The fascists are more honest about it: they say openly—at least the Nazis did—that democracy is nonsense. Lenin was equally frank only in his more mystical moments; otherwise the communists use Newspeak. But as soon as they grow strong enough, they finish off democracy just as efficiently as the fascists, and usually more so.

All this is rather abstract, however, and since individualistic Anglo-Saxons usually demand concrete, individual examples, let me offer you a few.

In Canada there lives an old professor by the name of Vladimir Krajina. He teaches at the University of British Columbia in Vancouver and is an eminent botanist who has received high honors from the Canadian Government for his work in the preservation of Canadian flora. But in World War II, he was also a most courageous anti-Nazi fighter. He operated a wireless transmitter by which the Czech underground sent vital messages to London, information collected by the members of the Czech Resistance in armament factories, by "our men" in the Protectorate bureaucracy who had access to Nazi state secrets, and by Intelligence Service spies such as the notorious A-54. The Gestapo, of course, was after Professor Krajina. For several years, he had to move from one hideout to another, leaving a trail of blood behind him, of Gestapo men shot by his cofighters, of people who hid him and were caught and shot. After the war, he became an MP for the Czech Socialist party. But his incumbency lasted for little more than two years. Immediately after the communist coup in 1948, Professor Krajina had to go into hiding again, and he eventually fled the country. Why? Because the communists had never forgotten that he had warned the Czech underground against cooperating with the communists. And he was right: he was not the only one who had to flee. Hundreds of other anti-Nazi fighters were forced to leave the country, and those who would or could not ended up on the gallows, in concentration camps, or, if they were lucky, in menial jobs. Among them were many Czech RAF pilots who had distinguished themselves in the Battle of Britain and then had returned to the republic for whose democracy they had risked their lives. All this is a story since repeated in other Central and East European states. It is still being repeated in Cuba, in Vietnam, in Angola, and most recently in Nicaragua.

In a recent article in the *New York Review of Books,* V. S. Naipaul tells about his experiences in revolutionary Iran. He met a communist student there who showed him snapshots of communists being executed by the Islamic Revolutionary Guards and then told him about his love for Stalin: "I love him. He was one of the greatest revolutionaries. . . . What he did in Russia we have to do in Iran. We, too, have to do a lot of killing. A lot. . . . We have to kill all the bourgeoisie." For what purpose? To create a Brezhnevite Iran, perhaps? To send tens of thousands of new customers to the Siberian Gulag? But obviously the bourgeois don't count. They were useful when they fought the Shah, as the Kadets had been in 1917 while they fought the Czar. Now they are expendable. They have become "fascists," just like the Barcelonian anarchists denounced in the Newspeak of the communist press decades ago in Spain, as described by Orwell in *Homage to Catalonia*. They have become nonpeople. James Jones once wrote: ". . . it's so easy to kill real people in the name of some damned ideology or other; once the killer can abstract them in his own mind into being symbols, then he needn't feel guilty for killing them since they're no longer human beings." The Jews in Auschwitz, the zeks in the Gulag, the bourgeoisie in a communist Iran. Symbols, not people. *Revolutionsfutter.*

When Angela Davis was in jail, a Czech socialist politician, Jiři Pelikán, a former communist and now a member of the European Parliament for the Italian Socialist party, approached her through an old American communist lady and asked her whether she would sign a protest against the imprisonment of communists in Prague. She agreed to do so, but not until she got out of jail because, she said, it might jeopardize her case. When she was released, she sent word via her secretary that she would fight for the release of political prisoners anywhere in the world except, of course, in the socialist states. Anyone sitting in a socialist jail must be against socialism, and therefore deserves to be where he is. All birds can fly. An ostrich is a bird. Therefore an ostrich can fly. So much for the professor of philosophy Angela Davis.

So much for concrete examples.

In his *Notebooks,* Albert Camus recorded a conversation with one of his communist cofighters in the French Resistance: "Listen, Tar, the real problem is this: no matter what happens, I shall always defend you against the rifles of the execution squad. But you will have to say yes to my execution."

Evelyn Waugh, whom I confess I prefer to all other modern British writers, said in an interview with Julian Jebb: "An artist must be a reactionary. He has to stand out against the tenor of the age and not go flopping along; he must offer some little opposition."

All I have learned about violent revolutions, from books and from personal experience, convinces me that Waugh was right.

This is my little bit of opposition.

THE IMAGINATION AND
THE WILL TO CHANGE

EDUARDO GALEANO

I SHOULD BEGIN by asking if there is any literary piece that is not political and social. In my opinion, all are social, because they belong to human society. All are political as well, to the extent that "political" always implies participation in public life, whether the author of a book or an article or a short story wants it or not, or knows it or not.

Writing makes a choice by the simple fact of its existence. In directing itself to others, it inevitably occupies a position and takes sides in the relationship between society and power. Its content, whether liberating or alienating, is in no way determined by its theme, by its subject. The literature that is most political, most deeply committed to the political process of change, can be the one that least needs to name its politics, in the same sense that the crudest political violence is not necessarily demonstrated by bombs and gunshots.

Frequently, books, articles, songs, and manifestos, with social and political themes, written with the most revolutionary intentions, do not achieve the results desired. Sometimes they agree, unintentionally, with the system they wish to defy. Those who approach the people as if they were hard of hearing and incapable of imagination confirm the image of them cultivated by their oppressors. Those who use a language of boring, stereotyped sentences, who create one-dimensional, papier-mâché characters, without fears, doubts, or contradictions, who mechanically carry out the orders of the author, are blessing the system they say they are fighting. Is not the system specialized in disintegration? Literature that shrinks the soul instead of expanding it, as much as it might call itself militant, objectively speaking is serving a social order which daily nibbles away at the variety and richness of the human condition. In other cases, no less frequent, the attempt to communicate and to spread ideas fails beforehand, because it is directed at an already convinced audience in the language the audience wants to hear. However revolutionary it pretends to be, work undertaken without risk ends by being conformist in fact. Even though it arouses fervor, it provokes drowsiness. It is said to be directed at the multitudes, but it really converses in solitude, with the mirror.

I believe that literature can recover a political, revolutionary path every time it contributes to the revelation of reality—as Rick Salutin has said—in its multiple dimensions, if in some way it nourishes a collective identity or rescues the memory of the community that created that memory, whatever the themes were. From this point of view, a love poem can be more fertile than a novel dealing with the exploitation of miners in the tin mines or workers on the banana plantations.

In interpreting reality, in rediscovering it, literature can assist in acts of comprehension that nourish human creation. Like a two-way mirror, literature can show both what can be seen, and what cannot be seen but is there. And since nothing exists which does not contain its own negation, literature often acts as a sort of vengeance and as a prophecy. Imagination opens new doors to the understanding of reality and the prescience of change. The dream anticipates the world to be conquered and at the same time defies the stagnation of the bourgeois order. In a system of silence and fear, the power to create and to invent and to imagine attacks the rootedness of obedience. The masters of the social order say that it is a natural order, an orderly world internally consistent no matter what angle you view it from, like a police photo. The creative imagination reveals that its presumed eternity is temporary and that there is no face without its counterface.

The revolutionary value of a text can be measured by taking into account the things it triggers in the person reading it. The best books, the best essays and articles, the best novels, the most effective poems and songs, cannot be read with impunity. Literature that is directed toward consciousness acts upon it, and if accompanied by purpose, talent, and luck, it sparks the imagination and the will to change. In the social structure of the lie, to reveal reality is to denounce it. It implies its own denunciation.

It is said that one book does not change the world, and that is true. But what does change the world? A fast or slow process, depending on the situation, but always incessant, and with a thousand dimensions. The written word is one of them, and not merely an auxiliary wheel. To deny literature which is not part of an emergency is as serious a mistake as to despise the literary forms of expression which escape the boundaries of genre or which have no place on the altars of academic culture.

—Translated by Mariana Valverde

PART FOUR

FORMS OF OPPRESSION

Repressive Tolerance

A DISNEYLAND OF THE SOUL

MARGARET ATWOOD

THE SUBJECT we have come together to address increases in importance as the giants of this world move closer and closer to violent and fatal confrontation. Broadly put, it is: what is the writer's responsibility, if any, to the society in which he or she lives? The question is not a new one; it's been with us at least since the time of Plato; but more and more the answers of the world's governments have taken the form of amputation: of the tongue, of the soul, or of some other part of the body, such as the head.

We in Canada are ill-equipped to come to grips even with the problem, let alone the solution. We live in a society in which the main consensus seems to be that the artist's duty is to entertain and divert, nothing more. Occasionally, our critics get a little heavy and start talking about the human condition. But on the whole, audiences prefer that art be not a mirror held up to life but a Disneyland of the soul, containing Romanceland, Spyland, Pornoland, and all the other Escapelands which are so much more agreeable than the complex truth. When we take an author seriously, we prefer to believe that her vision derives from her individual and subjective and neurotic, tortured soul—we like artists to have tortured souls—not from the world she is looking at. Sometimes our artists believe this version too, and the ego takes over. *I, me,* and *mine* are our favorite pronouns; *we, us,* and *ours* are low on the list. The artist is not seen as a lens for focusing the world but as a solipsism. We are good at analyzing an author's production in terms of her craft. We are not good at analyzing it in terms of her politics, and by and large we do not do so.

By "politics" I do not mean how you voted in the last election, although that is included. I mean who is entitled to do what to whom, with impunity; who profits by it; and who therefore eats what. Such material enters a writer's work not because the writer is or is not consciously political but because a writer is an observer, a witness, and such observations are the air she breathes. They are the air all of us breathe; the only difference is that the author looks, and then writes down what she sees. What she sees depends on how closely she looks and at what, but look she must.

In some countries, an author is censored not only for what he says but for how he says it. An unconventional style is therefore a declaration of artistic freedom. Here we are eclectic; we don't mind experimental styles; in fact, we devote learned journals to their analysis; but our critics sneer at anything they consider "heavy social commentary" or—a worse word—"message." Stylistic heavy guns are dandy, as long as they aren't pointed anywhere in particular. We like the human condition as long as it's seen as personal and individual. Placing politics and poetics in two watertight compartments is a luxury, just as specialization of any kind is a luxury, and it is possible only in a society where luxuries abound. Most countries cannot afford such luxuries; this North American way of thinking is alien to them. It was even alien in North America not long ago. We've already forgotten that in the 1950s many artists, both in the United States and here, were persecuted solely on the grounds of their presumed politics. Which leads us to another mistaken Canadian belief: the belief that it can't happen here.

It has happened here, many times. Although our country is one of the most peaceful and prosperous on earth, although we do not shoot artists here, although we do not execute political opponents, and although this is one of the few remaining countries in which we can have a gathering like this without expecting to be arrested or blown up, we should not overlook the fact that Canada's record on civil rights issues is less than pristine. Our treatment of our native peoples has been shameful. This is the country in which citizens of Japanese origin were interned during the Second World War and had their property stolen. (When a government steals property it is called "confiscation.") It is also the country in which thousands of our citizens were arrested, jailed, and held without warrant or explanation, during the War Measures Act, a scant eleven years ago. There was no general outcry in either case. Worse things have not happened not because we are genetically exempt but because we lead pampered lives.

Our methods, in Canada, of controlling artists are not violent, but they do exist. We control through the marketplace and through critical opinion. We are also controlled by the economics of culture, which in Canada still happen to be those of a colonial branch plant. In 1960 the number of Canadian books published here was minute, and the numbers sold pathetic. Things have changed very much in twenty years, but Canadian books still account for a mere 25 per cent of the overall book trade and paperback books for under 5 per cent. Talking about this situation is considered nationalist chauvinism. Nevertheless, I suppose we are lucky to have any per cent at all; they haven't yet sent in the marines, and if they do it won't be over books but over oil.

We in this country should use our privileged position not as a shelter from the world's realities but as a platform from which to speak. Many are denied their voices; we are not. A voice is a gift; it should be cherished and used, to utter fully human speech if possible. Powerlessness and silence go together. One of the first efforts made in any totalitarian takeover is to suppress the writers, the singers, the journalists, those who are the collective voice. Get rid of the union leaders and pervert the legal system and what you are left with is a reign of terror.

As we read the newspapers, we learn we are, right now, in a state of war. The individual wars may not be large and they are being fought far from here, but there is really only one war: the war between those who would like the future to be, in the words of George Orwell, a boot grinding forever into a human face, and those who would like it to be a state of something we still dream of as freedom. The battle shifts according to the ground occupied by the enemy. Greek myth tells of a man called Procrustes, who was a great equalizer. He had a system for making all human beings the same size: if they were too small, he stretched them; if they were too tall, he cut off their feet or their heads. The Procrustes of today is the international operator, not confined to any one ideology or religion. The world is full of perversions of the notion of equality, just as it is full of perversions of the notion of freedom. True freedom is not being able to do whatever you like to whomever you want to do it to. Freedom that exists as a result of the servitude of others is not true freedom.

The most lethal weapon in the world's arsenal is not the neutron bomb or chemical warfare but the human mind that devises such things and puts them to use. But it is the human mind that can also summon up the power to resist, can imagine a better world than the one before it, can retain memory and courage in the face of unspeakable suffering. Oppression involves a failure of the imagination: the failure to imagine the full humanity of other human beings. If the imagination were a negligible thing and the act of writing a mere frill, as many in this society would like to believe, regimes all over the world would not be at such pains to exterminate them The ultimate desire of a Procrustes is a population of lobotomized zombies. The writer, unless he is a mere word processor, retains three attributes that power-mad regimes cannot tolerate: a human imagination, in the many forms it may take; the power to communicate; and hope. It may seem odd for me to speak of hope in the midst of what many of my fellow Canadians will call a bleak vision, but as the American writer Flannery O'Connor said, people without hope do not write novels.

WHAT IS REPRESSIVE TOLERANCE?

JOSEF ŠKVORECKÝ

I MUST confess that I signed up for this panel out of curiosity, and in the hope of learning from the other participants what oppressive tolerance is. Only when it was too late to withdraw did I learn that each of the discussants was expected to make a statement. So I am now faced with the necessity of making a statement about something that is a deep mystery to me.

First of all, repressive tolerance is a case of what the old logicians called *contradictio in adjecto*. In what sense can one be oppressive when one is tolerant? The only sense I can think of is that kind of spineless tolerance some people display toward any nonsense or provocative stupidity whatsoever. An encounter with that kind of tolerance is always irritating and therefore, to me, oppressive. But such oppression is not dangerous, and can even be a source of inspiration when it makes one mad.

Governments, and governmental institutions, can also be spinelessly tolerant and permissive of any outrage. I must confess I like such governments. They may irritate me, for in their tolerance they permit the dissemination of opinions and propaganda I know to be false, or even dangerous. But they do not oppress me; and out of that irritation come nice letters to the editor, articles, and even fiction. If they do oppress me, then it is only very indirectly: for I am oppressed by the thought of what would happen if the bearers of those false and dangerous ideas were to overthrow the tolerant government and introduce a regime of oppressive intolerance.

But should such tolerant governments ban the spreading of false and dangerous ideas, they would involve themselves in the inescapable quagmire of censorship. Who shall draw the line, and according to what criteria? Years ago, when I was young and foolish as all young and some old people are, we were discussing the achievements of the communist regime in Czechoslovakia in our field—that is, in literature. The achievements were negative, for the communists, more than the Nazis, managed to prune the blossoming tree of fiction and poetry until it had become a telegraph pole. But to give the communists the benefit of the doubt, I said to my much older friend: "All right. But at least they have suppressed the offensive trash—all those dime novels and tearjerkers that used to be sold on every corner." My old and wise friend said: "I wonder. There seems to be a natural law. If you want to have a Kafka or a Joyce, you must also have tons and tons of penny dreadfuls." Later on I realized that we still had the penny dreadfuls, only they were called socialist-realist novels; and strangely enough, although we had tons and tons of them, no Kafka emerged, except in the underground. And in authoritarian societies, the underground does not have access to printing press; not even to a duplicating machine.

So I say: Three cheers for hospital romances! For the ladies who let themselves be photographed as if the photographer worked for a gynecological journal! For the detectives who manage to break seven jaws and mutilate and murder seven people in the course of fifty pages! Without them we would have no D. H. Lawrence or Ernest Hemingway. Without repressive tolerance we would have neither.

Sometimes one hears Western writers expressing envy for the writers who have come out of the cold or even for those who still pine away in the cold, for they—say the Western writers—have ready-made, dramatic subject matter. Writers in our tolerantly repressive society seem to be suffering from writer's block half the time. Some people, including some of the writers expressing such opinions, think this is meant only as a joke, not to be taken seriously. But I wonder. Hemingway believed war to be the best school for a writer, and I think he was absolutely right—of course, on the condition that the writer survives the war, which cannot be guaranteed. Life in the cold certainly contributed greatly to the making of a Dostoevsky, a Solzhenitsyn, a Kundera, a Malaparte or a Günter Grass—but it also killed Mandelstam, Babel, Pilnyak, von Ossietzky, Gramsci, Vladislav Vančura, Závis Kalandra, and obviously hundreds, if not thousands, of nameless artists. I have never heard of a tolerantly repressive society killing a writer, except, perhaps, with booze or drugs.

So I shall stop here and listen attentively to my colleagues on this panel, because they apparently know immeasurably more about the subject than I.

THE UNENDING STRUGGLE

MARIE-CLAIRE BLAIS

IF WE are sometimes conscious of being part of a privileged society, where we can live as we like, where we are intellectually and politically free to live and write, with rights that are generally respected, we are conscious too that a kind of repressive tolerance is present in the experience of certain writers and their work. All it takes is a general atmosphere of denunciation and intolerance in which people begin to say, "This person is not one of us," and our creative freedom will be threatened, even where we are said to have complete intellectual liberty.

It was not long ago that society decided what a writer should say and write, particularly in a work of fiction which was supposed to reflect an ideal image of a bourgeois society, a society which was exclusively white, restrained in thought and in form. This is far from the conception we now have of a universal writer who writes books that belong to everyone. Nor was it long ago that the writer of fiction was generally supposed to restrict his choice of subject and characters to those that would please without being shocking or revealing the truth, and was at the mercy of the prejudices governing his time and of a complacent society which thought only of its physical and moral comfort.

Balzac, like many others, suffered from this invisible tyranny which one senses in his work. He sometimes yielded, in spite of his great genius, to the complacency that the times demanded. We are lucky to have been preceded by a generation of writers who were concerned with every aspect of tyranny in modern life and who revolutionized the arts. Thanks to Joyce, to Virginia Woolf, to Sartre and Camus and Beckett, we are free to write and think in new ways. Just a short time ago, black writers like Richard Wright and James Baldwin showed us how far from our understanding we had kept the terrible reality that they described.

One should speak too about a subject which is part of human rights, namely the rights of women, and about every kind of sexual discrimination, which results from deeply rooted prejudices. Women writers have spoken out courageously against these prejudices, sometimes taking men's names to protect themselves against men's rage: Charlotte Brontë, George Eliot, Olive Schreiner, and Radclyffe Hall —all did that, both for women and for homosexuals. *The Well of Loneliness* was condemned to death as an obscene book; Radclyffe Hall spoke of it as "the exiled child of my brain," though she continued to defend the book and to denounce the ignorance of her times. It is painful to think that these writers, who woke a new social conscience in their readers, saw themselves as pariahs and were compelled to defend themselves in the face of incomprehension and intolerance, even having to delay the publication of certain books until after their death, when they would have liked to see them published without suffering the outrage of public condemnation.

This was true of Forster's *Maurice,* which was published posthumously. In a letter to a friend, Forster spoke of *Maurice* in these words: "The man in my book is, roughly speaking, good, but Society nearly destroys him, he nearly slinks through his life furtive and afraid, and burdened with a sense of sin." He says, "My defense at any Last Judgment will be, I was trying to connect up and use all the fragments I was born with." It is as painful to think about the weight of society's judgment against Forster as it is to think of the accusations of vilest immorality leveled against the work of Wilde and Gide.

Gide, Proust, Wilde, and Radclyffe Hall fought to give us the relative freedom we have now. They fought against the slavery imposed by prejudice, just as Dostoevsky, Dickens, and Zola fought against wage slavery and the reduction of women, men, and children to slavery in factories, in mines, in domestic service. We can write more freely now because of them, but the struggle against every aspect of oppression must go on in every part of the world. For some writers are less free today than writers were fifty or one hundred years ago, and even in the Western world, our liberty is threatened by a reactionary tide. All those writers who are part of the resistance in totalitarian countries are fighting for an ideal of liberty which they think we have here, but we cannot be wholly free until we have helped them attain it.

MYTHOLOGY AND MARGINALITY

GASTON MIRON

ALONG with the ideals of liberty, justice, and equality, the concept of tolerance and individual rights was one of the principles put forward by the liberal democracies which were established in Europe in the second half of the nineteenth century. In France, for example, Alexis de Tocqueville earlier made himself one of the greatest propagators and defenders of this concept.

Since that time, tolerance has been part of the ideological arsenal of different bourgeoisies. They have used it subtly, and the writer has always played a game of entrapment with the idea and with the power which both uses and abuses it.

Once its power was established, the bourgeoisie invoked certain concepts to prevent its power from being questioned. Individual liberties were among these concepts.

On the one hand, a mythology of the writer was created: he was firmly located in the irrational, he was marginalized; often enough he internalized this image of himself propagated by the bourgeoisie. Sometimes he glorified his bohemian life-style and marginality, often out of derision or impotence.

On the other hand, the liberal democracies glorified pragmatic, utilitarian values. The writer was someone with his head in the clouds, outside day-to-day reality, while everyone else was occupied with the serious, necessary things of life. Art was beauty, noble leisure. This idea was current in the nineteenth century and opposed the writer in his irrationality to the rational bourgeois order.

However, little by little, the writer began to rebel, to become conscious of the dead end in which he found himself, particularly in the second half of the nineteenth century. Since the technical production of books became easier and public education was making considerable strides, the writer acquired ever more readers. These readers threatened to constitute—and did, in fact, for a period of time—a counterweight of opinion capable of ruining the power of bourgeois society.

In the early 1930s Louis Aragon wrote: *Feu sur les chiens savants de la social-democratie/Feu sur Léon Blum*. Immediately, the radical socialist party brought a suit against Aragon for incitement to murder. Numerous poets gave testimony by stating, "Your Honor, it is only a poem, it doesn't mean what it says, it's an image, a metaphor. The referent of literary language is not reality, it's the world of art, the text itself." The judge was quite pleased to see everyone fall into the trap: "Not guilty, exonerated of all blame." Ironically, these statements correspond to the bourgeois idea of the writer and of art. It was quite clear: writers were irresponsible. They could say whatever they wanted, they could threaten everyone, but it meant nothing. They had the leisure to be "freer" in their actions than did others: they were artists.

It was against this sort of image that the writer started to rebel. The writer had to demythologize himself, since the bourgeois mythology completely neutralized him.

I will say a few more words about the contemporary and most pernicious form of tolerance: the recuperation of the writer. In his rebellion, the writer at least constituted a counterpower, a counteropinion. But different strategies were developed to deal with this counterpower, which often questioned the very basis of bourgeois society.

For many years now, we have seen the spread of recuperation in the bourgeois democracies. As Roland Barthes has pointed out, recuperation is one of the great laws of history. Eventually, if not during one's life then after one's death, the process of recuperation is always completed. Thus, writers are invited to colloquia; they are given many honors; they are subsidized. Tolerance ends up by engendering tolerance: "It's not really so bad as all that. We have privileges. We do quite well, actually." The writer is recuperated and becomes, in turn, "tolerant."

Another form of recuperation is the power which conditions minds: the power of propaganda, of the educational system, which are auxiliary bourgeois powers capable of absorbing subversive discourse. In fact, this form of oppositional discourse is even highlighted.

In smaller cultural communities, the question of tolerance makes itself felt all the more acutely. Writers often feel themselves to be accomplices of tolerance. The writer cannot radically place himself in opposition to his culture if it is in danger of disappearing. Small cultural communities, small linguistic groups, are in a precarious position and must struggle daily for their existence and development. This state of affairs creates many problems for the artist and the intelligentsia in general in regard to the problem of freedom and tolerance. This tolerance sometimes even inspires guilt in us: the writer experiences this because he cannot eradicate himself with his culture, he cannot self-destruct. There is a threshold of tolerance which he must observe in relation to himself and to the collectivity. If not, it all becomes a process of self-destruction. This is the problem of small cultural communities and linguistic groups.

What should the writer do? I believe that the writer must try to escape the bourgeois mythology which has been formed around him for the last two centuries. In addition, the writer must involve himself more and more in the world around him: he must affirm the legitimacy of his creative and critical discourse, which is also a discourse of reality and rationality.

We all ask ourselves these questions and search for answers in a maze of traps: who is who? who is fooling whom? who is opposed to whom? It is really a game of mirrors.

—Translated by Donald Bruce

THE MARKET OF ANONYMITY

NAIM KATTAN

WE ARE familiar with forms of tolerance in societies which are not openly repressive. They marginalize the writer, leaving him the freedom to shout, howl, laugh, or cry. He can set his conscience at rest. Does he not say what he feels like saying? But what if there is no one to hear him? Out of ignorance, vanity, or the need to survive, the writer can address himself to invisible readers who hide themselves in order to read him, or better yet, to that reader "somewhere else" who ends up by uniting with him. He can also dream of future generations who will be able to flush him out, bring him out from the shadows, and display him before the universe. This phenomenon is so familiar, we tend to consider it as traditional.

I would like to speak about more recent forms of tolerance, more subtle and also more insidious, products of a postindustrial society and subproducts of a society which, if not free, is at least liberal.

The book is an article which is made and sold. It is subject to the laws of the market. This is not new, but in the nineteenth century, and even until twenty or thirty years ago, the book attracted only small business interests and artisans. Entertainment technology brought the book into medium-level industry and attracted big business to its production and distribution. The consequences of this development are numerous, and they do not favor the writer's freedom. If the book is an object which generates profit, the laws of the market can be applied to it. It is turned into a mass-produced object for undifferentiated audiences. In order to reach the largest possible audience, the book must be anonymous. And what is new is the volume. The book is but a starting point for films, television, and all the other vectors of the entertainment industry. Publishing becomes, if not in itself big business, at least an appendage of big business. The truly different, solitary writer finds that his terrain is shrinking. That which is not anonymous is reduced to peculiarity. The lure of success is often irresistible, and many writers hasten toward the new anonymity. They discover that even their names become commercial values in the market of anonymity. The others no longer find takers. Readers do not look for their books or ask for them, for the simple reason that they are not even aware of their existence.

An anonymous product is quickly exhausted. Of course, certain formulas create a dependency and a loyal and lasting public. The others must find new "trademarks." This phenomenon is already well known in the soap, cigarette, and beer industries. Within the multinational market, particular tastes must be catered to or created if necessary in order to stimulate the market. From this comes the propensity of the book market to create fashions to exploit the peculiar, the unconfessed, to expand it and banalize it so that it may become anonymous. After the horror story comes witchcraft; the sentimental novel is side by side with the pornographic one. Even then it is necessary to find new ingredients. Group sex gives way to sadomasochism which, in turn, moves over for incest. This extreme liberty is only apparent; in fact, it is governed by the laws of the market.

Everything which creates literature—the questioning, the complexity, the uncertainty of a quest—seems too difficult to sell. This encourages uniformity. The author who refuses the commercial imperatives condemns himself in the long run to marginality and isolation. He will always be free to write what he wants, and he may even find a publisher and readers, but his book will have no access to the market. There is no conspiracy here or even calculation. Rather, it is a conjuncture between freedom of production, mass culture, and entertainment technology. This is not some sort of organized repression. But the writer—isolated, abandoned, and despised because his writings are situated on the edge of the market—can justifiably feel that he is simply tolerated. In his mind, the word "tolerance" has a detestable connotation. To tolerate means to accept "otherness" or difference, by placing oneself in a position of acceptance or refusal. The person who tolerates considers himself endowed with a certain superiority because he can reject "otherness." The very notion of tolerance is an attack on the dignity of men. A work and a thought, by their free presence, establish their place in the hierarchy of art. The laws of the market establish a false and detrimental hierarchy according to the sales figures. Liberal society creates this subtle form of repressive tolerance. But because it is liberal, it provides the possibility, if not the means and the instruments, of denouncing this type of repression and consequently of combating it.

—Translated by Donald Bruce

A SITUATION OF PRIVILEGE

HANS MAGNUS ENZENSBERGER

I COME from a country which is rather like Canada in one respect: Germany has never made a revolution. It is unlike Canada, however, in that it has a history of profound counterrevolution. Democracy was imported to one half of Germany after the war by the Allies—or as some people would say, it was inflicted upon the country after the fall of fascism. In the other half of the country we have had imported revolution, not a self-made one. I'm not going to say much about Eastern Germany; it is a one-party dictatorship and therefore the question of civil liberties is clear-cut. About Western Germany, I could entertain you with a long list of incidents of police harassment and persecution, of searches without warrants, of police violence in demonstrations, but we are not talking here about the general civil liberties situation. Our question is, what is the place of writers, the role of writers, the situation of writers, in this context?

Here I must say that writers historically have never had it so good. Their situation has never been as good as it is now in my country, and we ought to think twice before complaining too much. Some people like to adduce the concept of repressive tolerance. This is a very dubious concept. To start with, it has a vaguely complaining sound. Of course, we all know what is *meant* by it, but what I feel uneasy about is the tendency to feel yourself the victim of something or other. The only way for a writer to deal with repressive tolerance is to exploit it fully, and not to complain, no matter what the man or the system giving you this tolerance may think about it. Certainly there is a kind of tolerance which is tactical, granted for certain purposes from the point of view of a system or of a conspiracy, but I don't think we ought to be very interested in the motives for this tolerance; we should just take it and exploit it. And that's all there is to be said, as far as I'm concerned, about the concept of repressive tolerance.

We have had some worries in the wake of a wave of hysteria which swept over West Germany after 1968, and especially after the terrorist acts of the 1970s. At one point, a law was passed which penalized the advocating of violence in print. This was perhaps the only legislative measure aimed at narrowing freedom of expression for writers. Writers reacted very forcefully against this law, arguing that a state attorney could find instances of advocating violence in the better part of world literature, since the world is not free of violence. The better part of dramatic literature, for example, *is* about violence, and therefore, there will always be somebody on stage advocating violence. If you wanted to prosecute literature on that account, we wouldn't be able to produce any of this commodity. After two or three years of complaining about the law, which was actually used in just two or three instances as far as I know, it was repealed.

So we are back to the situation which has become normal for us in the last few decades. It is actually a situation of privilege for the writer, because we do not live in a society which is free in the sense that everybody is able to speak their minds. If you were on a factory floor, and you talked politics too loudly, you might find yourself without a job in no time at all. This is not true of the writer: the writer runs certain risks, but I think they are risks inherent in his profession. If you write about certain things in a certain way, you may lose subsidies or not win prizes or fellowships. In fact, many of us have been excluded for quite some time from big media like the major television systems. But our complaints should not be too vociferous, because these things just point to the risks inherent in our profession. We should not be pleased about it but see it as a completely normal reaction on the part of powerful people anywhere.

There is a tendency among writers to adopt a whining tone, as if they were the pets of society and should be given some kind of especially delicious dog food all the time. I have noticed this tendency in my own country, and I am violently against it. Our profession is inseparable from certain risks, and as long as these risks do not imply that I go to prison or that I'm persecuted by the police, or that I'm deprived of any means of production, some sense of shame should inhibit us from complaining too loudly at a time when we are in fact privileged compared to other citizens.

Our situation of privilege has some other consequences. Many intellectuals, many writers, have a sincere wish to help others. This congress is an example of this wish, the sincerity of which I do not want to put in doubt. However, there is something problematical about the position of the helper, especially when the helper is speaking on behalf of others. This is inevitable when the other is not able to speak for himself, but it also creates a certain ambiguity, because nobody will speak as well as the man who speaks on his own and for himself. As we can see in the welfare state, many helpers are bureaucrats, and many bureaucrats get paid for their job because they are considered helpers. So we ought to be very careful to distinguish the type of help—if any—which we as writers are able to offer, from that of the warden or custodian.

This is not only a moral problem but also a political problem, because the world is full of political bodies that think of themselves as representatives or authorities qualified to speak on behalf of others. One famous example is the Leninist concept of the working-class party: the working-class party speaks on behalf of the working class; the central committee of the party speaks on behalf of the party; and the politbureau speaks on behalf of the central committee.

If you really think hard about helping others, it's not as easy as it might appear. The man who is always on the good side and always signing the right paper may not do any damage to anybody else, but it is possible for him to do some damage to himself, because he runs the risk of becoming smug. In our type of society it has been up to now rather easy—perhaps too easy—always to come out on the good side; I think people, at least people of my generation, have not yet been put to a real test. History is quite likely to provide such a test for us, and there might be nothing wrong with keeping this in mind.

THE WRITER AND POLITICAL POWER

MICHEL TOURNIER

IT IS sometimes said that the French think on the Left but live on the Right. This is because in principle the Left represents imagination and generosity, while the Right represents security and the preservation of acquired advantages. Now as each of us knows, the heart is on the left and the pocketbook on the right. Conversely, however, it could be said that writers think on the Right and write on the Left. In any case, this is true of some of them—and a number of the greatest are among these.

Nothing is less "social" than the preoccupations expressed by Stendhal's career and life. Nonetheless, the speech made by Julien Sorel at the end of *The Red and the Black* seems to anticipate Marx and Engels's *Communist Manifesto,* which appeared eighteen years later.

For his part, Balzac stated: "I write between two torches, the Throne and the Altar." This remark would seem to indicate a penchant for furiously reactionary works; in short, the novelistic equivalent of de Maistre and Bonald. Fortunately, there is none of that in Balzac. The tableau of Restoration society which he created in the *Human Comedy* smells strongly of revolutionary gunpowder.

Flaubert's fulminating declarations against "the people" in general and the Communards in particular are well known. But the infinite respect with which he treats the poor in his works, for example, Félicité in *A Simple Heart,* originates in a generous spirit, indeed a utopian populist one.

Émile Zola reveals himself to be an even more contradictory figure. He defended the theory of the "naturalist" novel, which would lay out the heredity of characters—all of whom proceed from the same family tree—and from this he would deduce their behavior with a fatal rigor. Thus, we have the criteria of "heredity" emanating typically from the Right, indeed from the extreme Right. However, none of this carefully elaborated design comes to light from a reading of the *Rougon-Macquart* novels. Rather, the characters in these novels are all crushed, or at the very least dominated, solely by the pressure of environment—a characteristically leftist view. Moreover, we are all well aware of Zola's courageous actions in the Dreyfus Affair, a situation in which, for the rightists of the day, Dreyfus's alleged guilt stemmed from his race, in other words from his heredity.

Undoubtedly, one could enumerate many examples of this kind. Instead, let us simply observe that an important literary work is naturally infused with a leftist spirit, whatever the political ideas of its author. Now, it is quite another matter with politicians in power. Whether their thoughts tend to the Right or to the Left, the aim of their actions is the maintenance of their own stability and the conservation of their political domination, even when their origins are vaguely revolutionary. In reference to the recent events which have been shaking Poland, the following thought-provoking statement was found in a Soviet editorial: Solidarity was accused of wanting "to destabilize the socialist revolution." It is indeed an admirable sort of revolution which proclaims above all else its conservatism! Forty years ago, though I was quite young at the time, a slogan used by the Vichy government made quite an impression on me. It said more or less this: "The watchword of the National Revolution: Conserve!"

Consequently, one ought not to be astonished if the relations between political power and literary creation have always been delicate, often stormy, sometimes catastrophic. To be convinced of this, it suffices to evoke the names of some famous pairings, such as Molière and Louis XIV, Diderot and Catherine the Great, Voltaire and Frederick of Prussia, André Chénier and Robespierre, Mme. de Staël and Napoleon Bonaparte, Victor Hugo and Napoleon III, Solzhenitsyn and Brezhnev, Malraux and de Gaulle, Günter Grass and Willy Brandt. In these pairings, the writer is crushed by the politician in the short term, but the passage of time works in the writer's favor. Valéry observed that we speak today of "Stendhal and Napoleon." But who would have dared to suggest to Napoleon that one day they would say "Stendhal and Napoleon"?

The idea of this superior posthumous dignity should never leave a writer when he meets a great political leader. We suffer through

Molière's fawning on the King, which sullies some of his comedies. We detest Goethe's servility at the feet of Napoleon. And, closer to our own time, we do not particularly admire the eagerness, characteristic of an insignificant journalist, with which Malraux paid court to Stalin, Mao, Kennedy, or de Gaulle. The same Malraux groaned that Chateaubriand had not made the journey to Saint Helena in order to speak to the vanquished Emperor: the author of *Antimémoires* would certainly not have missed this "scoop"! We are free to prefer the noble confrontation, in all its terrible inequality, of Mme. de Staël with Napoleon, or that of Victor Hugo with Napoleon III, or even of Solzhenitsyn defying the Soviet apparatus.

A new word has forced its way into the political vocabulary, but it lends itself well to our subject—"recuperation." Formerly, one would have said "compromise." In other words, a writer can let himself be bought by political power. He will have peace, comfort, and maybe even riches, in return for which he will agree to wear a muzzle and leave his testicles in the cloakroom. Thus, there are "writers' unions" in the socialist countries, where one finds a whole zoo of stuffed, feathered creatures. I take good care not to cast stones at them, for were I to find myself in a similar situation, there is no proof that I would not prefer this solution to exile or the Gulag. Not everyone has the martyr's vocation.

Our Western societies also possess poisons which, though they may be milder, are nonetheless equally effective in taming the untamed writer. These poisons are the literary prizes, the academies, the official posts, and more significantly, the confidence and loyalty of a particular public of readers. The more a writer puts himself personally into his work, the more he is exposed to this sort of compromise. The incorruptibility of the writer of pure fiction has less merit than that of the author of essays, confessions, or diaries. The lineage of the great "intimists"—Montaigne, Rousseau, Chateaubriand, Gide—is evidently much more exposed to attack from the environment than that of the great "fictionalists"—Stendhal, Balzac, Hugo, Flaubert, Zola. This is why we can never do enough justice to André Gide's political commitments. During his long career, this man, who always sought to put himself totally into each of his books, never ceased to challenge society. First, by attacking, in *Corydon,* heterosexual tyranny—at the very moment when Victorian England was grinding down Oscar Wilde; then by sympathizing with the communists, and finally by denouncing Stalinism for what it was (Louis Guilloux, who had made the same trip to the U.S.S.R. and had seen the same things, preferred to enclose himself in the silence of coward-ice); then by compelling himself to be a member of an assizes jury in order to see how justice was dispensed; and above all, by under-taking the long and dangerous journey to Chad and the Cameroons, after which he denounced the misdeeds of colonialism. Rarely has such a privileged and refined bourgeois so obstinately poisoned his own existence and created for himself so many enemies, for the sole aim of fulfilling what he considered to be his duty. Those of his imi-tators who, in turn, sought to be "committed"—Malraux, Sartre, Ara-gon, Camus—appear singularly prudent in comparison.

Writers of pure fiction who do not base their work on their own tribulations can more easily establish a distance between themselves and their work, thanks to which they can claim to compromise them-selves while at the same time retaining what is essential. Erik Satie did not like Maurice Ravel. Upon learning that the author of *Boléro* had just refused the Legion of Honor, he said, "Ravel refuses the Le-gion of Honor, but his whole work accepts it." This was quite unjust toward Ravel, who was all the same no Camille Saint-Saëns. Con-versely, however, one can imagine a writer saying, "I can very well accept the Legion of Honor since my whole work refuses it." Such a writer's motto could be: Accept every compromise in the name of a life's work, itself incorruptible. I know some writers who, deep within themselves, feel so radically marginal that they could easily become President of the Republic or Pope without believing that they had conceded the slightest concession to the "system."

The important question of the writer's vulnerability vis-à-vis power and society could be related advantageously to thoughts con-cerning genius and talent. It could be said that genius is solitary cre-ation, while talent is rather more related to communication. A writer of genius who lacks talent will remain isolated, misunderstood, steril-ized by the absence of an echo. His work risks disappearing with him, or even before him, for he may, out of despair, destroy it with his own hands. For its part, talent makes the milieu in which the cre-ator is immersed conductive and it alone permits him to make him-self heard by his contemporaries. But this conductivity is not without danger, for it operates in both directions. That is why a talented writer who lacks genius soaks up like a sponge everything that passes within his reach. He is celebrated and runs from success to success because he understands everything, he imitates everything—or better yet, he gives form to the raw material society provides him with. This is not negligible, but he risks becoming nothing more than an echo chamber. On the whole, this sort of writer takes more than he gives. This reminds us of the terrible rivalry between Michelangelo and Raphael. One day Michelangelo, being somber both of humor and of dress as was his custom, remarked on a brilliant and joyful procession going by. It was Raphael and his friends. "Always surrounded like a prince," muttered Michelangelo. Raphael, who had heard him, exclaimed, "Always alone, like an executioner."

Certainly, genius is condemned if it is not attended by a minimum of communicability. But conversely, we suffer to see writers whom we truly admire disfigured by negative traits, by mutilations and deformities which betray their belonging to society, indeed their shameful complicity with it. I am thinking now of a particular pair of writers, both exemplary and damned, provided by the example of Victorian England.

First Rudyard Kipling. We cannot evoke without some tenderness the author of *Just-So Stories, Kim,* or the two *Jungle Books,* which are a delight of the imagination and the spirit. On the other hand, we can accept only with some difficulty the official eulogist of the English colonial empire, and Kipling's secular arm, Lord Baden-Powell, the sad hero of the Boer War. In Kipling there is indisputably a pathological horror of sexuality and—fatally—an apology for the Army and war, the school of the "virile" virtues, accompanied by its corollary, the "scout" pedagogy, the aim of which is to combat "bad thoughts" by means of exhausting physical activity. "Kill, don't make love. Disembowel your neighbor; that will keep you from caressing him."

And inexorably arises the shadow, the countercheck, the fraternal enemy, just as much a caricature but in a diametrically opposed sense: Oscar Wilde, the anti-Kipling, the monocled salon hero, the round, fat-bottomed dandy whose chicken-assed mouth and black teeth exude ferocious words.

I admire these two writers equally; I owe something to the work of each. But I lament the hideousness inflicted upon their genius by the Carabossa-like stepmother, bent over their cradle, this Queen Victoria, obese but without guts, without feeling. Her callous eye did not see the ten-year-old children that the society of which she was the symbol sent to labor in the depths of the Yorkshire mines. Kipling and Wilde let themselves be trapped in this society. It would have been preferable had their genius unleashed itself against it.

These are only two examples among many. Actually, the relationship between the politician and the writer is mediated by public opinion. But this public opinion must first exist. Molière could not hope to shake royal power by his comedies. A hundred years later Beaumarchais succeeded. In the lapse of a century, an enlightened "clientele" constituted itself, a clientele without which nothing is possible. Since then its importance has not ceased to increase, and with this the political importance of writers. This evolution is all the more remarkable for proceeding at the same rate as the constant reinforcement of the material means placed at the disposition of tyranny. Formerly, a ragtag band having nothing more on its side than desperate courage was able to measure up victoriously to a regular army. Between the scythes of the peasant rebels and the soldiers' sabers, the forces were not too unequal. In the missile age, the people do not have the slightest chance of winning against the regular army.

However, these last years have been marked by some resounding "downfalls." In the U.S.A., the president was forced from office by two journalists. Only the intellectuals are capable of shaking the Kremlin. In Latin America, in Africa, and in Iran, tyrants tumble down under the shock of words. What must be stressed here is not the idea of writers being involved in an ephemeral and accidental *fronde,* but rather the idea of writers exercising a fundamental social function. "Order and disorder, these two scourges," as Paul Valéry wrote. It is, in effect, a question of two equally redoubtable poles between which human societies have always oscillated. The constant in all literary creation is to remind us that human society must not, under pain of death, become the equivalent of a beehive or a termite colony. Society must ceaselessly put itself into question and evolve. It is the writer's task to break the existing frameworks, tear down the barriers, and create a new vision and sensibility. A literary masterpiece always has the same ring to it as a call to disorder.

It is therefore inevitable that the tyrant should consider the writer to be a troublemaker and persecute him accordingly. And, indeed, the great mythological figures—whose constant renaissance and common usage in society constitute the ultimate success of literary creation—are without exception the rebels and the damned, from Prometheus to Don Juan, not to mention Tristan, Faust, and Robinson Crusoe.

The wise and lucid political leader knows—as the tyrant most certainly does—that it is necessary to leave society a margin of evolution and revolution, for that is life itself. We would not be giving a false idea of democracy if we were to say that it is a regime under which it is possible to change everything without breaking anything.

I would have liked to close these reflections without mentioning my personal situation. But it is my duty to say that, on those occasions when I have met with contemporary political leaders, I have rarely felt anything "special" in their presence. An obsessional attention and rigorous obedience to the imperatives of the social and economic conjuncture leave no room in them for the distance, the nobility, the humor, the eroticism, and the playful aggressiveness which are the cardinal virtues of the literary perspective.

It is an entirely different situation with a member of the opposition, for he is condemned to imagine, and by this, he becomes the writer's privileged interlocutor. It is certainly a very strange dialogue which can establish itself between these two "opponents": the politician who hopes soon to possess the reality of power, and the writer who here and now possesses power, though the writer's power is imaginary by its very nature and destined to remain so. Their fragile alliance is based on the notion of the "possible," understood in two different ways: on the one hand it is an aspiration, and on the other, an imaginary fact.

—Translated by Donald Bruce

DISCRIMINATING TREATMENT

HANS CHRISTOPH BUCH

IN East Germany after the expulsion of the popular singer Wolf Biermann, a wave of repression began against writers critical of the regime; most of them have been expelled to West Germany by now. There was an exodus of the most talented and the most interesting writers. At first they were really expelled. Later the government changed its tactics and gave them visas for a limited time of three years; but practically, these writers have been banned from their country because they cannot go back. If they go back, for instance to visit relatives, they have to undress at the border and are searched in a humiliating way for manuscripts or whatever goods they could carry or hide on their bodies. This happened to a friend of mine, Klaus Schlesinger, a well-known writer; after he complained to the government, however, it suddenly stopped.

The East German Government is skillful in dealing with these dissidents, because they are not all treated the same way. First of all, those who are internationally famous can permit themselves almost anything. They can speak out, abroad or at home, and they are only mildly warned or told to be more careful. But they would never be expelled because the government fears the noise that such a step would make. For instance, Stefan Hermlin, vice-president of International PEN, whom I recently met in Paris, said in a French TV broadcast that it was a shame that the works of Günter Grass were not being published in East Germany; in Poland, he added, they were published. And he could make this remark without fear of consequences.

Another famous writer, Stefan Heym, and a famous dissident who is more a philosopher than a writer, Robert Havemann, were sentenced because they had violated a law against the transfer of foreign currency. This is a clever tactic, because it sounds like a real criminal act, although everyone who knows socialist countries knows that Western currency is constantly brought in and that it circulates even on an official level. So Havemann and Heym were sentenced to pay a ransom of a few thousand marks, which didn't hurt them much, but it was a symbolic warning, and at the same time a humiliation, because they were put on the same level as smugglers of Western currency.

The case is more severe with writers who are known only within the two Germanies, writers who have no international fame. These writers are either expelled or get visas limited to three years, and are told more or less openly that the government does not want them to come back. And this is still a mild kind of treatment in comparison to what is happening with dissidents in other socialist countries.

The situation is far more serious and bloody for unknown writers, young writers who have not published in the West, who have no fame, no protection, no lobby, no friends. In most cases, their names are not even known to Amnesty International. These people are really the victims of cultural repression, and· they are defenseless. For instance, a writer by the name of Manfred Bartz, born in 1934, who has contributed short stories to the satirical magazine *Eulenspiegel* and written for cabarets, but never published a book of his own; his name is almost unknown outside of the GDR. He was arrested for having violated Article 106 of the East German constitution, which is directed against what is called "antisocialist propaganda." Although he was a regular contributor to satirical cabarets and magazines, which to a certain extent can criticize what are called "errors" or "mistakes" in East Germany, this writer was condemned to a six-year sentence in prison. First he was expelled from the writers' union and had to work as a manual laborer on a construction site; later he was condemned to the six-year term, which he is still serving. His case has only recently become known in West Germany, and he will probably be released soon, because the West German Government pays a sort of ransom to free people from East German jails. It's a real business, which has been going on for quite a long time. There is also a chance he may be exchanged for a spy, since there is a constant exchange of spies between the two Germanies.

Another case, even less known, is even more revolting: it's the case of a young woman, Barbel Sänger, who was arrested simply because of a manuscript she had written. It was a play, a radio play, I think, about a family trying to escape from East to West Germany. She did not describe the conflicts within this family in order to denounce the state and its repression, but she was naïve enough to think that such a play could be put on stage, or at least discussed, in East Germany, because she wanted to explore the subject, which was a common fate in East Germany: many people try to escape and are sentenced to jail. She mailed the manuscript to a publisher, who immediately handed it over to the secret police. The young woman was arrested, but when PEN intervened we were told that this person was not a writer since she had never published anything.

This is a very important point: many of these young people are not professional writers; they have no books published, which means that they are less protected and more vulnerable. However, I would like to cite a famous example from Nadezhda Mandelstam's book, *Hope Against Hope*. It's a memoir, in which she tells the story of Osip Mandelstam, her husband, and Pasternak. One day, after Mandelstam had been arrested by Stalin, Boris Pasternak got a personal phone call from Stalin. And Stalin said, "Comrade Pasternak, I have one question. Could you tell me whether this man Mandelstam is a talented poet, a poet of genius?" Now, Pasternak's answer was really daring and it still sounds very convincing to me. He said, "That's not the question at this moment," although Mandelstam was at that time, and probably still is, one of the leading poets of his century. But the question is not whether someone is talented or not; that's another question to be decided by literary critics. When someone is being persecuted, we should all be on his side and try to free him. That applies to many unknown writers, who maybe are not *great* writers, in Susan Sontag's sense, but they are being persecuted and arrested, and therefore we should all be on their side.

Postscript, 1983: Robert Havemann died in April 1982, in East Berlin. His funeral, although not open to the public, became a symbolic manifestation against the communist regime; hundreds of people demonstrated, under the eyes of the secret police, for freedom from political repression and censorship. Barbel Sänger and Manfred Bartz have both been released, under pressure from PEN, Amnesty International, and the government in Bonn. Other young writers, artists, and intellectuals have been arrested in their place.

Censorship and Self-censorship

THE WRITER IN CHILE

SERGIO MARRAS

To UNDERSTAND the conditions surrounding literary creativity in Chile, one must understand the context in which writers who have decided to stay in the country must evolve in order to develop their creative work. Therefore, I shall first describe the legal, political, and economic parameters influencing and limiting our literary community.

Since March 11 of this year, a new political constitution has ruled Chile. The natural and exclusive right of Chileans to govern themselves is not recognized there; the constitution denies ideological pluralism, it grants excessive powers to the President of the Republic, it minimizes the role of Parliament, it gives unlimited power to the armed forces, and lastly, it subordinates fundamental human rights to the arbitrariness of the government. If this be little enough for a state constitution which pretends to be democratic, it establishes the framework by which the economy of the country will be ruled.

Not all clauses in this constitution have full force and effect at this time, but all will in 1989. Now a temporary legal regime governs, and it allows for even less popular participation than those clauses that will take effect in 1989. For example, without consulting anyone, the President of the Republic can decree a state of emergency whenever he believes there might be a disturbance of the peace. Other powers permit the arrest and detention of persons for a twenty-day period without having to bring them before a tribunal; the restriction of the right of assembly and freedom of information; the prohibiting of entry to the country and the expulsion of those considered guilty of certain conduct or, generally, of those considered dangerous; the confinement of any person to a location inside the country as determined by the government. All of these measures can be taken without the right of appeal, according to the private will of the chief of state.

Today Chile lives under a state of emergency, and therefore all that I have just stated prevails.

With respect specifically to the role of the writer, we must examine the right to freedom of expression. A law exists requiring a special permit from the Ministry of the Interior before any book, new magazine, or any other printed matter may be circulated. The penalty for transgressing the law consists of a large fine and/or imprisonment. It should be noted that the government rarely refuses a permit for explicit reasons. Its method, rather, is not to respond to the application. Since the law does not establish a time limit for the ministry to reply, years may pass before a denial or authorization arrives. Recently, one of the few remaining opposition journals was notified that it did not have authorization to publish news on Chile, which this journal had been doing for two years; it was restricted to the publication of international news only. The journal had to suspend operations entirely and take the case before the tribunals for a decision on its future.

This is the legal framework within which the writer living in Chile must exist.

A second infringement on the freedom of expression comes from the economic policies the government is attempting to impose constitutionally: the adoption of an extreme free-market philosophy, by which the state loses a large part of its control of the economy, leaving it in the hands of the large economic consortiums. As well, the state abandons such functions as the development and assimilation of national culture. In adopting this philosophy, the regime has made the decision that all ventures, including artistic literary activities, must be profit-making, or at least self-financing wherever possible. Artistic activity in Chile had traditionally been in the hands of the universities, the latter being relied on for funding books, theatrical works, and films out of budgets designed for such projects. The universities were also counted on to provide air time for cultural programs on television channels that they owned. Today this phenomenon has virtually disappeared. These channels have become strictly commercial. Artists must finance themselves, or fall into the hands of what has been termed "corporate art," receiving bursaries from large corporations and thus assimilating only acritical art, exclusively formal and almost always ahistorical, art that can be completely controlled.

With respect to literary activity, this regime, like no other experienced before in our country, has imposed a high tax. Together with the high printing costs and the low economic means of the average Chilean, this tax makes books an almost unattainable good for the majority. According to Chilean publishers, the industry has become depressed from heavy taxes and the excessive printing costs of limited editions—never more than two thousand volumes.

According to these publishers, the limited editions are also made necessary by the drastic change in the reading habits of Chileans in recent years. This change is not only the result of low salary levels, but also of the failure of educational institutions to require reading. Further, there has been an excessive rise in commercial television, which the government has done nothing to counterbalance. For example, exactly one half the number of books published in 1973 was published in 1976. If we take the total number of books in the editorial market in 1970, including imports, we see that in 1975 the number was reduced to less than one half the previous volume. Lastly, a survey done by the government determined that the influence of books on 70 per cent of Chilean men and 90 per cent of Chilean women was either negligible or nil.

By this point, you are probably wondering what a writer in Chile today is doing. The change has been as great as that required of a fish which has to learn to live outside the water in minutes. She or he has to learn to write in another form, in an ambivalent, ambiguous language, breaking molds and genres, mixing, at times, prose and poetry, permanently stimulating his creativity in both form and content. Young writers who began their creative work after the advent of the regime have been learning to express themselves from within censorship, knowing that most likely nothing will be published. Thus is reborn the writer who writes but does not publish, having to share his work through recitals, literary workshops, or very limited and modest editions. A submerged literary activity is created, one that seldom materializes in book form.

And if there are no books, what does the writer live on? In some cases, they work as journalists, for the cultural pages of magazines and newspapers, without being able to say what they want and describing an authorized cultural world that hardly exists. In other cases, writers become advertising writers in spite of themselves. The enormous advertising boom in recent years has absorbed a great deal of the creativity of the young. Sometimes the writer is a professor of literature, and thus must hold himself to the assigned programs, in fear of losing his job if he attempts to teach differently. But we could say that these are the lucky ones. The majority live by being underemployed, or on low salaries as civil servants or employees of private corporations, able to devote only a minimal amount of time to literature.

But, in spite of everything, literature survives. Somehow, the new languages that have had to be created have strengthened it. A new creative power is beginning to take its first steps. Poetry has undoubtedly benefited the most. A new poetic language has planted itself which goes farther from the frontiers of its own genre, to be transported into other fields, such as music.

I would like to reaffirm that artistic evolution in Chile continues, for now through musicians and composers who create songs that will not be recorded for a long time, nor listened to on the radio, nor seen on television; through dramatists who present their work on improvised stages, or on the street; through books printed in modest editions or never published, or through books without the possibility of mass circulation; and through readings and recitals among friends. I wish to reaffirm that while in the official Chile democratic culture is obstructed and limited, in the basements of the country—in the Chile that doesn't have a public face, with limited or no access to the means of communication—a new art and a new literature grows and develops. As a philosopher of ours once said, "In spite of everything, the act of thinking allows intelligence to breathe." I would like to add that intelligence in Chile has still not been totally suppressed.

FORMS OF SELF-CENSORSHIP

ZDENA TOMIN

I'D LIKE to take up the issue of self-censorship and to talk as clearly as I can about the forms of self-censorship I know best. Having lived in the West for only one year, I really have not penetrated the depths of censorship or self-censorship as it functions here, so I will talk about the self-censorship in Czechoslovakia, the country where I lived for forty years.

I think you can distinguish three forms of self-censorship. The first is the fight against censorship. This form of self-censorship was very popular and developed to quite an extent in our country during the sixties, especially in the latter half, when writers knew that writing all they wanted to write, saying all they wanted to say, would never get their books, plays, or essays past the censors. Don't forget that this was the period of liberalization, which reached a peak in 1968 in the Prague Spring, and so censorship was not as strong as it had been, but it still existed. Writers were using allegory, absurdity, and fantasy, to express—under a rather thin disguise—their true feelings about their society. And, because they could count on a shallow education on the part of the censors, using figures from medieval literature, or from Greek tragedy or comedy, was relatively safe. They wrote in such a way that everyone immediately understood what they were trying to say. So there is a form of self-censorship that may be positive under certain conditions, because it can get ideas past the censors to the people who are eager to understand and to perceive.

The second form is what I call self-censorship as a means of either survival or success. This is a very complicated, tricky and rather sad form of self-censorship. It's hard to say something against it, when it's used as a means of survival. Who are we to tell other people, "Die or go to prison, or lose your position, your house, your family, your wife, forever"? The price paid for it is that you survive, but lose your integrity. We see this kind of sad, disintegrating, crippled writer in our country nowadays. These are the writers who are not banned, who have decided to perform the ritual of writing, either because they are not brave enough, or because they know they are not good enough, or because they were really put under pressure and are fearful—even today in our forests and our small towns there are still barracks and military camps of the Soviet army—and they have decided to impose censorship on themselves.

Censorship was abandoned in Czechoslovakia in 1968, but after the occupation of the country later that year, especially in 1969, the primary demand of the new regime, backed by the official army, was that total control be imposed on the mass media, and on literature, as soon as possible. But this total control, this total censorship, was to remain without an official name. So this kind of censorship was known as self-censorship. This means that every writer, every editor, is himself responsible for what he writes; but he is responsible to the people, which really means to the censors, and ultimately to the state police. He knows very well that whenever he writes something which will be considered politically unacceptable, or even merely uncomfortable, he has to cope with losing his job, losing his membership in the writers' union, and eventually being put into prison. And the price being paid for this kind of self-censorship is a sad disintegration of integrity.

The third form is self-censorship as a responsible action on the part of the writer. It is perhaps the trickiest as far as literature goes. I have had experience with both sides of the problem.

Banning a writer—not just censoring his works, but banning him as a person, as a citizen, making him an outcast—can be at the same time a rather profound liberation. Being banned, you don't have to think any more about self-censorship as a means of success or survival, because you've already been thrown deep into the gulf: there is nowhere else you can fall. You don't feel responsible for struggling with some form of censorship; you suddenly feel responsible for yourself, for your work, and for the society you are now looking at from the bottom. That's a strange point of view to experience, and it is liberating, in a way. You suddenly write everything you want, everything you feel really deeply; you write only if you must, knowing that each page you write can put you in prison. You write the way you have to—not paid, not commissioned, not thinking of publishing, but because you have to.

So this was a period in my life when I did not impose censorship on myself at all. But there was one catch: I was not sure about the quality of my writing. The deep freedom of being banned, of being stripped of your own self-censorship, is so exhilarating that you cannot really control the quality of your work. You circulate the *samizdat* among your colleagues, and you may reach several hundred of the general public, but you have no critics, you have no criticism. That's the catch to this kind of freedom.

And then, as I said, I went to the West, where I suddenly experienced a very strong self-censorship. Not because of Western publishers or anything like that, but because I felt I had a duty, being here now, physically free, not hampered, nor intimidated by the police, nor being in prison, to write something. I decided on a play, which would throw light on the people I had left behind. There is a guilty feeling you have—you feel like a bloody deserter, leaving your wounded fellow soldiers lying on the field, but that is another deception. We are not an army, we are each individuals living for ourselves, but you feel it nonetheless.

So I felt this kind of duty, and suddenly I knew that I could *not*, in this first play, tackle all the problems which are so painful for the human rights movement, all the disagreements we have, all the terrible gossip, all the envy. I felt, I cannot *deal* with it, I have to *celebrate* them. And the first draft I wrote was impotent; it was a celebration without conviction. I tried to do better the next time but a kind of censorship still applied; I have only a limited time, and I want to show what is most important for the people in the West to know: that the dissidents are not professional troublemakers, that there is a lot of joy, that they make love, that the secret police are not grim murderers but rather betrayed small people—not the less dangerous for that. I hope you understand: I just wanted to show you a totally different picture from what I usually read in the newspapers under the heading, "dissidents," or "Czechoslovaks." It's what I would call self-censorship from a certain responsibility.

CENSORSHIP IN SOUTH AFRICA

NADINE GORDIMER

I ONCE wrote that the best way to write was to do so as if one were already dead: afraid of no one's reactions, answerable to no one for one's views. I still think that is the way to write. Insofar as no one forces a writer to visualize an "audience" (unless he has one eye on the bank), to imagine who it is who is going to be moved, shocked, delighted, incensed, perhaps illuminated by the piece of work in hand, it is possible to keep to this ideal of a writer's freedom. But in the circumstances of political and social pressure applicable to writers under consideration at our conference, this basis of the writer's basic freedom is beleaguered from without and psychologically threatened from within.

In the society in which I live and work—apartheid South Africa—the legal framework of censorship affects the work even of dead writers; so there's no freedom to be gained, there, in my dictum of writing as if from beyond the grave. A banned work remains banned, even if the writer is no longer living, just as it does in the case of the exiled writer, who is alive but civically "dead" in his own country.

Censorship of literature is procured chiefly by two statutes, the Internal Security Act of 1950 and the Publications Act No. 42 of 1974. Together these statutes aim to ensure that the South African reader is deprived not only of sexually titillating magazines, books, and films, but also of serious works that question, radically, the institutions and practices of a society based on racial discrimination. Together these statutes are designed to preserve political orthodoxy according to the ruling color and class, by isolating the public from radical political thought and contemporary literary trends.

The Internal Security Act of 1950 is primarily aimed at suppressing overtly political writings, but its legislative tentacles have also strangled a substantial body of creative writing since, in the words of Thomas Mann, in some eras and some countries, "politics is fate," and imaginative writing has always been occupied, in one interpretation or another, with human fate. This Internal Security Act functions as a censor by providing for the banning of both publications *and* writers. In the first instance, the act authorizes the banning of any publication which expresses views "calculated to further the achievement of any of the objects of communism." That qualifying "any" means that those precepts of human rights which are common to the whole spectrum of progressive thought, from liberalism to communism, are lumped together, along with the actual advocation of violent overthrow of the state, under the general heading of subversion.

It was under this act, and not the Censorship Act, that the moderate, wide-circulation black daily newspaper, the *World,* was banned in 1977. The relevant clause invoked was that the newspaper had served "as a means for expressing views or conveying information the publication of which is calculated to endanger the security of the State or the maintenance of public order." What the *World* had indeed been publishing was an accurate account of the actions and state of mind of the black population of South Africa, and in particular Soweto, in the year of school boycotts that followed the black children's and students' uprising against second-class education in 1976, and the labor unrest which gathered momentum in 1977.

Other provisions of the same act have the power to impose a ban not merely on a single publication such as the *World* but on *all* the utterances as well as the writings of certain individuals. Persons whose views may not be quoted at all in South Africa in terms of Section 11 of the act fall into several categories. First, members of organizations outlawed under the Internal Security Act itself; second, persons banned by the Minister of Justice, under Section 9, from attending gatherings, on the ground that in his opinion they have engaged in activities which further the achievement of any of the objects of communism. In the sixties, a whole generation of black South African writers living abroad was listed under the third category, which bans ex-residents of South Africa who, again in the opinion of the Minister of Justice, "advocate or engage in activities abroad calculated to further the achievement of any of the objects of communism." These writers include Alex la Guma, Dennis Brutus, Ezekiel

Mphahlele and the late Can Themba. Of them all, only the works of Mphahlele, with the passage of time and his return to South Africa under a restricted academic dispensation, have been released from this type of ban. A few white writers in exile, notably Ruth First, Albie Sachs, and Mary Benson, are prevented from being read in South Africa by a similar type of ban.

With the rise, during the seventies and eighties, of the Black Consciousness movement, with its strong emphasis on the cultural arm of the black struggle for human rights, a number of young black writers and aspiring writers have been prevented from publishing their work because they are banned under Section 9, the second category of the act, which prevents attendance at gatherings. A ban of this nature would seem to have little to do with writers, since they don't do their writing at public gatherings. But these young writers see their literary activity as an integral part of their political activity. Most are active as speakers at political meetings as well as poets or short story writers at home. If the ban that prevents them from attending gatherings usually is not imposed because of anything they have written but because of their platform or organizational activity, or the part they have played in boycotts or strikes, nevertheless that ban falls also upon their writings, since it implies that nothing they say or write may be quoted or published. Thus, a fairy tale or a love poem by one of these writers may not be published any more than a political statement one of them may have made.

Other writers are silenced by a ban in the first category of Section 11, because they are or are alleged to be members of organizations outlawed under the Internal Security Act. Since 1976–77, this has meant the Christian Institute, a nonracial radical church organization, as well as the various Black Consciousness movements and, of course, the mass liberatory movements of the fifties and sixties— the ANC (African National Congress) and PAC. Among individuals recently banned are Zwelakhe Sisulu, a prominent journalist and son of Walter Sisulu, a great ANC leader imprisoned with Nelson Mandela on Robben Island, Phil Mtimkulu, Joe Thloloe, Charles Ngakula, Mathatha Tsedu, Mari Subramoney, Vuyisile Mdleleni, all journalists and/or writers. A woman writer, Amanda Kwadi, was detained for some weeks and released just before I left South Africa a month ago. And the writer Don Mattera was served with a renewal of his five-year ban.

Needless to say, South Africa's infamous practice of detention without trial has effectively silenced various black writers, sometimes for long periods. Of those who have been brought to trial, few have been charged on the evidence of their writings, with the notable exception of the famous SASO (South African Students' Organization) trial in the 1970s, when the chief evidence led was plays and poems written by some of the accused. Yet all detained writers without exception are prevented from writing; some, released without ever having been charged with any offense, are nevertheless served with bans upon their release, which then silence them outside prison as well. All prohibitions under the Internal Security Act are characterized by the absoluteness of their terms and by the arbitrary nature of their imposition.

The Publications Act of 1974 replaces the Publications and Entertainments Act of 1963, which banned not only books by South African writers but also books by Edmund Wilson, Mary McCarthy, Roth, and Updike, in addition to those one might expect, such as Cleaver and Fanon. Under the old legislation, action was taken against writers by a Publications Control Board, but there was a right of appeal to the Supreme Court. Although relatively few appeals against the board's decisions were brought into court, a number of its decisions were reversed by the Supreme Court. This led to the present Publications Act of 1974, which excludes the right of appeal to the courts. Under this act, Kurt Vonnegut is one of the most recent American writers to join the list of foreign writers banned in South Africa.

The 1974 act established a government-appointed Directorate of Publications, which is responsible for the overall administration of the act. The directorate appoints committees which are given the task of deciding whether publications, objects, films, and public entertainment generally, referred to the committees by the directorate are "undesirable" within the meaning of the act. Appeals, now barred from the courts, can be made only to the Appeal Board set up by the directorate itself.

"Undesirability" is defined thus:

A publication, object, film or public entertainment is deemed undesirable of it:

is indecent or obscene or is offensive or harmful to public morals;
is blasphemous or is offensive to the religious convictions or feelings of any section of the inhabitants of the Republic;
is harmful to the relations between any sections of the inhabitants of the Republic;
is prejudicial to the safety of the State, the general welfare or the peace and good order of the State.

In the application of the act, it is laid down that "particular regard" is to be paid to "the constant endeavour of the population of the Republic of South Africa to uphold a Christian view of life"—this in a population where there exist the claims of traditional African, Muslim, Hindu, and Jewish religious and secular moralities. Moreover, for the purpose of determining undesirability, the motive of the author is irrelevant. A work may be found undesirable if *any part of it* is undesirable—a principle that reached its apogee when a Gore Vidal novel was banned on the ground that one passage compared the Holy Trinity to the male genitalia.

The production and distribution of works declared undesirable is a criminal offense. Sexual candor aside, the most dangerous ground the writer treads is the area of open or implied trenchant criticism of the institutions of state, in particular the police and defense, the administration of justice and the politicolegal apparatus of so-called separate development for people of different colors, sympathetic treatment of black liberation movements and radical opponents of the status quo, and explicit accounts of interracial sexual relations. More and more, in the last five years, sympathetic or even simply open, honest treatment of black liberation movements, and the activities of all other radical opponents, of all colors, of the union between capitalism and racial oppression in South Africa, have increasingly become the areas to which censorship reacts most strongly.

Under the strictures of these repressive acts, how does a writer work?

In the twenty years since censorship was introduced in South Africa, writers' attitudes have changed and evolved to meet it in different ways, and in relation to the different contexts of their lives in a grossly unequal society.

At the beginning, black writers were little interested in censorship.

White writers were concerned with the one area where apartheid limited the lives of black and white alike, but black writers saw the suppression of freedom of expression as the least tangible and therefore the least of the different aspects of oppression experienced in their daily lives. Without freedom to sell their labor, without freedom of movement, without freedom of association—in a phrase, "with the passbook in their pockets"—the risk of having a book banned seemed trivial. At the beginning of the sixties, it was difficult to get black intellectuals to sign protests against censorship. But after the banning of the mass black movements with their populist appeal, the renaissance of the black spirit of liberation was cupped in the hands of young blacks who saw, in a police state situation where overt political consciousness-rousing was impossible, the importance of cultural consciencization. They looked to writers to imbue the new generation with a sense of identity and pride in that identity through song and story rather than taboo political doctrine. They saw those writers, as I have already said, as the cultural fist of liberation. It was then that censorship no longer seemed irrelevant. This coincided, roughly, with a hardening in the attitude of progressive white writers, who changed their tactic of, in a sense, cooperating with the hated censorship by appealing when a book was banned, to the tactic of noncooperation with any functions of censorship. The principle of "publish and be damned" ran up its flag.

This principle has been implemented, to a surprising extent, by the formation of small publishing houses, mainly by people who are themselves writers. These publishers, unlike the rich British publishers operating as a fossilized colonial outpost in South Africa, were prepared to lose the little money they had, if a book should be banned from sale, in the hope that at least some copies would be circulated before the ax fell. This is the way many books reach readers in South Africa today, and the way in which writers tread the dangerous ground of subjects I have referred to.

Conscious and unconscious self-censorship, and stylistic defenses are questions with which I have dealt in the panel on Isolation and Commitment. There remains to be said that as the situation in South Africa has become more and more crisis-ridden, painful, and dangerous, the fear that prompted self-censorship has been cast out. And so something of the writer's innate freedom has been regained.

Banned

Zwelakhe Sisulu   (*journalist*)
Phil Mtimkulu   (*journalist*)
Joe Thloloe   (*journalist*); on trial, April 1983.
Charles Ngakula   (*journalist*)
Mathatha Tsedu   (*writer*)
Mari Subramoney   (*writer*)
Vuyisile Mdleleni   (*writer*)
Don Mattera   (*writer*); ban lifted, May 1982.

Detained then released

Amanda Kwadi

Recently banned books

Amandhla!   Miriam Tlali
Sing for the Fatherland   Zakes Mda
Egoli   Matsimela Manaka
Divide the Night   Wessel Ebersohn

POLAND: LITERATURE AND CENSORSHIP

STANISLAW BARANCZAK

Note: This paper was received in the summer of 1981. Since then the recent "thaw" described by the author has been followed by another "frost."

I WILL speak about the problem of censorship in contemporary Poland and about censorship's influence on various forms of Polish intellectual life in the seventies. I will also try to tell you how Polish literature, education, the humanities, and political thought dealt with censorship and how they finally began an open fight against it. Why do I focus on this particular topic instead of telling you in more general terms about Poland and the events of the last year, which have put Poland at the center of the world's attention? First, I suppose I may say that I know the problems of literature's resistance against censorship from the inside, from the point of view of a participant. I was (and still am) a coeditor of two Polish magazines published beyond the reach of censorship, and I cooperated with the first independent publishing house (NOWA). In the late seventies, my name was included in the censors' blacklists, and thus I was compelled to publish my work beyond official circulation, either through the émigré press or the uncensored Polish publishing firms.

Second, the very existence of numerous and flourishing magazines and publishing houses completely independent from censorship and, at the same time, working almost entirely in public, seems to be something unprecedented in Eastern Europe. It therefore deserves our undivided attention.

And third, it's not only my opinion that in Poland the question of censorship and freedom of speech was and still is one of the central points of conflict between the people and the regime. The restrictions put upon free speech by state censorship became one of the most important causes of the political and economic crisis which led to the

Polish August; it's no wonder that the shipyard strikers' demand for a strict limitation on censorship was one of the first on their list of "21 postulates." We should also take into account that certain forms of breaking the state's monopoly of information—constructing an independent information network or publishing certain magazines and pamphlets directed to the public, but especially to the workers—played a significant role in the mental preparation of the society for the approaching changes. That preparation brought about the astounding efficiency of a "bloodless revolution" in August. We may say that the fight against the abuses of censorship was the most distinct manifestation of the intellectuals' role in the general protest movement which emerged several years before 1980.

I will start with a short survey of the history of censorship in twentieth-century Poland. In many respects, this history resembles that of other communist countries, but in some other important respects, it seems to be unique.

In the last sixty years, Poland has experienced a striking contrast between two different forms of state censorship. The borderline between them was the Second World War. While the censorship of prewar Poland was more or less based on democratic principles, postwar censorship can only be described as totalitarian, especially during 1949–53 and 1976–80.

This doesn't mean that prewar censorship was spotless. When Poland regained its independence in 1918, one of the first tasks of the government was to issue a decree defining the system of censorship. It was one of the most urgent matters because Poland inherited as many as three different administrative systems from the era of the partitions. This decree, issued in January 1919, established a form of *repressive* censorship: a censor could interfere only with the dissemination of a published text—not with the publication itself. Moreover, authors and publishers could vindicate their rights before an independent court; that is, each decision of a censor had to be considered by a judge. Thus, there was freedom to publish, and only in certain circumstances could a censor's decision lead to the confiscation of a previously published text.

During the thirties, however, as the dictatorial tendencies of the state leadership grew stronger, one could notice many informal attempts to establish a kind of *preventive* censorship. If, for instance, an oppositional newspaper was confiscated as often as two hundred times a year, this created economic pressure for the publisher. In consequence, he sometimes "voluntarily" asked state officials for preventive censoring just to avoid financial losses. Although unconstitutional, this practice was silently supported by the government. Nevertheless, in a formal sense, until 1939 only a repressive (confiscational) censorship existed. At least this was the case for printed publications, because movies, radio programs, and theatrical performances submitted to their own preventive censorship, which was very mild indeed and limited mostly to matters of "morality."

The imposition of communist rule in 1944 brought a dramatic change. In July 1946, the authorities issued a decree creating the so-called Central Office for Control of the Press, Publications, and Performances. The Central Office was supposed to take under its *preventive* control all means of public information and was responsible only to the Prime Minister. It should also be emphasized that the decree of 1946 defined the concrete tasks of the Central Office very vaguely and ambiguously, which was probably intentional, since it gave the censors the unstated power to make quite arbitrary decisions.

It didn't take many years to understand that, whatever could be said about the dictatorial tendencies of the thirties, the postwar system of censorship accomplished much better the totalitarian ideal of complete control of information. Let us enumerate the most outstanding differences between the prewar and postwar systems:

1. A repressive censorship gave way to a preventive one (more precisely, to a combination of both, since a book is usually censored twice: as a typescript and as a printed volume). In other words, in postwar Poland there is no "freedom to publish" any more; a system of "general tolerance with the reserved right of a ban" is replaced by a system of "general ban with the reserved right of permission." (I am using here the terms of a sociologist, Ulla Otto.) To publish something was no longer a natural right. One had to get permission, which became a kind of privilege, granted reluctantly—or not at all—by state authorities.

2. In opposition to the prewar system, the postwar censors didn't have to give anyone the reasons for their decisions or be personally responsible for them. As a rule, a censor's decision was anonymous and based on instructions "from above," which were kept secret from an author or a publisher.

3. After 1944 there was no possibility of an appeal against a censor's decision. It was impossible to take any legal proceedings against the censor—which had been a standard and often very successful practice during the prewar years. Even such means of protest as leaving a "white patch" in place of a deleted text became strictly prohibited in People's Poland.

4. In postwar Poland, state censorship had a complete monopoly of control. It controlled virtually every means of public information, from newspapers and TV programs to rubber stamps and printed invitations to weddings. This is a great difference because, even in the thirties, censorship was not able to control every printed word, nor did it have at its disposal so many forms and means of suppression.

Everything I have said so far referred to postwar censorship as an abstract notion. However, in the historical reality of contemporary Poland, censorship—like almost everything else—went through many changes. It also had its own occasional phases of "thaws" and "frosts." During the last thirty-five years, the activity of the Central Office depended on changing instructions proceeding from the party superiors and was molded by the various concepts of state cultural policy of the state.

In the case of Poland, it seems particularly significant that the postwar history of censorship is somewhat parallel to the history of anticensorship protests. The latter were sometimes quite helpless, but there were moments when resistance against censorship had a great influence over culture as a whole.

Let us recall some of the basic facts. The establishment in 1944 of a communist dictatorship didn't have an immediate effect on cultural life. Exaggerating slightly, we might even say that the years 1944–48 constituted a period of relative cultural pluralism. For instance, the authorities tolerated a small number of private publishing houses as well as some formally independent journals (especially Catholic ones). Publicly expressed opinions, although suppressed by censorship, ranged from the conservative defense of traditional values to ultraleftist postulates.

However, it didn't last very long. In the first months of 1949, some drastic changes occurred as a direct result of earlier political events (for example, the "unification" of the Communist and Socialist parties, and the official condemnation of a "rightist-nationalist deviation"). This was the beginning of a strict, monoparty rule and the end of cultural, not to mention political, pluralism. In January 1949, the Polish Writers' Union Congress officially proclaimed "socialist realism" as the only admissible direction for literature. Anyone who opposed this direction was consequently subjected to restrictions or even repression. It is no wonder that "socialist realism" with its narrow choice of subjects and journalistic style produced an astonishing decline in literary quality.

Fortunately, that period didn't last very long either. In 1953 Stalin died, and 1956 was the year of Khrushchev's famous speech denouncing Stalin's crimes, of the Polish October, and of the Hungarian Revolution. In Poland, 1956 marked the beginning of the great "thaw," the general break with the literary uniformity of "socialist realism." Censorship grew much more tolerant as its previous "errors" became the target of public opinion. There was a spontaneous outburst of new expression in all domains of creativity. The literary scene witnessed the birth of the so-called literature of "settling scores" which actually started much earlier (with Adam Wazyk's famous *Poem for Adults,* published in 1955) and was written mostly by disappointed writers who previously contributed to "socialist realism." There was also a great wave of literary debuts, some of which were the "late" debuts of writers who, during the Stalinist years, had written "for their desk drawer." Hence the Polish October wrought a great revolution in aesthetic consciousness: the monopoly of "socialist realism" was replaced by a multitude of individual styles.

It would, however, be difficult to claim that the monopoly of Stalinism was similarly replaced by a great variety of political opinions. Real political pluralism was still impossible. In the general intellectual atmosphere of the period, only one position was dominant: the so-called "revisionism," a revision of communism from within Marxist positions, the attempt to democratize the system without rejecting its fundamental principles.

This was the main intellectual weakness of the Polish October, and from today's perspective, we can clearly see that this weakness prevented intellectuals from successfully counteracting the new freezing of the cultural atmosphere. This freeze did not occur as abruptly as in 1949, but imperceptibly, step by step. Gradually, all "controversial" initiatives of intellectuals were put down or simply destroyed. By 1958 it became clear that the authorities were aiming once again at limiting freedom of expression. Their approach this time was, however, different from that of 1949–55. Before 1956 no one restrained "formalist" tendencies or avant-garde experimentation. The aim of censorship's increasing control was rather to suppress the "revisionist" tendencies in literature, the arts, the humanities, and political thought.

But after 1956, a new social phenomenon emerged: the suppression of free speech was more often countered by collective protests. As early as 1957, the closing of a courageous weekly, *Po Prostu,* was immediately met by street demonstrations. This was quite a symbolic event, but brutal suppression of the demonstrations by the police made intellectuals seek other forms of protest. In the sixties, the number of protests grew constantly. The year 1964 brought the famous "Letter of 34," the first document in which the intellectuals openly protested the abuses of censorship. This letter, though timid, was very important. After the start of a bitter countercampaign against those who signed the letter, intellectuals realized that Polish culture was again developing under abnormal conditions. No wonder that successive congresses of the Writers' Union were presenting a growing number of critical speeches concerning censorship and the cultural policy of the state. The culmination of that criticism was caused by the infamous ban imposed in March 1968 on the Warsaw performances of the masterpiece of Polish Romantic drama, *Dziady,* by Adam Mickiewicz. This ban—which was probably police provocation—resulted in a direct confrontation between the state and the protesting intellectuals, including students. This time Polish culture suffered a terrible loss. Some of the student leaders were imprisoned, and many intellectuals were slandered by the government press and punished by restrictions or prohibitions, or even forced to emigrate. But in the long run, March 1968 brought some good as well as evil to Polish culture: it marked the end of "revisionist" illusions and signaled the final crystallization of the liberal and democratic consciousness of intellectuals' opposition to the system. In March 1968, the system revealed its true face.

Now what can be said about the seventies? The so-called "Gierek decade" apparently mirrors very faithfully the old pattern: once again we have a short "thaw," after which comes a long "frost." Analogies may be tempting, but there are also many differences. The dismal experience of March 1968 and the tragedy of December 1970 marked, as I said, a new phase in the consciousness of Polish intellectuals. After such events as the anti-Semitic campaign in the press and the bestiality of the police during the student riots, and especially after the December massacre of the demonstrating workers, it was difficult to preserve any faith in the possibility of improving the system from within. Eminent writers, artists, and scholars were ever more frequently assuming a dissident stance. Many of them signed petitions—for example, the famous "Letter of the 59," which protested the planned changes in the constitution and demanded the introduction of basic civil rights. In particular, the June 1976 events —another wave of workers' demonstrations and another show of police brutality—attracted many intellectuals to the side of the growing opposition. I think 1976 was a crucial date for modern Polish history. It was the date of the creation of KOR (the Committee for the Defense of the Workers), which was the first organization aimed at the defense of human rights in genuine cooperation with all social strata. And 1976 is also the starting point for the activity of the underground printers who organized the first independent publishing house, NOWA.

Why did NOWA have to be created? First, let us remember that in 1976 there was no trace left of Gierek's "short thaw" of 1971–72. On the contrary, censorship's control over information and culture was never so strong as in the second half of the 1970s. It became especially clear after the notorious affair of the "Strzyzewski papers." Strzyzewski, a censor from Kracow, escaped to Sweden in 1977, carrying with him a set of the secret instructions issued by the Central Office for Control of the Press, Publications, and Performances. He sent a copy to Warsaw, asking KOR to reprint it and make it known to the people at large. Thus the *Black Book of Censorship* was published and it revealed to the shocked public that in the preceding few years it had been practically forbidden in Poland to publish anything truly essential to society. Information about catastrophes in Silesian coal mines, statistical data concerning the growth of alcoholism, critical remarks on Marxist ideology, warnings against the dangerous effects of pesticides used in agriculture, texts about the problems of national minorities, criticisms of the state's policy versus the Catholic Church, names of writers, artists, and scholars who "fell into disgrace"—all these "had to be eliminated" (as the censors' instructions put it) from all the media. And in the late seventies, they were eliminated very meticulously indeed.

But these restrictions achieved a result quite contrary to their aim. This time it wasn't so easy to subdue the people's need for real information and genuine culture. But in the fall of 1976, a new phenomenon emerged in Poland: an independent and uncensored press. It didn't differ very much at the start from typical East European *samizdat*. The first bulletins of KOR and of such magazines as *Biuletyn Informacyjny* or the literary quarterly *Zapis* were copied on ordinary typewriters and circulated from hand to hand. There was only one difference: all the names and addresses of the publishers were published openly in their magazines, as if to show that their activity was completely legal, as indeed it was.

But this was only a beginning. After a very short time, the technical base improved: the typewriters were replaced by mimeograph and Xerox machines; the magazines began to resemble a "normal" press; the first pamphlets and books appeared. This was connected with the creation of NOWA. The history of NOWA deserves a special account, although we must remember that today there are several other independent publishing firms, some of them with a very impressive output.

Although the independent press started, as I said before, in the fall of 1976, NOWA emerged exactly one year later. It was a very significant moment. Only a few months earlier, in May 1977, the communist authorities had tried to intimidate the democratic opposition, arresting several members of KOR. After a wave of protests—in the country and abroad—the authorities were forced to retreat: in July they released those arrested and, what was even more important, they also had to set free the workers jailed after the June 1976 riots. In this way, the authorities reluctantly accepted the opposition's right to exist. In practical terms, it meant that people who fought for human rights—among others, for the freedom to publish—now risked only some petty annoyances (forty-eight-hour detention, dismissal from work, no passport to travel abroad, etc.), but they could be relatively sure they wouldn't get a prison sentence. Of course, this encouraged the independent press a great deal. As Miroslaw Chojecki—a KOR member and NOWA's chief manager—recalls, "The founders of NOWA . . . had a vision of a quasinormal publishing house, related to the market and with a regular output of books and periodicals with a circulation running into thousands of copies. But in contrast to official publishing houses, they lacked not only the necessary infrastructure (printing, storage, bookshops, etc.), but also the very means of printing." One has to remember that in communist countries—and Poland in the late seventies was no exception—access to every duplicator or Xerox machine is strictly guarded. The independent publishers had only one alternative: either to construct their own means of printing or to smuggle them into the country from abroad. The first way proved insufficient: the home-made screenprinting machines, though inexpensive and easy to re-construct after police confiscations, were very primitive, and their output was too small and hardly legible. Thus, only the other way remained: to smuggle into the country some more sophisticated ma-chinery, bought with money collected by émigré supporters or by foreign NOWA sympathizers. There is no need to say that this was also not easy, because of the strict control on the borders.

But the printing machinery was not the only problem. The NOWA publishers had to obtain numerous materials necessary for produc-tion, from paper to metal clips—and once again we should remember that in communist countries every private person who wants to buy in a shop a larger quantity of such articles is automatically suspect. Another thing was the problem of security. Although NOWA's activ-ity was perfectly legal, the police possessed the power to confiscate its output or machinery on the basis of, for instance, some fictional investigation in a fictional crime case. That's why, even if the pub-lishers' names and addresses were made public, the printers' where-abouts had to be kept secret. They worked mainly in private apart-ments or cellars, changing the location as often as possible, working several days in a row without leaving the room, sleeping and eating among the piles of newly printed sheets.

One more problem was distribution, which also required a good organization and the ability to throw the police off the trail. Distri-bution had to be at the same time public and secret: the readers should know where they could buy new books, the police shouldn't know where they could confiscate them. It's certainly a kind of bal-ancing act, but in spite of these difficulties, NOWA managed to form an extensive distribution network covering almost the whole country.

In such circumstances, it's obvious that NOWA's activity has been made possible only by the fact that it has had many collaborators and supporters. Their number is still growing, and the cooperation ranges from a full professional involvement (as in the case of some printers and editors) to occasional help (when somebody, for instance, loans his car or cellar for distribution or printing).

Let us say a few words about the final product of all that complex activity—the books and magazines published by NOWA. In the beginning, NOWA wanted to act mostly "as a sort of rescue service for Polish culture," filling the gaps in information, literature, and social sciences caused by state censorship. But the creation of an independent press offered writers, journalists, and scholars a much better chance: a chance to think and speak freely, without self-censoring and with an opportunity to publish their works however unorthodox they were. The case of *Zapis* can serve as the best example. *Zapis* was supposed to be a magazine in which writers could publish work prohibited by censorship. This idea changed very quickly: in the second issue of *Zapis,* almost half of the material was written especially for that magazine and without any attempt to submit it to a censor. The next issues attracted other writers, not necessarily present on the censors' blacklists, and thus, *Zapis* became a normal literary magazine, with only one small difference: that it didn't bother to be censored by anybody.

The history of NOWA is very similar in this respect. Today it not only fills the gaps in national culture but also offers facilities for all possible kinds of new creative initiatives. NOWA's output is really impressive, if you consider that it has existed only four years. It has published almost 150 books, among them classical—and still forbidden by official censorship—works by Stefan Żeromski, and Witold Gombrowicz. NOWA was the only publishing house in Poland which managed to publish several books by Czeslaw Milosz even before he was awarded the Nobel Prize. It published the novel of one of the most famous Polish writers, Jerzy Andrzejewski, which had ten years of censorship troubles. The most outstanding works of contemporary Polish literature—novels by Tadeusz Konwicki and Kazimierz Brandys, poems by Jerzy Ficowski and Wiktor Woroszylski, essays by Pawel Jasienica, Andrzej Kijowski, and Witold Wirpsza—were also published by NOWA, along with many translated works (for example, by George Orwell, Osip Mandelstam, Josef Brodsky, Bohumil Hrabal, and Günter Grass). NOWA also printed collections of historical documents, appeals and leaflets, academic books and journals and magazines.

August 1980 marks the newest phase in the history of independent publishing in Poland. The connection between the uncensored press and the new union movement is quite obvious. On the one hand, we have such workers' newspapers as *Robotnik* and many leaflets, magazines, and books which circulated in Poland before 1980; on the other hand, it's very significant that among the demands put forward by striking shipyard workers in August, there was a demand to stop the persecution of the independent press and a demand to work out a new law on censorship.

The year 1980 proved that the importance of free publishing is obvious to everybody. Such incidents as arresting an independent publisher under a false indictment (which happened to Miroslaw Chojecki only a few months before August) are unthinkable now. When the authorities tried to arrest one of NOWA's printers who was working for Solidarity, their decision was met immediately by a warning strike.

The future of relations between the free publishers and censorship is still unclear, but one thing seems certain: as long as censorship exists in Poland, there will be a need to fill the gaps in national culture and to secure its further development. Independent, uncensored publishing is still the only solution for that dilemma.

SECRETS AND MYTHS

IAN ADAMS

I HAVE to admit that when I first sat down to think and write about the subject of this panel, I was a little uncomfortable. First, because I was nudging up against the myth that we live in a totally free society in Canada and we can say and write anything we want; and second, because I realized that no one was suing me because of anything I had written. The first uneasiness comes from the fact that we tend to confuse censorship with persecution; and when I thought about it, the reason why I hadn't (been sued, for the first time in fifteen years) is that I've spent the last six months preoccupied with writing a book.

To my mind, the most successful kinds of censorship exist on three levels in our society. And those are the ones that I can talk about.

I think there is a state censorship that exists and that permeates our society. And apropos of that point, I think that this book was probably the most successful work of "fiction" published in Canada this fall. It's titled *Commission of Enquiry Concerning Certain Activities of the Royal Canadian Mounted Police*. The subtitle is *Certain RCMP Activities and the Question of Government Knowledge*. It's a nice title for the criminal activities of our secret police. It's also quite a successful novel in the sense that it's experimental: while the essential characters are supposed to exist, they have no names, so that the people responsible for wrongdoings never actually get mentioned in the book. Of course, the authors could afford this kind of experiment because they had $15 million to spend writing and experimenting with different kinds of approach.

My point is that state censorship exists on a massive scale in our country. And it's historical. The first investigation of the RCMP Security Services was in 1947. That report became known as the "Taschereau Papers." They were immediately sealed and, under the

Official Secrets Act, were not allowed to be opened for thirty years. On September 15, 1977, I presented myself at the offices of the National Archives and said, "Thirty years is up, I want to see these papers." There is a great deal of information in them which has destroyed people's lives, because in the years after the war, the secret police went around intimidating and investigating a lot of people, and especially many in trade union organizations. The guy in the archives said, "Sure." He went to look for the boxes these papers were stored in, and they weren't there. Twenty-nine phone calls revealed the fact that someone from the Privy Council office had come over a few days earlier and taken the boxes away. And two weeks later the Cabinet, in a special session, passed an order-in-council which would at their discretion have these papers sealed, so we will probably never have access to certain key documents.

The question is why governments do this. I think the answer is that of course all governments lie, it's an axiom, and that they do it to cover up the brutal things, the truly monstrous things that are happening in our society. I'll just touch briefly on two of those.

In about two weeks from now, the Quebec Government will open an inquest into the death of a former Canadian ambassador, John Watkins. It was seventeen years ago that he died, and finally his inquest is going to begin. When the information of his death was first published, it said that he died of a heart attack, having dinner at his home in Montreal. This was the official story for many, many years. It was only three months ago that I discovered his death certificate in Montreal, in the Quebec Coroner's Office. And on the death certificate was the name of a witness. The witness was a man I recognized as being a high-ranking intelligence officer. He had given his name, but he had not identified himself as an intelligence officer. And so for the first time it became possible to ask, well, what was an intelligence officer who had not identified himself as an intelligence officer doing as the witness of the death of an ambassador? More investigation revealed the fact that John Watkins had been investigated by the RCMP, simply because he was a homosexual and had served for a period of time in the Soviet Union. The secret police put these two facts together and think automatically they have a spy.

They interrogated John Watkins for a long time. At first they told us, "It was only a few days, and we had a couple of chats with him, and we flew over to see him in Paris." Then gradually, after a lot of digging, the story unfolds: Watkins never had a house in Montreal; they went to see him in Paris, where they began a long and arduous interrogation. John Watkins was a sick man, a *very* sick man; he'd had two heart attacks that year. They talked him into going to London to continue the interrogation, and there he was probably also interrogated by MI5. And finally they brought him back to Montreal. He was under interrogation for twenty-eight days. He died "just as we were finishing up a few details," they said. I know now that the only reason they continued the interrogation for that long was because the CIA insisted on it. For many years the CIA has been obsessed with the idea that our External Affairs is part of the international communist conspiracy.

I don't think that much of this information is going to come out in the inquest.

Another monstrous thing that has to be talked about is that in the sixties the CIA and the Canadian military intelligence services entered into a collaboration with certain psychiatrists to found a program called MK Ultra. This was a program of mind control experiments on two groups of people. The first group were psychiatric patients. The second group were prisoners who were seeking remission of sentence and wanted to volunteer for these things, and signed a vaguely worded consent form. The mind control experiments were a combination of sensory deprivation sessions with very heavy drugs —LSD 25, amyl nitrate, pentothal—and the object was to totally break down an individual's personal and intellectual defenses against interrogation, so that they could adopt these techniques for the interrogation of people who they thought were intelligence agents working against the security of the state.

Some of this is known and has been published in fragments, but what is not generally known is that after a few years the intelligence forces involved, both the CIA and the Canadian Defense Department, abandoned the experiments because they were disastrous. They turned some of these people into vegetables, and others who were psychotic became increasingly violent. Some of the prisoners were turned loose in society and no real attempt was ever made to follow up on what has happened to them. This information about MK Ultra and the degree of Canadian intelligence involvement will probably never emerge.

There is another kind of censorship in our society, and that is the legal apparatus. Many of you probably know of the case I was involved in, and about *S, Portrait of a Spy,* the book I published about the security services. I don't want to go into it in great detail, just to talk about the aftereffects of that case. As you know, the editor of one of the leading Toronto newspapers collaborated with a former intelligence officer to bring a suit against me to stop distribution of the book. He was successful in that for about three years. But because of the massive support I got from writers and writers' union organizations, we were able finally to free the book and get it published again.

There are some interesting consequences to this. One is that the publisher is saying that he would never publish that kind of book again, or that if he did, he would demand that the writer put up a ten-thousand-dollar bond first. I know that now when I seek to do magazine work, editors don't want to deal with me because they assume the overheads will always be too high. So you can see how the courts are effectively used against the writer and to intimidate publishers. The way the legal establishment can be used to punish writers and to prevent them from getting their work published in our society is quite effective.

Then there is the self-censorship of society itself. When you live in the belly of the beast of capitalist society, as a writer you come to understand that people have an enormous resistance to information about poverty, injustice, or about the activities of their own secret police. They just don't want to listen. And so it becomes even more impossible for them to accept information about what has happened in Argentina. That is a criminal kind of self-censorship that is built into society. People don't want to hear about things. They want to have a "quiet life" because they really don't care about other people. And there's a lot of self-righteousness in that, and also a lot of anxiety.

This is one of the continuing problems for all of us. It forces writers like myself to grapple with the kind of myths and fantasies that society does absorb. I've come to understand that the most powerful fantasy figure in our society is the spy. There are many reasons for this. One is that in a time when we are conditioned more and more to believe that we have no control or responsibility for our own lives, the spy survives as a kind of anima, a fantasy figure who is licensed to plan and commit all those violent, antisocial acts we would like to perform when we are threatened or oppressed by the stresses of this life. That spies can act with such freedom and sanction from the authorities, under the guise that it is for the protection of us all, makes their world all the more enticing.

In some ways, the powerful fantasy figure of the spy is connected with the rhetoric of national security. I would like in my work to try to demystify that. Because, you see, I've come to the conclusion that both governments and secret police forces understand this connection between the fantasy figure of the spy and the politics of national security. If we don't break down that kind of fantasy, we will have to start to accept their rationalizations of why it was necessary to interrogate John Watkins for twenty-eight days until he died of a heart attack. Or why it is in the interest of national security to destroy all the files on those human guinea pigs in the MK Ultra experiments.

There is no difference between that kind of rationalization and the kind of official statements we hear every day coming from Argentina or Chile or South Africa, because the same justifications are used there to kill writers and artists. If we don't come to understand that, then we're not very far, ourselves, from that situation.

THE TESTIMONY OF
ANATOLY MARCHENKO

NATALYA GORBANEVSKAYA

I WOULD like to talk about a particular case, about a writer whose destiny is, in two senses, representative of the problem of "The Writer and Human Rights" in the U.S.S.R. On the one hand, he has ardently defended human rights and liberties by his writings. And on the other, his own destiny is a terrible example of the repression exercised in the U.S.S.R. against those who attempt to realize their freedom of speech.

I am going to talk about Anatoly Marchenko, who, in 1967, after six years in political camps and prisons, wrote his first book, *My Testimony*. The book would not be unique if it were not also the first testimony about the post-Stalinist camps in the Soviet Union. The period when Marchenko made his first "sojourn" in the political camps was when Soviet literature began, officially, to speak of the recent past, of the camps under Stalin. The press campaign around the publication in 1962 of *One Day in the Life of Ivan Denisovich* attempted to suggest that the camps described by Solzhenitsyn no longer existed, that all this was in the past—admittedly a very sad past—but nonetheless, definitely in the past. For a brief moment, Solzhenitsyn's story opened a breach for the publication of numerous memoirs concerning the Stalinist camps. But there was no other work which equaled Solzhenitsyn's for its denunciatory force. The Soviet authorities had already gotten a grip on themselves; already they were aware of their mistake in allowing Solzhenitsyn to publish; already other works by Solzhenitsyn, by Varlam Shalamov, or by Eugenia Ginsburg had no chance of being published in the U.S.S.R., and so they began to be distributed in numerous typed copies, in *samizdat*.

Obviously, at no time was there a chance of publication for someone who wanted to relate contemporary cases of oppression. But, paradoxically, during the Khrushchev years, content of this nature did not appear in *samizdat* form either. Much later Marchenko described this period in his unfinished book, *Live Like Everyone:*

> I have spent six years in the political camps and prisons. But never, anywhere, has anyone said one word about the political prisoners in the U.S.S.R. The whole world was uneasy, anxious about the situation of the political prisoners in South Africa and in Portugal, in Franco's Spain, and in South Vietnam, but not in the U.S.S.R. We simply did not exist. Because of this injustice, we were on the verge of insanity. It was the despair of those condemned to oblivion. . . .
>
> I was also indignant about the shameful silence of public opinion in this country and in the world towards the Soviet political prisoners. We ought to have at least loudly protested. I saw so many people leave the camps at the end of their sentence. Among them, how many there were who were capable of thinking, even of writing. They spent time behind barbed wire; each of them suppressed his indignation and accused the whole world of being Khrushchev's, and then Brezhnev's, accomplice.
>
> But, hardly had they been released and recovered their freedom than they forgot the sufferings of those who remained behind. Is it possible that everything can be explained by ordinary human weakness, by cowardice? At that time, as much as today, I did not doubt and I do not doubt the large number of intelligent and honest people among those who have been released. But even now, at the time of writing this, an old question arises for me: why? Of course, each one of us can reply sincerely: "I am not a writer." But I, for my part, am not a writer at all.

If I have read you such a long passage, it is not to follow Marchenko in his search for a response to the question, why have others not written? Rather, it has been to underscore the actions of a man who was not at all a writer—and yet became one because others were silent.

Released from camp in 1966, Marchenko devoted several months of the following year to his book, to his testimony. He confronted several difficulties—traps in the act of writing. Again, from his recent memoirs:

Formerly, I considered the writer's work to be of the easiest kind: to invent something to write about, to try to write correctly. As for myself, I did not even have to invent anything.

Once he began to write, this simplistic notion was shattered:

In the course of writing these pages, which I was writing for the first time in my life, I understood one thing: you have to write sentences in the same way as you speak, and not squeeze into a sentence everything that you mean, as if it were the last chance to express yourself. I did not merely understand this, I "saw" it.

Perhaps his literary credo may seem naïve, but I can say with full knowledge of the facts that Marchenko correctly grasped this quasi-stylistic danger which is, in fact, an existential one. It threatens many of our writers, both professional and self-taught, when they set out to describe the truth. You really seek to squeeze into a sentence or a book everything you have to say, because it could actually be your last chance to express yourself. And what is more, even what you have succeeded in expressing could be suddenly confiscated or destroyed.

In his latest book, Edward Kuznetsov describes the tricks he used to write it in the camp, and how he tried to make the administration believe that he was no longer writing. What ingenuity he had to resort to in order to hide the manuscript and have it smuggled out of camp! Thus, the manuscript passed over the barbed wire.

On the other side, it is easy. You are not frisked every day, but every day you expect to be searched or maybe even arrested. I remember well my own situation when I was working on my book *Red Square at Noon*. Every night I dreamed of being searched. With the book completed and a first edition of seven typed copies distributed, I regained my calm.

In similar conditions, Marchenko fought against time and his own sense of haste, sought his literary form, and completed his testimony before the invisible tribunal of public opinion. The effect of *My Testimony* was like an explosion, even in those circles that are now called "dissident," where the existence of political camps was known. Only his concrete presentation of dozens of prisoners' destinies and of the atmosphere of the camps was able to come to grips with the vastness of the problem.

The authorities perceived this book, written and widely distributed in *samizdat* form, as a slap in the face. Yet in persecuting Marchenko and preparing severe reprisals against him, they did not want to reveal publicly the true reason for their hate. A KGB agent once told him directly: "Don't expect that you will be judged for your book. You will be judged as a common criminal."

Two years after his release, Anatoly Marchenko was sentenced to one year of camp detention for allegedly having broken the regulations concerning his internal passport. His arrest for this nonpolitical offense occurred just after the open letter in which Marchenko expressed his indignation over the Soviet press campaign against the Prague Spring. His trial, also nonpolitical, took place on August 21, 1968, the day of the Soviet invasion of Czechoslovakia. These facts in themselves are eloquent.

However, one year, which is the maximum penalty under the article of the penal code used against Marchenko, was too little for the authorities. In the camp for common criminals where he was serving his sentence, they found so-called "witnesses" to his "slanderous" statements against the Soviet regime. He was sentenced to an additional two years of detention (in 1966 he had left the camp, seriously ill and almost deaf as a result of meningitis). Three supplementary years of camp detention did not improve his health. Though he had been classified as a trained worker before his arrest, both in the camps and after his release he was restricted to working as a common laborer.

His life outside prison was also filled with privations and limitations. For years after his release from camp in 1971, he remained under administrative surveillance. That meant he was not permitted to leave his home after eight o'clock in the evening, to change his place of residence, to enter a public place such as a cinema or bar, and so forth. The long and unlawful prolongation of this administrative surveillance had only one purpose: at a given moment, the authorities could declare a violation of the rules of surveillance and imprison him. This took place at the end of 1974: Marchenko was sentenced to four years' internal exile and deported to eastern Siberia.

This experience was the subject of his second book, *Hunger Strike*. Marchenko maintained a hunger strike for months, from the time of his arrest until his arrival in the place of exile. During the hunger strike, he was transported without any medical care in the famous railway car used for transporting political prisoners. This, too, he survived.

Last spring, Marchenko was arrested again. He was sentenced to ten years' camp detention and five years' internal exile. We are justified in doubting whether he will ever go into exile, whether he will survive until the end of his ten years of camp detention. This sentence is equal to a death penalty, even though it was not formally pronounced.

The book *My Testimony* was not mentioned once in the four trials Marchenko has had since its completion. Nonetheless, we may rest assured that it constitutes the principal reason for the Soviet authorities' eagerness to muzzle Anatoly Marchenko. Marchenko was the first witness to their crimes, crimes which have only become worse. The present Soviet power is terribly frightened of its own Nuremberg trial, which has been under way since the publication of Marchenko's *My Testimony*. The number of witnesses is now growing. For all Soviet prisoners of conscience—past, present, and future—Marchenko's defense has been and will remain a prime concern, even in the face of the incredible wave of repression which is presently striking the human rights movement, and all the national and regional movements in the U.S.S.R., and which is particularly severe toward ex-political prisoners.

This congress is honoring Vasyl Stus, the Ukrainian poet who has already spent seven years in the camps and three years in exile, and who has been sentenced to a further ten years of camps and five years of internal exile.

At almost the same time, Viacheslav Chornovil, the Ukrainian literary critic who had spent eighteen months in the camps in the 1960s, six years in camp in the 1970s, and who had been deported to three years' internal exile, was arrested in his place of exile and sentenced to a further five years' imprisonment. This sentence was based on false criminal charges.

Levko Lukyanenko and Ivan Kandyba, two Ukrainian jurists, were sentenced to ten years' camp detention and five years' exile after having already spent fifteen years in the camps.

Mart Niklus, an Estonian translator and biologist, was also sentenced to ten years' camp detention and five years' internal exile after his eight years in the camps.

All these people were members of the Ukrainian Helsinki Monitoring Group.

The same punishment was reserved for the Lithuanian human rights militant, Viktoras Petkus, founder of the Lithuanian Helsinki Monitoring Group; he had already served seven years in the camps. This was also the punishment for Balis Gajauskas, who had spent twenty-five years of his life in the camps.

All these people, exhausted by their previous periods of detention, are prime candidates for burial in the camp cemeteries, without a cross, without a name. Whether writers or not, they provide us with the courageous example of those who struggle, with no thought of turning back, for the elementary rights and liberties of all men.

I believe that it is our duty, as writers living in freedom, to follow their example and, if at all possible, to protect them from arbitrary punishment.

—Translated by Donald Bruce

Imprisonment

THE RE-EDUCATION OF A VIETNAMESE WRITER

CHUONG TANG NGUYEN

I BEG your permission to introduce myself. My name is Chuong Tang Nguyen, and my usual pen names are Bang Nguyen or Truong Hai Au. I am now the editor of *Ban Viet,* a Vietnamese magazine published every month in Toronto.

My life of suffering cannot be detached from the destiny of my country and my people, or from that of my fellow Vietnamese writers. So I hope that my experiences will help you to understand some aspects of the tragic life of Vietnamese writers, not the communist writers but the ones who are now victims of the communists.

From the first day of their takeover, the communists have unceasingly proclaimed, "From now on, every Vietnamese is the master of his life." Nothing could be more ironic. We left our country for one simple reason: to resume the right to be masters of our own lives. Everyone knows that escaping by boat is very dangerous. We had to cope with prison, with storms and tempests, with pirates, and even with death. But when I set my feet on free land, it was not easy to answer the question why I left my country. If I answered simply, "I left my country for freedom," nobody would understand what I meant. The word "freedom" by itself does not mean anything. It is hard for people who have always lived in freedom to understand completely the meaning of the word.

When I put my feet on Indonesian soil, my first place of asylum as a refugee, they asked me "Why did you leave your country?" I felt at a loss for an accurate answer. The truth is very complicated, and I had to answer not only for myself but for all the boat people. The communist propaganda network has rudely distorted the truth, inside the country as well as outside it. Ho Chi Minh, the father of the Viet-

namese Communist party and the present Vietnamese regime, proclaimed, "Nothing is worthier than independence and freedom." But
because the communists praise freedom, we had to leave our country; because the communists praise freedom, hundreds of thousands
of people had to go to the "re-education camps" located in faraway,
dangerous mountains and forests. The communists' ways of reasoning and of using words are not the ways we are used to. They are
shaped by political purposes. "Democratic" means democratic for
the people but not for the enemy, and if someone does not obey the
communists, he becomes an enemy. So in Vietnam, when the government says "freedom," we understand "jail"; when they say "voluntary," we understand "compulsory"; when they say "happiness,"
the people see only poverty and distress; when they say "prosperity,"
the people have to suffer hunger; and when they say "peace," war
will certainly come.

On April 30, 1975, like almost all people who had been connected with the old regime, I was very scared. Some days later, a
rumor ran through Saigon that there were many suicides. When I arrived in Canada, I read some magazine articles about the communist
regime in Saigon, and I found that a number of writers and journalists seemed to be skeptical about the suicides. But I can confirm that
the rumor was true: two of my friends committed suicide. One killed
himself, leaving his wife a widow and his four children orphans; the
other gave orders to his wife and children to take sleeping pills and
commended to his eldest son, twenty years old, the terrible duty of
putting an end to all the sleeping family before killing himself with
his father's automatic.

But from the first hours of communist rule, the propaganda network spoke of forgiveness, humanity, and respect for human rights.
The fear of the people was soothed little by little, because at that
time the South Vietnamese were unfamiliar with the communist way
of reasoning and the special meanings of the words they used. Some
days after the takeover, General Tran Van Tra, President of the Military Executive Committee of Saigon, proclaimed in a radio broadcast
speech that "between the Vietnamese, there are no victors and no
defeated; only the American imperialists were defeated." I was very
naïve then, so this speech impressed me. I decided to remain in the
country, happy to see Vietnam being reunified and pacified, with
many prospects for the future. I was willing to accept a hard life and

expected to cooperate with my fellow citizens in the rebuilding of our homeland. I hoped that from now on the Vietnamese people would enjoy liberty, justice, equality, and peace. I felt pity for those people who had committed suicide. I thought they had been senseless and narrow-minded. I did not want to go abroad and live in exile.

But I could not enjoy for long the liberty and pardon so solemnly promised by the government. As a writer who had cooperated with the old regime, I was "invited" to go "to study." I needed "to be re-educated" to deserve to live in the new society. I had to become "a new man." On June 23, 1975, obeying the order of the Military Executive Committee, I went with a little bag of clothes and presented myself for re-education. After being incarcerated with some thousand other people, I was taken to a military camp located in a forest about sixty miles from Saigon, close to the Cambodian border.

There they taught us to live the life of the jungle people, cutting wood, building houses under the supervision of armed guards. The *can bo* (communist cadres) called us "brother students"; many guards called us "prisoners"; in official documents we were called "criminals." There were "political courses" which lasted many whole days. They were endless lectures to remind us about "the crimes of the American imperialists and of the puppet government, their lackeys," and about the "immense forebearance of the revolutionary organization."

After each lecture given by a cadre, there was a discussion. Everyone had to relate his past and brand himself a criminal, a traitor. People who spoke of their misdeeds were praised as sincere; people who could not find anything wrong in their past lives were criticized as liars, incapable of remorse. So everyone tried to invent a misdeed for himself.

All the people who had had some connection with the old regime— military officers, high-ranking civil servants, deputies, congressmen, even politicians and writers who were not involved with the communists—had to be re-educated. The cadres explained to our families that we needed "re-education" to become good husbands, good fathers, good citizens. But in the camps, they told us that we had to be isolated from good society because we were undesirable, dangerous elements, the scum of the people, cancerous tumors of society. However, we had to be grateful to the party and the government, whose tolerance was as immense as "sky and ocean," who loved us, took care of us, protected us from the wrath of the people because every one of the people was resentful of us, hated us, and wanted our heads!

In the re-education camp, we learned the most bitter lessons of life. We had to work hard all day, from Monday to Saturday, and our daily ration was two bowls of rice, together with some poor vegetables, leaves, and salt. Each month we were allowed some thirty grams of meat or fish. It was a great feast for us when we got one or two slices of meat or fish. Poor nutrition weakened everybody and we fell sick easily. Each time we were sick, the cadres said to us, "There is no medicine better than willpower, courage, and patience." So we were rarely given medicine. We tried to overcome disease with our "willpower, courage, and patience," which were called Vitamins WCP. With those vitamins, tens of thousands died in the re-education camps. Although I was only six months in the camp, I witnessed many people dying from "study." I also witnessed with my own eyes some suicides.

Fortunately, I was released after six months. My release certificate stated: "This man is temporarily released and allowed to return to his family. The local administration should be involved in helping and following him." Note the meaning of the word "help" according to the communist way of reasoning. For example, "help" might mean to criticize or blame, but it might also mean to report me to the authorities if I did something suspicious, or simply to incarcerate me when necessary. To follow me and "help" me, the local police agent came to my house twice every month, to say hello to me, to ask about the happiness of my family. There were many questions he never forgot to repeat to "help" me: "What did you do under the old regime? What re-education did you come back from? What authority released you?" These questions were to remind me that I was always a "re-educated," that I was not like ordinary people. So like everyone in the same case, I was very shy. I never dared express my thoughts openly, for fear of "help," for fear of returning to the re-education camp. I was told that I was given back all my rights as a citizen, but I understood that I was a man to follow, a man under supervision. There was an invisible mark carved on my forehead. I was "a re-educated."

How could I continue to live such a life? I had only one choice—to go abroad on a boat.

After many failed attempts to escape with my whole family, I had to go alone. My eldest son had left before me with one of my friends. On June 10, 1979, I escaped Vietnamese waters. Four months later, my wife succeeded in escaping with my three other sons and arrived in Singapore. We arrived in Toronto on April 1, 1980, after having lived ten months in Indonesia, in two different refugee camps.

At present, my situation is that of a writer living far from his homeland. But I do not consider myself in exile, because the ones who are really in exile are my countrymen in re-education camps, suffering an extremely painful life, expelled from society; and also the others who, although they are allowed to live in society, have lost their right to express themselves. Their society has become foreign to them: even though they are living in their homeland, they miss it, because their homeland is no longer theirs.

MOVING OUR LIPS

NATALYA GORBANEVSKAYA

I CANNOT say precisely who was the first writer to be imprisoned by the Soviets. Perhaps it was Boris Savinkov, a novelist, but better known as one of the leaders of the revolutionary socialist party. Perhaps it was Mikhail Prishvin, a populist writer, who was arrested simply because he had friends at the center of this same political party. We could also cite the names of the oldest journalists who were members of—or at least closely associated with—the Bolsheviks' revolutionary political parties, and imprisoned during the first months after the Leninists seized power.

In August 1921, the Cheka, the predecessor of the present KGB, arrested dozens of intellectuals in Petrograd and accused them of conspiracy. A few days later, more than sixty people, including eight women, were shot. Among them was the great figure of the Silver Age of Russian poetry, Nikolai Gumilev. Since then the history of Russian literature and of the literature of the many Soviet peoples has been stained by the blood of its writers.

Under Stalin, at the time of the Terror, anyone could become food for the hungry prisons, camps, and firing squads. Victims of persecution and yesterday's executioners were piled into the same prison cells by the NKVD, another name for the Cheka/KGB. Perhaps it was in the same transit camp barracks near Vladivostok that the great poet Osip Mandelstam and the apologist of Stalinist terror, Bruno Jasienski, perished. Those who had relentlessly denounced their colleagues were, in turn, denounced by an even more vigilant young guard. They were transformed, as we say, into camp dust.

At the present time, there is *one* advantage. As long as a writer keeps in his place, as long as he does not protest or contest the status quo, he no longer risks anything. Today those writers who end up in the camps and prisons have wanted to sin against the total and totalitarian ideology. They have used their freedom of speech and creation as if this ideology were not all-powerful, as if it were not the owner of their freedom and of their souls, of their pens and of their typewriters. They have violated the ideological and even psychological monopoly of the state. They have dared to be free under a regime of slavery.

A couple of days ago, I spoke here about those who are presently incarcerated in Soviet camps and prisons. I spoke of men such as Lukyanenko, Kandyba, Mart Niklus and Petkus, members of the Helsinki Monitoring Group, who, as so-called habitual offenders, were all eventually sentenced to ten years' camp detention and five years' internal exile. I said that for them this sentence is equal to the death penalty.

And yet physical death is not the worst thing that can happen to the political prisoner, to the writer, to the individual. Even worse is spiritual death, the death of the soul, of intelligence, of reason: a form of death in which the body subsists but the individual as such no longer exists. Having undergone arbitrary medical treatment in the Kazan prison, I can speak as an expert on this matter.

During his exile at Voronezh in the 1930s, Osip Mandelstam told his persecutors: "You have not succeeded in depriving me, in making my lips move." In the psychiatric prison, you are deprived of everything. If you move your lips yourself, it is a case of schizophrenia. If you claim to be a poet but have never been a member of the Writers' Union, that is paranoia.

Today, present in this room, is Roman Finn, who recently left the U.S.S.R. and lives in Toronto. A biophysicist, he dared to write a work of political philosophy. Biophysicist and essayist: for the psychiatrists of the KGB, this is an obvious case of a split personality.

In all such cases, you are cured of schizophrenia, of paranoia, of "reform" lunacy, of religious madness, of the schizoid wish to think differently. You are cured of your personality, your opinions, your convictions, your memory, your knowledge. You are cured by means of neuroleptics, by electric shock, by insulin shock. You are cured by the "walls of prison." This is not a bad joke, but rather a dictionary term used by Soviet psychiatrists: "the walls of prison that cure."

Through chemotherapy they change the way your brain functions. You are administered the famous haloperidol, whose secondary effects are normally associated with Parkinson's disease. Even if you are given permission to write, you are unable to do so. Your trembling hands cannot hold the pen. You cannot remain seated for more than a few minutes. You are not capable of concentrating your thoughts. You cannot even read. After having read a page, you ask yourself, astonished, "What have I just read?"

They deprive you by means of strong tranquilizers. In Soviet psychiatric slang, this is called "medicinal stunning." At first, you awake every morning and ask yourself, "Am I already insane? Or will it be tomorrow, or the day after?" Sooner or later you risk becoming truly "stunned," no longer yourself, and your lips will not move again.

Mykola Plakhotniuk, the Ukrainian poet, was arrested solely because of his poems and sentenced to seven years in Soviet prisons. More recently, the Russian poet Valentin Sokolov, called Zeka (a prisoner), who had barely been outside the camps since his adolescence in the 1940s, was sent to a psychiatric prison. Though his poems have never been published in his native country and are little known in the West, they are spread in the camps by word of mouth. This living legend of the Stalinist and post-Stalinist eras had not been successfully crushed by the camps. But they found another solution. He is in a place where, each time he moves his lips, he is given a sulphur injection until his lips forget to move.

The prisoners of the Soviet system are missing nonpersons; they are the unburied living dead. We are aware of only the smallest part of their world. Even when word reaches us, we can seldom keep informed about their fate. In 1972 Aishe Kekilova, a Turkmenian poetess, disappeared into a psychiatric prison. Since then neither dissident groups in the U.S.S.R. nor Amnesty International has succeeded in obtaining the slightest piece of information about her: did she spend time in prison? Was she released? Is she still alive? Nothing; no response. We do not know how many prisoners of conscience there are in the Soviet psychiatric prisons. We do not know how many writers are among them.

For the writers and public of Toronto I can suggest a field of action. There is an action group here in Toronto called "Psychiatrists Against Psychiatric Repression." But the very useful work of this group, necessarily limited by the professional environment, and without the help of writers, journalists, and the general public, will not be as effective as it could be. I propose that all interested persons contact this group, through Amnesty International.

In closing, I would like to stress another aspect of the problem we have discussed. We are inclined to consider the theme of the writer and imprisonment in terms of the imprisoned writer. But there remains something even more important: the writer vis-à-vis the imprisonment of others, be they writers or not.

I hope that the period when the intellectuals of the free world saw only one face, one color of fascism, and were the accomplices of Russian fascism's concentration camps, is over. But even today, if writers limit themselves to professional solidarity, they betray their profession. Our profession is to move our lips for those who cannot. From this point of view, the prisoners of the psychiatric prisons are certainly the most deprived.

Let us not forget them.

—Translated by Donald Bruce

THE ENEMY WITHIN

JOY KOGAWA

THE IMPRISONMENT of my people during my childhood is a story I would rather not dwell on. It is a story of the forced expulsion of twenty-two thousand of us from our homes, of governmental theft of our properties, of deportation for no crime, of years of hard labor, of disenfranchisement. It is a story of official racism and shame, of disillusionment and suffering.

Whenever I am asked about it, it is like being plunged headfirst into my bowels. I feel I am being asked to bring out handfuls of dung to share. I would rather be in a tree house in the clean, clear light of morning. But we are here together because the fact of our imprisoned kin today throughout the world draws us down and down to search for clues to a way up and out and into the day.

There are two questions that are sometimes asked of me. First, how could Japanese Canadians have let those monstrous events take place? Why did they not resist? Second, how could such things have happened in—of all places—Canada?

Let me address the first question. We, from our modern vantage point, often presume that if we ourselves were threatened with eviction, we would resist or, at the very least, protest. We would organize, we would lobby, we would badger our members of parliament and city hall—but the Japanese Canadians in 1941 had neither voice nor access to any effective voice. And protest, such as it was, was dealt with swiftly and efficiently. Those who resisted—and many who did not—were put behind barbed wire. Men were sent to road-building camps. Women and children were herded into animal barns and then sent to the ghost towns of British Columbia.

During those early days, the leaders and thinkers and activists in our community must have struggled with the question of whether to fight with the authorities or to fly from confrontation, whether to struggle for our rights or submit to fate.

The passive path must have been chosen for a variety of reasons:

You can't fight city hall. The odds are overwhelmingly against you.

Or: it's better to give in today and live to fight another day. If you bend like a willow tree in the storm, you will not snap.

Or: submission is emotionally easier than confrontation. To fight is to lose.

Or: trust the government. They say they are protecting us by sending us away, and they say our businesses and homes are being kept safely for us.

Or: God is our champion. Our call is to trust, not to fight.

Or: the world is illusion, and struggle folly.

Or: suffering is constant in the human condition and is to be accepted.

Those given the burden of choice must have weighed variations of these pragmatic and political or spiritual and private considerations. But for the majority of us, I suspect that the crisis we faced gave rise to a herd instinct, to a blind and sheeplike faith that there was safety in numbers.

History tells us little of the wisdom of the choices our leaders made. We did follow them; we were obedient. Had they advocated other than peaceable action, had we resisted with force, I have little doubt that we would have encountered bloodshed. Certainly the will to make us disappear was in the country and was voiced and recorded in newspapers and government documents.

Our legacy today is a mixed one. On the one hand, we are viewed as one of the most successful ethnic groups in the country. We are seen to be a people who overcame great odds and established ourselves by dint of being upright, law-abiding, intelligent, and industrious people. Among Japanese Canadians, there is a high level of education, of professional expertise and middle-class affluence. Our crime rate is almost nonexistent. We have prestigious individuals who excel in a number of public fields and in the arts. On the other hand, we have obeyed the injunction never again to live in close proximity to one another, and we are scattered across the country. There is no Japantown in any city in Canada, no corporate visibility. This political weakness is reflected in, for example, the fact that there is for the

Japanese in Canada not one nursing home or hospital to care for the aged pioneers who lost everything to this country, and are now left to die in white-run hospitals and nursing homes without the diet they need or the staff to interpret for them.

Our psychological legacy is equally mixed. We have gained determination and endurance, but on another level, we have refused to confront the past, and we mask and deny the results of the ugly social environment we imbibed. We do not name the roots of the many forms of self-betrayal and self-alienation that we exhibit today. We are not at home in our own land and this "dis-ease" is passed on to our children. For many of my fellow Nisei, it is a point of pride—a way of life—not to know other Japanese people, not to speak and understand Japanese. Secretly, many of us want to be "the only Jap in town." The intermarriage rate among the Japanese in Canada is 80 to 90 per cent. The injunction to disappear has been highly successful. The loss of our culture gave us no cause for alarm, since we were given to understand that our culture had no value.

The second question is, how could these events have happened in Canada? The story of the Japanese in Canada tells us something about universal corruption, universal greed, universal ignorance, blindness, and fear. We are at one with other countries of the world, dancing the same dance in our stained underwear.

In Canada we have still not tried our leaders for these crimes of war and beyond war. We have still not named and publicized the creators of those unjust policies and orders-in-council. We have still not redressed the wrongs that were done to the Japanese Canadian community. Among us are some who dread being reminded of the past and wish to hide in our continuing silence. There are others who believe we serve neither ourselves nor the country by such silence. In fact, by becoming part of the silent and oppressive majority, we show that yesterday's victims often become today's victimizers.

In Canada (unlike in the U.S.) the decision to send us to concentration camps was not a military but a political one. The decision to confiscate our property—which is something that did not happen in the U.S.—was again a political one. The decision to deport us, the decision to disenfranchise us, the decision to deny us the freedom to work or travel within this country, the decision to implement the dispersal policy, were all made by our elected politicians, who were supposedly voicing the will of those they served. Racism in Canada was therefore as official as ever it was in any racist regime in the world, and we cannot lay claim to moral superiority or be smug and complacent about our adherence to high principles and ideals of justice and equality.

Given all this, how do we begin to become clean? How do we name the enemy with clarity, and once the enemy is named, do we attack and destroy it or do we seek its transformation from enemy to friend?

We begin in our own backyards by plunging headlong together into our common mud. We begin by an examination of our own internal enemies—our own Canadian greed, our own personal greed, our own prejudices, the ways in which we betray and hurt each other each day of our lives. Only as we recognize the face of the enemy within can we see clearly the face of the enemy on the outside. Only as we wrestle within and recognize that which redeems us can we recognize the authentic voice calling us away from the helplessness and despair so many of us feel in North America today.

But we can no more will our salvation than we can will to fly. Our journey is not so much a matter of choosing a path as it is a matter of expectant waiting and an exercised readiness for the path to be uncovered. The secret is in our eagerness to see and recognize that which beckons us to health, and in our longing to walk down the path that is made visible. Our main task, I believe, is to make ready our hearts, and our hearts will be informed as well as our limbs and our minds. Our task is a rigorous exercise of our imaginative compassion.

I am not here speaking simply of a privatization of concern or of a negation of our public responsibility. I am not saying that political, public, and corporate action are not primary tasks. What I *am* saying is that I believe our private and public realities are coextensive, and that the accuracy of our actions is dependent on our being grounded in our spiritual resources.

In North America today, we do not identify clearly the common enemy that threatens our survival. That is perhaps because our enemy is legion. Much of our academic discussion dilutes our action and maintains our various oppressions and oppressors in their positions of power. A bedlam of voices cries out many types of victimization, and often the loudest voices are guilty of victimizing others. This babble of sound drowns the calls of any unifying voices, and people of goodwill often find themselves flung into counterproductive causes in a growing chaos of blind activity.

If I dare add another voice to the din, it would be to plead for quietness—to ask that we learn to listen rather than to shout out, that most of all we heed the ones who are so oppressed they cannot speak at all.

At this conference, we have many who have come to speak for those who cannot speak. They have exercised their imagination by considering those whose needs are greater than their own.

How do the rest of us begin to exercise this imagination? We must begin in a new silence. Not the silence of oppression or fear, but the silence of attention—until we are able to hear that which moves within our silences.

There is a saying attributed to Jesus which declares that if we bring forth that which is within us, that which we bring forth will save us. If we do not bring forth that which is within us, that which we do not bring forth will destroy us.

The writing of my novel *Obasan* was a bringing forth of my heart's labor. And since it has been done, I have been awakened and released to the ways in which I have been guilty all my life of collaborating in the betrayal of my people. I have become aware of another face of the Judas and Hitler within me. I now seek to embrace that face, to transform the enemy within to friend.

Recently, my father and I visited an old Japanese man in an all-white nursing home in Coquitlam, B.C. His long, loud weeping and loneliness are now within me as part of my own voice. I am now both compelled and determined to identify with that cry. My betrayal of my people is beginning to end, and I share that cry with you, which is to say also that you and I and he, and those in prison everywhere, are deeply at one with one another.

A COMMENT

NATALYA GORBANEVSKAYA: Joy Kogawa's presentation has explained something to me which I did not understand before. In the Soviet Union too, during the war, whole populations were deported. In 1941 it was the fate of the Volga Germans, who had lived in Russia since the eighteenth century; then in 1944, it was the fate of about ten different peoples: the Chechens, the Crimean Tatars, and others. I was always astonished that the West remained silent in the face of these crimes of genocide. Now I understand it better; for if, in the West, peoples can be accused of real or imaginary crimes, naturally there will be no reaction to crimes committed against peoples in other parts of the world, particularly in the Soviet Union.

Exile

BREAD FOR A STARVING CITY

TIMOTHY FINDLEY

TODAY, it so happens, is the anniversary of a great event which has received hardly any publicity. It should have continuing publicity; it is an event that we should none of us ever forget took place.

On October 3 of 1931, fifty years ago, a young Italian poet, whose name was Lauro de Bosis, took off in an airplane from Marseilles in France and flew to Rome in Italy, knowing that he could not possibly carry enough fuel in his airplane either to escape beyond Italy or to return to France. In other words, it was virtually a suicide mission. He had escaped from Italy, gone to America, raised money, and raised his voice against the fascist regime. He had printed many leaflets and booklets, and carried four thousand of these in his airplane. He flew over Rome—so low, it is said, that it appeared the airplane was climbing the Spanish Steps. All the while, he cascaded into the streets his pamphlets and his books, which spoke out against the fascist regime and on behalf of his personal friends and fellow writers who were imprisoned.

In an article he wrote, which was to be published after his death, he stated that the purpose of his act was to throw down bread upon a starving city. He was throwing down bread for the minds of people who were starving under absolute censorship.

And on this day, since it *is* the anniversary of that flight, it must be remarked that it is astonishing and appalling and outrageous that if *one* person, only one person, had ever in our time performed an act of that kind, we should not now have to be gathered in this room. I do not mean an act where a death is involved—but an act of creative, nonviolent "aggression" against the silencing of writers and the word.

LABELS

ROBERT ZEND

In 1921 two babies were born in a Budapest hospital, from two mothers who were in the same room of the maternity ward. One child was Catholic, the other Jewish. Since the babies were born within the hour, the nurses were so busy that they exchanged them.

Before continuing the story of the two babies, I have to explain how in 1921 a Catholic and a Jewish mother could be placed in the same hospital room. It was possible not only because it happened just a few years after the end of the First World War, in which the assimilated Jewry of Hungary fought without any discrimination, but because in those times the labels under which people were categorized were so numerous. The amount of hatred fed into the population by the rulers, in order to divide and conquer, had to be distributed in so many directions that the Jews, for the time being, had to settle for a small dosage of hatred—as did the other label owners, such as the ethnic groups living in the country (Serbians, Croatians, Saxons, Swabians, Rumanians, Valachs, Czechs, Slovaks, Ruthenians, Italians, Gypsies, etc.), or like minority religious groups (Calvinists, Lutherans, Greek Orthodox, Evangelists, etc.) who were all incited against one another. This is the main reason why in 1921 the swap of two babies was still possible.

About one decade later, when totalitarian governments took power in several countries of Europe, they began simplifying the labeling of people. Hatred was no longer divided democratically because the radical rulers were in a hurry. They needed one favorite scapegoat to concentrate on in order to strengthen their grip on the people, so they selected the most suitable subjects according to their needs. In Spain it was the communists, in the Soviet Union the capitalists, in Germany, the Jews. All labels—whether they were dignify-

ing or humiliating—were meted out to certain groups not because they
deserved a reward or punishment for something they did or failed to
do, but merely for circumstances beyond their control, for given facts
they couldn't help, such as having been born into a rich or a poor
family, into an Aryan or a Jewish family. In those years, the label
makers of Europe were strongly visual types; they preferred colors to
go with their labels. Thus, the German Nazis wore brown shirts, the
Italian fascists black shirts, the Hungarian Nazis brown shirts. The
color of the communists was red; the Jews were identified by yellow
(stars on their chests, or bands on their arms). Europe in the thirties
was very much like a Rubik's Cube in the eighties (except, perhaps,
for the missing color white—symbol of purity and innocence).

When the two babies of my story were ten years old, the swap was
somehow discovered. But by then, neither of the families was emotionally capable of correcting the error: during a decade the bonds of
love grew unbreakable. While keeping their secret, both the parents
and the boys remained close friends despite the changing times. That
is how it happened that when the babies became young men, the
Jewish boy who had been labeled a pure Aryan since birth saved the
life of the born-Catholic boy whose freshly gotten label predestined
him to extermination by the racists of his own race. More forcefully
than anything else, this story proved to me, in my early youth, the
complete senselessness of labeling people according to nationality,
place of birth, date of birth, religion, class origin, sex, age, the color
of skin, the color of hair, the color of eyes, the length of nose, the
number of pimples, or whatever. No matter which boy would have
been killed, the Aryan or the Jewish one, according to or despite the
law of those times, it would have been a criminal murder of an innocent human being.

Among the many Hungarian writers of that age, quite a few kept
their integrity. There was one in particular who wasn't willing to accept any label, either for himself or for others. His name was Fri-
gyes Karinthy. He didn't identify with any group. He belonged nowhere, but for him this nonbelonging meant an extremely strong
belonging to man, to mankind, to humanity. As a humorist, he was
tremendously popular, but as a philosopher, he had hardly any fol-
lowers then. Today most Hungarians are enthusiastic about his ideas.
He was (and is) my spiritual father, the master who first inspired me
to feel, to think, to express myself, to be considerate, to have high

ideals, to understand others as if they were me: in other words, to write. That's what writing means to me. It means many other things too, but those other things are built on this foundation.

Getting rid of the labels so fashionable in Europe was not the last reason I left my country in 1956. But the free world didn't deliver me from labels. For the first five years, I was in limbo, because I wasn't yet a Canadian citizen but I was no longer a Hungarian either. Not a British subject yet, I called myself a British object.

Years later one of my supervisors called me a "bloody Hungarian." Since this incident happened just two weeks after I received my Canadian citizenship, I sent to him an office memo in which I requested to be called in future a "bloody Canadian" instead.

During these years, I couldn't write for English publications because I didn't speak the language, nor could I write for publications in Hungary because I was considered an enemy for having left the country illegally.

The only thing I could do was write for Hungarian ethnic papers in Toronto. But I had to choose among them, for each served a special group in the Hungarian subsociety. One of them was a weekly for old communists who in 1919 had fled the so-called White Terror in Hungary, after the defeat of the so-called Red Terror. The readership of another paper consisted mainly of latent fascists and war criminals who escaped when the Nazis lost the Second World War against the Allies. A third was geared to the Hungarian-speaking Jewish businessmen who left Hungary when the new communist state began nationalizing private enterprise. Since I was simply a poet and writer who expressed his thoughts and feelings in his mother language, none of these organs suited my integrity; and they wouldn't have accepted me, since I did not match any of their labels. For a while, I wrote articles and humorous sketches for a fourth newspaper. Not because I shared its ideology but because a friend of mine, Andrew Achim, who was an editor of this paper, almost laughed himself to death upon hearing my funny stories read at my weekly house parties. He simply grabbed them and published them. For the sake of fairness, I must note here that in the last quarter of a century, all the aforementioned press organs were either dissolved, or sold to new owners, or changed their views because of the "melting pot" boiling within the Hungarian "tile" of the Canadian "mosaic."

Later, I wrote, drew, designed, edited, laid out, and published my own monthly literary magazine which, after about a year, collapsed, partly because it was aimed at the general Hungarian-speaking public. This mandate confused my advertisers, who—unable to think except in labels—kept asking me, "But tell me, is this magazine for leftists or rightists, for Catholics or Protestants, for Jews or gendarmes, for junior or senior citizens, or for whom?" My answer, "For Hungarians," left them in a deep quandary. Not for the first and not for the last time in my life, I realized that I was a misfit. Without the Hungarian labels, I was a Hungarian misfit.

When I approached Canadian publishers with the idea of publishing one or two of my books, they asked me if I was a well-known writer or poet in Hungary (which I was not). My pen name had been extremely popular among children, for whom I wrote, but the revolution broke out just as I was about to publish my first book of poems under my own name, with a dissident publishing company. After the revolution's defeat, I chose to leave my country rather than publish party-line poetry or publish dissident poetry—and be jailed, or deported, or silenced afterward. In the first years of my exile, I wrote only in my mother tongue, so translation into English was another (if not the greatest) problem.

When, several years after the revolution, the Hungarian Government realized its need for hard currency, it changed our labels from "counterrevolutionary hooligans" to "our beloved fellow countrymen living abroad," and opened to us the gates of the Iron Curtain. During my visits as a tourist in my own country, I did my best to explore the possibilities of publishing my Hungarian works there. The editors liked my work, but they had a problem with labeling me: "If you are a Hungarian poet, why do you live in Canada? If you are a Canadian poet, why do you wish to publish in Hungary?" In vain did I try to explain that being a poet does not depend on the geographical location of the poet's body, or on the political system under which the publisher functions, but on the linguistic and literary value of the poems. I have to mention here that the poems I tried to publish in Hungary were not at all hostile to Hungary; they spoke about the change, the culture shock, the homesickness, the schizoid emotions of an exile between two worlds. After reading my work, a writer friend of mine in Hungary told me, "You are a bigger Hungarian patriot in Canada than we are here, in Hungary."

But one sympathetic publisher there finally proposed a compromise: "Let's pretend," he said, "that you are a Canadian poet who wrote your poems in English, and we will call the poems we publish in Hungarian the Hungarian translations of your original English poems." "But I cannot lie about this," I said, "these are my original Hungarian poems!" "I understand," he said, "but there is no precedent. We have never done such a thing. We can publish Hungarian poets living in Hungary, either in Hungarian or in English translation. We can publish English poets either in English or in Hungarian translation. We can publish the English work of Hungarian poets living in exile, in Hungarian translation. But we have never published the original Hungarian poetry of Hungarian poets living in exile, in Hungarian, in Hungary. We just cannot start a new trend! Try again in two or three years; perhaps the political atmosphere will change by then." This was the day when I defined for myself what a misfit was: "A misfit is a human being who tries to remain a human being despite the surrounding pressure called mankind."

So far, I have been talking in the first person singular, yet most poets and writers who come from behind the Iron Curtain face similar problems. If you are an Italian, a Swedish, a French, a Spanish, or a German author, you can publish your work both in Canada on the one hand, and in Italy, Sweden, France, Spain, or West Germany on the other.

If you are a Hungarian, Czech, Bulgarian, Albanian, Polish, East German, etc., author, behind the Iron Curtain, you cannot write what you want: you have to write what others want you to write.

If you are an exile, you can write what you want, but you cannot publish your original work back home unless it criticizes the country which gave you shelter and accepted you. Nor can you publish the work written in your mother tongue in exile unless you can afford to be your own publisher. But here let me express my appreciation to the Multicultural Section of the Secretary of State in Canada. It has the power—unlimited politically, but limited financially—to break this rule.

"Are you as famous in Canada as Marshall McLuhan or Glenn Gould?" a publisher in Budapest asked me—like the Canadian one, twenty-odd years ago, who asked me if I was well known in Hungary. Before you are allowed to enter and enrich the poetry and literature of your native country, of your native language, you have to make a name for yourself in an alien country. You have to prove that you can speak and write in another language. You have to produce best-sellers for a culture other than that which nourished you from birth. This is what the cultural authorities of your native land demand from you, before even reading the first word of your poem that you wrote in your (and their) language. The same "cultural" authorities did publish manuscripts written by workers, peasants, and cleaning ladies who emigrated from Hungary to Canada and didn't make it. These books are called "life stories" and serve a double purpose: they are useful anticapitalist propaganda for the population of Hungary, and they also prove that in Hungary they publish books from Hungarians living abroad. This is the choice: you must become either a celebrated writer in non-Hungarian, or a failure as a non-writer, if you want to be published in Hungary.

It is possible that the greatest living poets and writers of the Iron Curtain countries, the greatest innovators of their languages, live abroad. Yet their works are sentenced to oblivion because of mindless discrimination, according to arbitrary and irrelevant criteria.

That is the unique cross that we are carrying. It is not shared by any other kind of artist, only by the handlers of the pen. A painter, a sculptor, an architect, a composer, a musician, a dancer, a performer living in exile is *not* banned from the public of the fatherland, perhaps because the label makers think (and they do think it quite erroneously) that their message *can* be interpreted in *many* ways. But a message, clearly expressed by the written word, seems too unambiguous to them. If you say something, it means exactly what you said. Therefore, it is more dangerous than colors, shapes, melodies, or movements, which are but the symbols of the Word, of Logos.

The cross we carry is unique also because the people of the written word who live under totalitarian systems can be translated into any language of the free world. Democracy is not revengeful: it does not set geographical or political conditions for its publications. There exists a great imbalance between authors living in dictatorships but being accepted in democracies and authors living in exile being rejected in dictatorships.

The elimination of this imbalance may be one of the tasks that the Human Rights Commission should deal with in the future.

Let me finish my speech with a poem I wrote recently:

> *In a country*
> *where everyone*
> *is searching for*
> *identity,*
> *I am*
> *an alien*
> *for I'm already*
> *identical.*

ON THE OUTSIDE

DANIEL VIGLIETTI

I WAS first invited to this conference to participate, with the Uruguayan writer Eduardo Galeano, in an event in which song and literature would work together, putting together a man like Galeano, who writes with a pen, and someone like me, who, if you will allow me, writes with a guitar. Later, the conference organizers asked if I would add some thoughts about exile. I agreed, since I have been living in that situation for eight years and one month. At these meetings, I have been handicapped by the fact that I do not speak English. For this kind of contribution, I need my mother tongue, Spanish. But today I have the assistance of a translator, and I am going to throw in some ideas about the exile in which hundreds of thousands of Uruguayans have been living for eight, nine, or even ten years. And our numbers are being increased by new waves of refugees. Instead of a generalization, I prefer to use a concrete experience. In this way, we can help one another to put together the thousand pieces of the puzzle of exile.

As an introduction, I would first like to read the translation of a song that I will sing in Spanish on Sunday. It is a fragment of a song that I wrote while in exile, entitled "Identity":

> *Who said "artist"?*
>
> *I am just a man*
> *that combats fear*
> *in his throat.*
>
> *A wounded man,*
> *in a wailing country,*
> *wood and air,*

neither a hero
nor a coward.

I am no singing banner,
but a human being,
no more, no less,
with day and night
right here in my body,
a contradiction singing affirmations,
somebody who doesn't believe it
when they announce the downfall of the New.

The Uruguayan dictatorship tried to defeat the New, to murder a proposal of change that manifested itself in several ways and was supported by different segments of our people at the end of the sixties and the beginning of the seventies. I am but one of the hundreds of thousands of Uruguayans condemned to live outside our country because of my opinions, because my songs are about ideas, words, that are not acceptable to the regime. We know that exile is a penalty less serious than death, than disappearance—which perhaps is the most perverse form of murder, because there is no body left to prove it. Exile is less serious than imprisonment, which is joined back to back with torture, its Siamese sister in Uruguay, where more than a hundred people have died from torture. We do not pretend to be the center of gravity: we are just a peripheral consequence of a genocide that also includes culture.

There is only one matter in which the Uruguayan dictatorship perhaps agrees with us. They too think that culture, when it is produced by healthy human coexistence, is a mirror that reflects clearly the social reality around it. That is why they break the mirror, trample on it, forbid its use. That is why we defend it. We fill it with images, with testimonies, with poems against that policy of genocide. "Culture means freedom," as José Martí said once.

The Southern dictatorships lock culture up when they cannot make it an accomplice of their politics of silence. We on the outside fight that silence with events, with concerts, films, dances, plays, paintings, and sculptures that are the aesthetic product of varied feelings and, at the same time, are acts of solidarity developed by what we call "the people in exile."

Our people are scattered around the planet, from Australia to Canada, from Mexico to Spain, from Angola to Nicaragua. This dispersion is at first traumatizing; later it becomes a tension that launches efforts of communication among us. On many occasions, Amnesty International has supported our concerns. And I and many other *compañeros* have taken concrete action for our country or for other countries whose realities we are aware of and can approach in a responsible manner. We try to heal the wounds of exile and to defeat sterile melancholy with the joy of creation. Those exiles whose names are publicly known because of their profession—for example, writers, musicians—attempt to rescue many other victims of repression from anonymity.

Mauricio Rosencof, a Uruguayan playwright, symbolizes many others; Haroldo Conti, an Argentinian novelist, symbolizes many others. "The militants of life are many, many," as Mario Benedetti, a Uruguayan writer, once wrote. We have to draw the faces of the disappeared and leave the prisoners to read their faces. We must sing to them to bring them out: in the midst of many losses, we must not lose our memory.

We who have the privilege of being able to practice our profession, while so many exiles are forced to change their tools, have to be demanding with ourselves in the development and enrichment of our intellectual discipline. We do not have to be in exile from our beliefs or our demands. The Argentinan writer, Julio Cortázar, once talked about the "internal fascism" that we antifascists may also have hidden within us. We could also talk of an "internalized exile": a voluntary abandonment of memory and hope, a suicide without a corpse. It is vital to recognize the link that exists between *me* and *us* in exile.

If we put these demands on ourselves, the exiled songwriter will progress from songs with a direct message and inflamed anthems to reflection and analysis. To a greater sensitivity about the rich processes that you face in an exile perceived as a workshop, as a challenge to our strengths. We lack the community, we lack the air in which we learned how to breathe, how to think, how to sing. But we should not add to that lack the carbon dioxide of despair and xenophobia disguised as maladjustment. It is true that we do not have around us many of the people, thanks to whom our song was born, the people to whom we should return, but we arc not completely cut off from them. To enter one's country, the only pass that songs and poems need is to be in someone's memory. At the same time, the resistance of the people and the birth of new cultural experiences in Uruguay go through exit control and confirm our feeling that we are working and struggling together, inside and outside our country, without being aware of it.

In presenting this picture of Uruguayan exile, which perhaps has many things in common with the exile of many other Latin American brothers and sisters, I do not want to forget an exile's objective difficulties in resettling in a foreign environment—for example, the difficulties of getting a regular job and legal papers. In that regard, the two Uruguayans attending this conference, Eduardo Galeano and myself, would like to point out that our applications for renewal of our Uruguayan passports were refused without explanation. And this has happened to thousands of our fellow countrymen and -women. We would like to denounce this arbitrary procedure, but we do not complain: it is the logical consequence of having worked with a guitar or a pen for a more just society in Uruguay.

This is all I have to say. I will say the rest by singing, which is my trade.

—Translated by Audrey Campbell

PART FIVE

THE WRITER'S ROLE

MORAL AUTHORITY

PER WÄSTBERG

WRITERS, having no power, have moral authority. Our responsibility is to ourselves and to the future. The thought of the future not as a Utopia where everything becomes better but as something infinitely fragile is new to our generation. As someone has said: we no longer look upon our world as inherited from our fathers, we look upon it as borrowed from our children. The earth is not the infinite resource it was thought to be; it has to be protected and treasured.

In such a world, perilous and vulnerable, the free flow of ideas matters. The visions of our great poets and thinkers are not for escaping reality, not for easy solace, but for nourishment and energy, for forging new links, for inventing new solutions. Today, freedom of expression can never be a luxury, because all sorts of ideas are needed, to be tested, to be discarded, even to be hated, for it is in the very process of choosing among them that we may take a step forward instead of stumbling another step backward toward destruction.

To put old knowledge together in new patterns is a task more necessary than ever—to persuade also through imaginative means the leaders of the world that war is unthinkable and peace our only hope; to give the young a mastery of imaginative language, which helps against despair and routine and insulates against the authoritarian temptations, against empty voices bellowing clichés.

It is the never ceasing quest to expand the knowledge of mankind through imaginative work that International PEN defends by its charter. The creative task which gives birth to new visions and unseen beauty may be the most effective form of protest for a writer.

Where the politician sees mass effects, the writer sees an individual and unique truth. While the politician sometimes speaks in order to conceal that he has nothing to say, the writer speaks in the fear that otherwise something will remain concealed.

To resist official decrees that go against your conscience is not always easy. There are better ways of living than to suffer exile, to be forgotten in labor camps and mental hospitals, or simply to be counted as one of hundreds of "disappeared." But as a Swedish poet said, "If we cannot avoid serving as hodmen at the domes now being built, let us at least carve our impotent 'no' in the bricks we carry." And that "no" may not be so impotent, as many recent actions of PEN have shown. There are writers who are free and alive today because of the efforts of International PEN. And thanks to the PEN Emergency Fund, there are writers' children still able to attend school while the breadwinner in the family is in jail. In this respect, PEN is the writers' Amnesty.

What sort of freedom does our charter defend? There are differing opinions about this. Our vice-president, Nadine Gordimer, answered:

> To me it is his [the writer's] right to maintain and publish to the world a deep, intense, private view of the situation in which he finds his society. If he is to work as well as he can, he must take, and be granted, freedom from the public conformity of political interpretation, morals and tastes.

André Brink, the South African novelist, said last year in Stockholm:

> Freedom becomes measurable, significant, and important to the extent in which unfreedom exists and hampers it. . . . Unfreedom is our condition; freedom is our desire; in between lies our nature, in which lies embedded the urge to transcend limits, frontiers, restrictions, barriers. . . . To write and to publish define and demonstrate man's need to transcend the limits of his unfreedom. . . . If a reader is denied access to a book, *his* freedom is jeopardized, *his* chances of glimpsing the truth are diminished, *his* right to know and to discover is denied.

And a Czech author said recently, "You cannot attain liberty through unfreedom, nor can you lie in order to reach the truth."

No common good can be founded on a common lie, and the lie propagated by many states and bureaucracies is that there is no truth in imagination. The debasement of words and concepts in official use is a special feature of our times, and the task of serious writers is to expose hypocrisy and raise the standards of world honesty. Where politicians—often rightly so—work in a spirit of pragmatism and compromise, writers, by being simple, unorchestrated voices, can afford another sincerity.

Thus, the author may be the only one who claims that the emperor is naked. A political regime can then do one of two things: put the clear-eyed writer in a dark jail cell, or go home and change into proper clothes. In either case, it remains the author's job to see to it that nobody is ignorant of the world's condition and can therefore claim to be innocent.

This is not to say that literature should attempt faithfully to document objective reality or that it be judged according to what is happening in society. Literature is not a simplified version of sociology or political science. The immediate usefulness of creative writers is uncertain. Perhaps it is rather their inutility that is so necessary.

Literature points to means of experience not easily expressed within institutions. It is like love: best privately enjoyed, but with social consequences. Literature, as I see it, proclaims that man is unpredictable and impenetrable, never to be entirely defined and thus never to be put to rational use by others. No geometry, no government or data bank can fully map out the needs of man, his dreams and fantasies. And so every work of art contains something liberating. That is why the censor hunts it, why so much energy is devoted to destroying such fragile things as dreams, thoughts, works of art— and their creators.

The writer's fight for freedom, his refusal to give way to censors, is something that most people will understand. But one other threat to that freedom is harder to grasp: the threat that comes from the very strength of the writer's opposition to repression. The freedom of his personal view of life may be undermined by the very awareness of what is expected of him. And often what is expected is that he conform to orthodox opposition.

Pressure for loyalty and unity may lead to self-censorship. The writer feels his freedom of action diminish, for he fears that his work will be misused by forces he is determined to fight. In the Third World, we have seen many writers, active in criticizing foreign domination, grow silent when their own countries become independent yet hardly free in the sense they had hoped for.

Finally, the threat against the writer's freedom comes from within: he likes to please, to gain readers, not to insult. He may be too embarrassed to express himself without inhibitions because of his family or his social commitments. An inhibited writer goes nowhere unless his very inhibitions are his subject matter. To write is to indulge in an intentionally promiscuous communication.

AGAINST IDEOLOGY

ALAN SILLITOE

As a writer, my task is to write, not so much to speak, and on such occasions as this, I become the master of the non sequitur, totally at variance with the theme to be expounded. For the next few minutes I will try not to be so, though I doubt if—being only a writer—I shall succeed.

Concerning the more practical details of what to do about all that we have heard during the last few days—reports of the horrors which have been and are being perpetrated on writers throughout many parts of the world—I have listened to some suggestions already. But writers are not practical beings. Let me first digress to say why I think this.

It is a disaster, in my view, for a writer to be expected to become a spokesman or spokeswoman for his or her people or ideology. Either before prison or during prison, or, often, after prison, the writer who was once free decides that he or she has to become "committed" to the cause. They feel they have no choice. Indeed, they do not, and one cannot but feel sympathy with the often agonizing decision they have to make in this respect. Just as they were not given the option of prison, so they are not awarded the choice of political commitment—with all that this means for their art. They have been robbed of that peace a writer needs to produce the best work.

In the same way, a creative writer—and I'm not talking about journalism or reportage—can never improve his art by aligning himself with any political cause. In spite of everything, he must keep free, because ultimately, the best propaganda is art.

Politics tend to dehumanize a writer. They are in a sense his greatest enemy, a way of silencing, confusing, or even corrupting him. They dehumanize because he thinks of people in masses, and not as individuals.

But there are such things as humane causes, and this conference is one. Political causes impede the work of the conference, which first and foremost must be that of trying to do something for writers throughout the world who are in prison. When an innocent man is behind bars, there is only the humane—and not the political—need to get him released.

This may be simplistic. But it is only a plea for us to become more effective in what we are trying to do. We must never lose sight of the essential fact of people being in prison, because after all, this is why we are attending this conference: for *the unfree*. That includes every writer imprisoned and prevented from following his occupation freely, from Anatoly Marchenko in Russia to whomever else you care in your hearts to mention.

As long as a writer remains in prison, I have no political ideology to color the efforts I think should be made to release that person. We should all keep our politics out of it, no matter what the temptation.

What can we do once we have scattered back to our various countries? As individuals we can stress all that we have heard, in any interview we give, in any essay or article or book review we may be called upon to write—and not be surprised that during the editing, before publication or broadcast, all mention of the imprisoned writer may be cut out!

In 1976 I was asked by the 35's Committee in London—a group of Jewish ladies who work for the good of their people in Russia, to write a play illustrating the plight of Ida Nudel, who had for many years been trying to obtain a visa to Israel. I did this, and the play has been produced in many places.

One of the speakers at this conference has already mentioned the appalling fact that in some countries it is only necessary to mention the name of an imprisoned writer to get him killed. In the case of Ida Nudel, she was sentenced in July 1978 to four years' exile in Siberia for so-called hooliganism.

But in my view—and this appears to be the consensus among those who have been released—one must always speak out, and in the great majority of cases, it does some good, eventually. It may not help the particular person you specify at that moment but someone else instead. The results are not always apparent when and where they should be.

Perhaps this is the only way writers *can* help—to write a play or story concerned with the plight of a particular author in prison, choosing someone for personal or geographical reasons rather than for political reasons. Perhaps the choice should be made by someone else, so as to prevent our politics from getting in the way. Thus the individual would prevail over the ideology, which would give the writer more objectivity, in whatever form his writing would take.

DRAWING THE LINE: A DISCUSSION

NADINE GORDIMER: The writer seems to have more responsibility for human rights than anyone else in the arts. Many more writers seem to run into trouble, to be banned or imprisoned, than visual artists or musicians. There are particular reasons why writers have this responsibility for human rights thrust upon them, and also why they accept this tremendous responsibility. I suppose it begins with the word, with the fact that language is used by everybody and that everybody has a sense of what can be said and what has to be left unsaid, even in normal situations. When we come to the relationship of writers to their society, to an oppressive society, the word carries tremendous weight. I don't know whether people who are not writers realize quite what a heavy responsibility it is. A gathering like this one will bring that home, we hope, to the outside world.

If we as writers have to accept this special responsibility for defending human rights, we must also claim, not some sort of special standing, but a special understanding that sometimes we have to go beyond the written word, to move away from writing to acting. I mention this because several of the writers whose names are on those empty chairs are people who have had to make this very difficult decision. And when one talks to people in the outside world, seeking help for writers who are imprisoned or oppressed in any way, one is often asked, "Oh, but was it for something that they wrote, or for something else that they did?" Since writers have this special responsibility thrust upon them, and since they take it up, they have a right to set this question aside, to claim that when the occasion arises they indeed do have to move from writing to acting, and that the world's opinion about who should be helped and who should not, the distinction between being punished for what you write and being punished for what you do, should be dropped. This question comes up often at writers' conferences. It came up at the International PEN conference in France, and it's a very important question indeed for writers.

Don Mattera, one of the writers whom we are honoring in absentia, is someone I know well. He has been banned not for anything he has written (although the ban means that nothing he writes may be printed and nothing he says may be quoted) but because the ideas that he has worked out in his writing he has carried over into the actions of his life. He is what is called in South Africa a "colored" person, somebody of mixed blood. The reason he is banned is that he tried to bring about, not only in his writing but in the actions of his life, a solidarity among blacks in South Africa.

So I would urge this conference to impress it upon the outside world that the writer, in taking on responsibility for human rights, also takes on the responsibility to act even beyond the act of writing —although writing in itself, under conditions of oppression, is a political act.

It is a mixed question, the line between what can be considered an extension of the writer's work as a writer and what must be considered direct political action. I think the line can be drawn at violence. The kind of action beyond writing that I have in mind is in places—probably the most obvious examples occur in South Africa where I come from, in Africa generally, and in Latin America— where intellectuals somehow get called upon to do more than simply write about the injustices that happen in their countries, so that they find themselves speaking, perhaps, on a public platform, or endorsing a protest against detention without trial.

Now, in my own native country, as in many of these Latin American countries, and indeed in the Eastern European countries, to appear at a protest meeting, and to demand the release of somebody who has been detained, is an offense of a different kind from writing. It would be an offense, perhaps, in my own country, under the Riotous Assemblies Act. You then become a common criminal. The line is very finely drawn between writing or signing a protest in favor of the release of detained writers or intellectuals generally, and appearing at a public meeting. But if you appear at that public meeting and speak, you have gone over from writing to acting.

This is the kind of thing that I have in mind. When a person like that comes up in court charged with having broken the Riotous Assemblies Act, or whatever the act is called in different countries, and that writer is detained or imprisoned, and you seek public sympathy and protest on his behalf, you get told, "Ah, but—he spoke at a public meeting: he has committed a crime against the Riotous Assemblies Act, it's not for something that he wrote." This is something that is in a sense ancillary to the act of writing. It's something that grows out of your life as a writer, out of your necessity to act upon the social fabric around you and to be acted upon by it, to be part of it, because a writer is, in a sense, his own material when he is writing about the society in which he lives.

A QUESTION FROM THE FLOOR: A couple of years ago, Amnesty International put out a report on South Africa, and as we all know Amnesty International always draws the line at violence. All its publications state that it is seeking to defend writers who are prisoners of conscience, people who have never at any time advocated violence. In its report on South Africa, Amnesty International describes the conditions for blacks. There is a detailed description of the arrests, the imprisonment, the banishment, the exiling; there are descriptions and photographs of torture and of the bodies of prisoners who have died in prison. And the report meditates that for a black South African living in these conditions, there is no alternative to advocating a revolutionary uprising. In fact, Miss Gordimer, you describe such an uprising in your latest novel. Now what I get from reading that report is that a black South African, to attain freedom, has in effect to advocate violence. So how can one draw the line at violence?

NADINE GORDIMER: It is indeed difficult to draw the line. But you have unintentionally confused the issue a bit by bringing in the question of state violence. Nobody would dream of questioning whether that exists or not; it does. What we're looking at is how, if state violence is answered by violent action on the part of a writer, we make the distinction between his action as a writer and purely political action of a violent nature. Perhaps a case in point is the poet Breyten Breytenbach, who is a convicted prisoner in South Africa, because he planned to start an underground organization whose aim was the overthrow of the state. He didn't succeed in overthrowing the state, and he didn't commit any act that harmed the hair of anybody's head. But I suppose we have to admit the intention was there. He had the intention to commit what people like myself would call a crime of conscience, which nevertheless did overstep the line between violence and nonviolence. It is very difficult in such a case to decide. But in general, I would stick to my original definition.

SUSAN SONTAG: There is a related issue, which came up during the recent International PEN congress in Lyon: some writers became writers while they were in jail. For instance, Armando Valladares, the Cuban writer who I wish had a chair on this stage as well. He has been condemned to a thirty-year sentence in Cuba and has already served twenty-one years of it. He is indeed a writer but became one in jail. And this bothers some people, who ask, shouldn't we be defending those who are being persecuted only for what they wrote? But what about the people who pass to action, what about the people who start from action and *then* go to writing?

I would like to add something else; it's as much a question as an answer. I understood you to be saying that Amnesty supports writers on the grounds that they are not advocating violence. But that's not my understanding of what Amnesty does at all. Amnesty supports the rights of prisoners of conscience, which includes many writers, and the right of these people to oppose the state. Surely the people who draw up these lists at Amnesty are aware that in certain countries people in opposition have in mind some kind of violent opposition to the state. If I understand correctly what Amnesty is about, there is no commitment on its part to excluding writers or prisoners of conscience who belong to revolutionary movements, which does imply at some point taking up arms against an unjust state. Amnesty is not committed only to pacifist writers. I don't think that Amnesty or any group working for the rights of imprisoned people is demanding a pacifist engagement from writers.

JULIUS TOMIN: Could I clarify that, and also do a little more justice to the question concerning Dostoevsky and the Grand Inquisitor? Petr Uhl is in one of those rotten prisons in our country. He is the person in Czechoslovakia most closely linked to the Fourth International, and could be labeled a Trotskyite. I don't know whether I was doing justice to him, but I said many times among my friends that if Petr Uhl became Minister of the Interior I would immediately emigrate. But when the regime put policemen in front of his door for more than a year, I felt it to be my duty—and my wife also felt it as such, and even my children felt it as such—to visit Petr Uhl, however great a risk we ran, despite the police at his door. Otherwise, I probably wouldn't have visited him. And now they have put him into prison. The problem is not what he professed or what he might have done. The problem is that for two years the police followed his every step, so he couldn't possibly have done anything against the law, and now he is sitting for I think five years in a very strict prison. Even in the case of people who openly profess something like violent revolution, the question is what they actually do and whether they transgress the law and for what they are imprisoned. You cannot draw a line, but it is possible to stand up for somebody with whom you absolutely disagree. You may find it extremely imprudent for yourself, but you would literally lose your own identity if you didn't stand up for somebody who perhaps directly opposes your own views.

A STATEMENT FROM THE FLOOR: My name is Joshua Rubenstein and I work for the U.S. section of Amnesty. I would like to clarify Amnesty's position on violence. Amnesty works for the release of prisoners of conscience, people who are in jail for their religious or political beliefs, who have not used or advocated the use of violence. Sometimes this issue becomes cloudy—for instance, when people are in a war and then years later get involved in this or that activity: their participation in violence in wartime does not in any way disqualify them from becoming prisoners of conscience later, like General Grigorenko in the Soviet Union. Amnesty has adopted a certain rule, because we don't see how any of these activities really were an expression of violence. But if people are in what are sometimes dubbed revolutionary groups, and these groups are engaged in violence, if they're actually members, then Amnesty has to decide whether their arrest is associated with specific incidents of violence or advocacy of violence. We actually have a committee to clarify these borderline cases. Amnesty is not a pacifist organization. It doesn't demand anything of anyone, except that prisoners of conscience be released, that there be no torture, that there be no executions. We are not judging a revolutionary's use of violence; we're simply saying that our organization cannot adopt them as prisoners of conscience. And we don't mean to deprive anyone of the right to self-defense. It may be that blacks in South Africa have no choice but to engage in violent revolutionary activity; but if they're caught, we can't define them as prisoners of conscience—they're something else. They may still deserve the support of many well-meaning people, but they're not prisoners of conscience by our definition.

CAROLYN FORCHÉ: My question also relates to violence and to drawing lines. I'm concerned about the harsh line that's being drawn between the writer and the nonwriter, between us as writers and all those "ordinary" people out there, in terms of our moral responsibility. I personally don't feel a difference between my duty as a journalist to write against atrocities and my duty as a human being to speak out and act out against atrocities. I think there is some danger in putting writers into a kind of special category; some writers, in my opinion, cross the line into pornography, which I see as violence against women. I can't defend what they are doing, even if they are, in terms of craft, great writers. To me it seems a more valid line to draw than what we're doing here: we're here because we have a common craft, but we're here to look into the struggle to maintain some sort of conscience instead of just sinking into a spiritual morass. And everybody, writers and nonwriters, shares in that struggle.

PART SIX

CLOSING STATEMENT

THE VIGIL

MÜMTAZ SOYSAL

RATHER than simply read the statement that was drafted late yesterday, I would like to underline the necessity of such a statement.

One has to make the world know that writers from different regions of the world, with different creeds, have come together to mount a vigil outside the walls, because this kind of affirmation is necessary at this moment.

I don't share the view of those who think that the human rights situation, as far as writers are concerned, is getting worse. I think it's improving, because governments are realizing that imprisoning writers is counterproductive. They have silenced some, but when they do so, humanity shouts at them. They are worried about their image. This change has come about thanks to the efforts of various organizations and of the writers themselves. So the more voices of protest there are, the more affirmations, the more the situation is likely to improve.

That is why I think some sort of voice should come out of this congress; it should not remain completely silent. And with this voice, we should recognize that we are still confronted by the evidence of suppression of the rights of conscience and expression throughout the world. We should affirm that the rights of the people are inalienable and universal; that the responsibility for the protection of these rights transcends boundaries, nations, and states; and that we commit ourselves, even if we are not committed to specific causes in our respective countries, to this universal cause of respecting the rights of writers in any country of the world. And we have to protest the cruelty imposed upon them.

That sort of voice issuing from a gathering such as ours will have a certain influence. Our statement doesn't have to be worked out like a legal text and precisely written; the voice coming out of this congress should be almost spontaneous. In the symposia and panels we have discussed the various issues concerning the writer and human rights. As a result of these discussions, there should be some direct protest, a demonstration, a certain vigil outside the walls, to make the world remember that despite the improvements, the vigil is still there, that we will not let the oppressors continue what they have been doing until now—silencing the human voice.

Having witnessed how the human voice is being silenced in so many countries of the world, we have to take a representative group of writers, not because the numbers they represent are equal, but because the forms of cruelty, the forms of oppression inflicted upon them, are quite representative of certain categories of oppression and cruelty. And then, giving their names as representative of these categories, we should appeal to those countries that are still putting their writers in prison, still silencing them, that they be unconditionally liberated.

On that note of protest, we could cite Haroldo Conti in this vigil, for all those who have disappeared, who have been the victims of abduction, secret and illegal detention. Conti was last seen in secret barracks, unable to speak, unable to eat.

And then we could mention the name of any of those who have been incarcerated for their dissent, treated as insane, or sent to the camps. We can mention the name of Vasyl Stus, facing more than a decade of hunger, forced labor, and utter neglect.

We can mention Yang Ch'ing-ch'u, for all those who have been convicted without justice, and for all those who have been condemned for sedition.

For all those who have been sent to prison for their defense of the rights of others, of the dignity of others, we can cite Vaclav Havel, denounced for resisting and defying the suppression of his own people.

For all those who have lived in cells again and again, being threatened, being hounded, we can cite Ahmed Fouad Negm.

For all those in exile, sent into desolation, proscribed, we can cite Jorge Mario Soza Egana, held in the hands of the secret police, subjected to torture, and banished.

For all those who have been silenced and confined, we can cite the name of Donald Mattera, who can write, but not to be read. Who can shout, but not to be heard.

We can cite these names—and then we can make our resolution known to the world: that they should be returned, that they should walk freely from their cells, speak with their voices and be heard again. For all those who are with them, we can again claim the inextinguishable rights of the human spirit.

PART SEVEN

SEVEN SILENCED WRITERS

LIKE A LION

HAROLDO CONTI

MY DAY always starts with the sound of the train whistle. It pene-
trates the houses still wrapped in shadows, bounces off the walls of
the railway warehouses, and finally loses itself in the city. It is a
grave sound and whines and moans like the trumpet of an angel
standing on a pile of ruins. I then open my eyes in the darkness and
say to myself while the sound still lasts, "Get up and walk like a
lion." I don't know where I heard this, maybe on the TV, maybe
from a pastor at the Salvation Army school, but that's what I say to
myself every morning and for me it has some sense, "Get up and
walk like a lion."

My old lady always asks what the devil I'm thinking. The poor
dear asks because she really believes I'm not thinking about anything.
But I always have my head so full of things that it wouldn't surprise
me if one day it might burst into small pieces. I'm sure that if she
found out what I am thinking she would be astounded. I say this just
when I hear the sound that passes over my head, because nobody
who looks at me has any idea that so much travels through my mind.
However, we are a family of thinkers. My father, with all his faults,
thought a lot and said things like that and maybe it was him I heard
say something like that.

Sometimes, like now, I wake up a bit before the whistle blows.
Stretched out in the bed with my head in the darkness, I feel like I'm
on a raft abandoned in the ocean a long time ago. Then I think of
everything about life. As if I were dead or just about to be born.
Even though in either of those cases I wouldn't be thinking, you understand, but I want to say that if I were on the side of the road, and
not on the road itself, I would be able to see things better. Or at least
see what is worth seeing.

My mother just got up and is moving around the kitchen. From here I can see her face thin and faded in the light of the little sputtering flame of the heater. She seems like the only living being in all the world. I'm alive too but I'm nothing more than a crazy head hanging in the darkness.

I think of my brother, for example. A couple of months ago they killed him. The uniform came with that son-of-a-bitch face they put on for such occasions and told us that my brother had had an accident. The accident was that they had beaten him to death. We went with the patrol to the 46th Division and there was my brother laid out on a table with a sheet covering him from head to foot. The uniform lifted up the sheet and we saw his face under the light of a lamp covered with a page of newspaper. I didn't allow one tear to fall for their enjoyment and anyway it didn't look like my brother. I really don't believe he has died. My brother was so full of life and I don't believe that a pair of uniforms could finish him off. It wouldn't surprise me that he would appear some day in some way, although he will never appear again, which also doesn't surprise me. For me he is still as alive as ever. Maybe more. When I say I think of him I really want to say that I'm sorry and until I see him most times it is my brother who tells me "Get up and walk like a lion." From the shadows. The words echo inside my head but it is my brother who says them.

—Translated by Florrie S. Chacon

HAROLDO CONTI: On May 5, 1976, the Argentine writer Haroldo Conti was abducted from his flat in Buenos Aires.

A novelist, playwright, and critic, Haroldo Conti was the first prominent Argentine artist to disappear after the military coup of 1976. He was far from the last.

The total number of disappearances attributable to the security forces since the coup of March 1976 has been put at fifteen thousand by human rights groups in Argentina. Many of the victims are now presumed dead. Amnesty International and many other organizations have received testimonies from victims of illegal detention who have been held incommunicado in secret detention camps and who describe the systematic brutality which takes place at these centers.

The government's only response to repeated requests for news of the disappeared has been to enact *Law 22.068—On the Presumption of Death because of Disappearance* in September 1979. No attempt has been made by authorities to tackle the question of whether these people arc alive or dead. The procedures which have led to "disappearances" have certainly not stopped.

Conti was born in 1925 in Chacabuco. "I am from the interior. I always saw Buenos Aires through the eyes of an outsider and this is the only way it functions for me." He entered a seminary but gave up his religious vocation and studied for an arts degree at the University of Buenos Aires. Although Conti studied and taught in Buenos Aires, he was drawn to the nomadic life in the interior of the country, and his most characteristic work breaks with the conventions of everyday life and the isolation of city life. His characters are usually wanderers, as in his best novel, *Mascaro el cazador americano* (*Mascaro, the American Hunter,* 1975), in which one of the leading characters is an intellectual who joins a traveling carnival. The carnival is seen as a threat to the established order, and the troupe is arrested; after their release, resistance groups form under the leadership of the carnival's "cowboy," Mascaro, the American hunter.

Conti was working on a sequel to this book when he disappeared. Nothing was heard of Conti following his abduction until someone who had been arrested soon after Conti and then released claimed to have seen him in a police barracks in Buenos Aires. Conti, he said, had been tortured so severely that he could not talk or eat or control his bowels.

The Argentine Government acknowledged his death at the end of 1981, without admitting their responsibility.

AHMED FOUAD NEGM

TWO POEMS

Prisoner's File

Name	Sabr*
Charge	That I am Egyptian
Age	The most modern age; (though grey hair in braids flows from my head down to my waist).
Profession	Heir, of my ancestors and of time, to the creation of civilisation and life-force and peace
Skin	Wheat-coloured
Figure	As slim as a lance
Hair	Rougher than dried clover
Colour of eyes	Jet black
Nose	Aquiline like a horse's
Mouth	Firmly in place (when I attempted to budge it, some mischief happened)
Place of birth	In any dark room under the sky, on the soil of Egypt.

* Sabr is a common Arabic name which means "patience."

From any house in the middle of palm
    trees,
where the Nile flows—
as long as it is not a palace.

Verdict

For seven thousand years
I have been a prisoner asleep,
grinding stones with my molars,
out of frustration,
spending the nights in grief.

The question of release

Someone asked me:
"Why is your imprisonment so long?"
"Because I am a peaceful and a humorous
    man.
I did not break the law,
because I am afraid of it;
the law holds a sword in its hands.

Anytime you want—
ask the informers about me
and you will hear and understand
my story from A to Z.

My name is Sabr,
*Ayyub,** patient with catastrophes,*
like a donkey,
I carry my share of the burden
and wait.
I drown in rivers of sweat
all day long.
At night I gather together my troubles
and upon them I lie,
do you know why?"

—Translated by Janet Stevens and Moussa Saker

** Ayyub—a personality in Arab folk literature known for his unending patience.

from *My Country and My Darling*

. . . The beautiful dream ended
and heavy anxiety started.
"Where is Imam?"
"Who are you?"
"We have been given responsibility;
if you come without resisting,
you will not be harmed.
We, of course, will be absolved."
"You are the worms of the earth
and a noxious plague."
"You are a grain of salt in the 'caliph's' eye."
"You are the cause of grief and tragedy.
You are a sickness in my country's body.
You are carrion."
"Make him shut up, that son of a dog.
Make him swallow dust.
Search everywhere,
pull out the drawers of the cupboard."
They handcuffed me, oh my darling,
they muzzled me, oh my darling.
They made me stand up,
they made me sit down.
They searched, of course, every hair on my body.
In madness
they even tore up the pillow.
The search came to an end.
Nothing.
Believe me.
Do not worry.
Have I anything to hide, oh Azza?
Except my love of people
and my hatred of silence?

One of the court-jesters peered into my eye
and you know that my eyes are clear and honest
(like all eyes in our country, oh darling),
—two windows straight to the heart.
He wished to see a simple sign of fear.
Well, where does fear come from?
He was a fool's son.
Which of us is the coward?
Or, which of us is the traitor?
The one whose heart is full of love and hopes
and the flowering of young spring and songs?
Or the "hunting dog" and his master, the emperor,
eaters of human flesh off royal metal trays?

—Translated by Moussa Saker

AHMED FOUAD NEGM: Egyptian "poet of the people," was arrested on April 29, 1981. Aged fifty-four, Negm is in poor health in a Cairo prison. He is reported to have been ill-treated during his interrogation and during the spring of 1981 was on a hunger strike against his conditions of imprisonment.

Negm has spent twenty years in and out of prison. His early experiences with trade unions in Cairo led to his first arrests. In 1959 he was beaten, tortured, and then imprisoned for almost three years. In 1962, Negm met his voice—Sheikh Imam, a frail blind singer, whose powerful voice has earned him the title of "tambourine." Imam set Negm's poems to music and sang them first in the streets of Cairo, then to students, then to gatherings of intellectuals and left-wing groups. The people of Egypt, and indeed the entire Arab world, heard them through their distribution on amateur cassettes and professional recordings.

In 1978 Ahmed Fouad Negm was convicted for "invading" the Ain Shams University in Cairo and for "assaulting" the police. Tried by a military tribunal, he was sentenced to a year at hard labor. Negm slipped through police hands and went underground, eluding police checks for over a year.

Negm is married and has children. His wife, Azza Balba, who deserted her "detestable aristocratic family" to marry Negm, thereby embracing poverty, harassment, and occasional detention, has remained loyal to him. They live in a sparsely furnished one-room apartment in the heart of the ancient Al-Ghourieh quarter of Cairo.

Negm's poetry is "of the people" in many senses: he writes in colloquial Egyptian dialect; his style is at the same time satiric and caustic in its humor, warm and human, drawing on traditional lore and idiom; his concerns are the corruption of official life, the corrosion of his beloved homeland; his total commitment is to the people. His work was regarded as a threat by the Nasser and Sadat regimes alike. All public performances, recordings, and broadcasts of his work are forbidden in Egypt.

VACLAV HAVEL

THE PROTEST (*excerpt*)

VANEK: (*Rummages in his briefcase, extracts the list of signatures from among his papers and hands it to Stanek*) Here you are, Mr. Stanek—

STANEK: What is it? The signatures?

VANEK: Yes—

STANEK: Ah! Good. (*Peruses the list, mumbles, nods, gets up, begins to pace around*) Let me think aloud. May I?

VANEK: By all means—

STANEK: (*Halts, drinks, begins to pace again as he talks*) I believe I've already covered the main points concerning the subjective side of the matter. If I sign the document, I'm going to regain—after years of being continually sick to my stomach—my self-esteem, my lost freedom, my honor, and perhaps even some regard from those close to me. I'll leave behind the insoluble dilemmas forced on me by the conflict between my concern for my position and my conscience. I'll be able to face with equanimity Annie, myself, and even that lad when he comes back. It'll cost me my job. Though my job brings me no satisfaction—on the contrary, it brings me shame—nevertheless, it does support me and my family a great deal better than if I were to become a night watchman. It's more than likely that my son won't be permitted to continue his studies. On the other hand, I'm sure he's going to have more respect for me that way, than if his permission to study was bought by my refusal to sign the protest for Javurek. He happens to worship Javurek, as a matter of fact. He's crazy about him! (*Sighs with some exaspera-*

tion) Well then. This is the subjective side of the matter. Now how about the objective side? What happens when —among the signatures of a few well-known dissidents and a handful of Javurek's teenage friends—there suddenly crops up—to everybody's surprise and against all expectation—my signature? The signature of a man who hasn't been heard from regarding civic affairs for years! Well? What? Let's think about it. My cosignatories—as well as many of those who don't sign documents of this sort, but who nonetheless deep down side with those who do—are naturally going to welcome my signature with pleasure. The closed circle of habitual signers—whose signatures, by the way, are already beginning to lose their clout, because they cost practically nothing. I mean, the people in question have long since lost all ways and means by which they could actually pay for their signatures. Right? Well, this circle will be broken. A new name will appear, a name the value of which depends precisely on its previous absence. And of course, I may add, on the high price paid for its appearance! So much for the objective "plus" of my prospective signature. Now what about the authorities? My signature is going to surprise, annoy, and upset them for the very reasons which will bring joy to the other signatories. I mean, because it'll make a breach in the barrier the authorities have been building around your lot for so long and with such effort. All right. Let's see about Javurek. Concerning his case, I very much doubt my participation would significantly influence its outcome. And if so, I'm afraid it's more than likely going to have a negative effect. The authorities will be anxious to prove they haven't been panicked. They'll want to show that a surprise of this sort can't make them lose their cool. Which brings us to the consideration of what they're going to do to me. Surely, my signature is bound to have a much more significant influence on what happens in my case. No doubt, they're going to punish me far more cruelly than you'd expect. The point being that my punishment will serve as a warning signal to all those who might be tempted to follow my example in the future, to choose freedom, and thus swell the ranks of the dissidents. You may be sure they'll want to teach them a lesson! Show them what the score is! Right? The thing is—well, let's face it —they're no longer worried all that much about dissident activities within the confines of the established ghetto. In some respects, they even seem to prod them on here and there. But! What they're really afraid of is any semblance of a crack in the fence around the ghetto! That's what really scares them! So they'll want to exorcise the bogey of a prospective epidemic of dissent by an exemplary punishment of myself. They'll want to nip it in the bud, that's all. (*Drinks. Pause*) The last question I've got to ask myself is this: what sort of reaction to my signature can one expect among those who, in one way or another, have followed what you might call "the path of accommodation"? I mean people who are, or ought to be, our main concern, because—I'm sure you'll agree —our hope for the future depends above all on whether or not it will be possible to awake them from their slumbers and to enlist them to take an active part in civic affairs. This is what really matters, isn't it? Well, I'm afraid that my signature is going to be received with absolute resentment by this crucial section of the populace. You know why? Because, as a matter of fact, these people secretly hate the dissidents. They've become their bad conscience, their living reproach! That's how they see the dissidents. And at the same time, they envy them their honor and their inner freedom, values which they themselves were denied by fate. This is why they never miss an opportunity to smear the dissidents. And precisely this opportunity is going to be offered to them by my signature. They're going to spread nasty rumors about you and your friends. They're going to say that you who have nothing more to lose—you who have long since landed at the bottom of the heap and, what's more, managed to make yourselves quite at home there—are now trying to drag down to your own level an unfortunate man, a man who's so far been able to keep from going under. You're dragging him down—irresponsible as you are—without the slightest compunction, just for your own whims, just because you wish to irritate the authorities by creating a false impression that your ranks are being swelled! What do you care about losing him his job! Doesn't matter, does it? Or do you mean to suggest that you'll find him a job down in the dump in which you yourselves exist? What? No—Ferdinand! I'm sorry. I'm afraid I'm much too familiar with the way these people think! After all, I've got to live among them, day in day out. I know precisely what they're going to say. They'll say I'm your victim, shamelessly abused, misguided, led astray by your cynical appeal to my humanity! They'll say that in your ruthlessness you didn't shrink even from making use of my personal relationship to Javurek! And you know what? They're going to say that all the humane ideals you're constantly proclaiming have been tarnished by your treatment of me. That's the sort of reasoning one can expect from them! And I'm sure I don't have to tell you that the authorities are bound to support this interpretation and to fan the coals as hard as they can! There are others, of course, somewhat more intelligent perhaps. These people might say that the extraordinary appearance of my signature among yours is actually counterproductive, in that it concentrates everybody's attention on my signature and away from the main issue concerning Javurek. They'll say it puts the whole protest in jeopardy, because one can't help asking oneself what was the purpose of the exercise: was it to help Javurek, or to parade a newborn dissident? I wouldn't be at all surprised if someone were to say that, as a matter of fact, Javurek was victimized by you and your friends. It might be suggested that his personal tragedy only served you to further your ends—which are far removed from the fate of the unfortunate man. Furthermore, it'll be pointed out that by getting my signature you managed to dislodge me from the one area of operation—namely, backstage diplomacy, private intervention—where I've been so far

able to maneuver and where I might have proved infinitely more helpful to Javurek in the end! I do hope
you understand me, Ferdinand. I don't wish to exag-
gerate the importance of these opinions, nor am I prepared to become their slave. On the other hand, it seems
to be in the interests of our case for me to take them
into account. After all, it's a matter of a political decision, and a good politician must consider all the issues
which are likely to influence the end result of his action.
Right? In these circumstances the question one must
resolve is as follows: what do I prefer? Do I prefer the
inner liberation which my signature is going to bring me,
a liberation paid for—as it now turns out—by a basically
negative objective impact—or do I choose the other alternative. I mean, the more beneficial effect which the
protest would have without my signature, yet paid for
by my bitter awareness that I've again—who knows,
perhaps for the last time—missed a chance to shake off
the bonds of shameful compromises in which I've been
choking for years? In other words, if I'm to act ethically
—and I hope by now you've no doubt I want to do just
that—which course should I take? Should I be guided by
ruthless objective considerations, or by subjective inner
feelings?

VANEK: Seems perfectly clear to me—
STANEK: And to me—
VANEK: So that you're going to—
STANEK: Unfortunately—
VANEK: Unfortunately?

—Translated by Vera Blackwell

VACLAV HAVEL: Havel is forty-six years old and a leading Czech
playwright. He has been imprisoned since October 1979, convicted
of subversion "in collusion with foreign persons on a large scale."
His sentence is four and a half years, which he is now serving in Her-
manice Prison near Ostrava. His work in prison (with oxygen cutting
equipment) is hard and he suffers from poor health.

Vaclav Havel has experienced discrimination since his youth. Coming from a wealthy family, he was labeled a "millionaire's son" and excluded from higher education. Havel has made a strong commitment to human rights for many years. In 1969 he signed the "10 Points Manifesto," a document protesting the repressive measures taken by the Czechoslovak government after the armed intervention by five Warsaw Pact countries in August 1968. In 1974 he worked in a brewery. In 1975 he wrote an open letter to the Czechoslovak President in which he strongly criticized the cultural, social, and political conditions in the country. In January 1977, Havel signed the manifesto of the unofficial human rights movement, Charter 77, and became one of its original spokesmen. Two weeks later, he and three other people prominent in Czech cultural life were arrested for "antistate activities." Brought to trial in October 1977, he was found guilty of sending writings abroad for publication in émigré journals and "attempting to damage the interests of the Republic." He was sentenced to fourteen months, a sentence suspended for three years. Arrested again in January 1978 after the police refused him and some friends admission to a railwaymen's ball, Havel was charged with "assaulting a public agent" and "obstructing a public agent from performing his duties." In April 1978, a group of Charter 77 signatories established the Committee for the Defense of the Unjustly Persecuted (VONS). On May 29, 1979, the state security police arrested ten members of the committee, including Vaclav Havel, on charges of preparing statements about people they considered to be unjustly persecuted and of circulating this information in Czechoslovakia and abroad. During the trial, Havel said he had been offered the opportunity to travel to the United States of America but refused to consider the offer as long as his friends were in prison.

OPEN LETTER TO
SOUTH AFRICAN WHITES

DON MATTERA

To YOU, I may be just another name. Just another number in a sea of black faces. To your government and to your secret police, I am a *persona non grata*—an enemy of the state who must be silenced or destroyed.

To those truly black people who share with me a destiny as children of Africa, I firmly believe that I am a spokesman for justice and freedom and equality—a man moved by the plight and pain of my oppressed brothers and sisters.

I am addressing you as a nation, and at the same time, I am also aware that many valiant white men and women have raised their voices, offered their lives and the lives of their families in the cause of freedom for all people. I am constantly mindful of their great sacrifice and I know and am convinced they will forever be enshrined in the hearts of black people.

I have chosen an open letter because your government has arbitrarily denied me my right to express my feelings publicly. My writings have been outlawed and nothing that I say can be published. My very thoughts are branded a danger to the security of the state, which in the final analysis is *really you.*

Since the crimes you and your government have perpetrated against my people are innumerable and since I lack the courage to rise up against you in their name, and most of all because I hate violence, I will confine this letter to the irreparable damage you and your government have personally caused me and my family.

Until this day, I have ever been united with those who suffer, are poor; with the sick and the dying. It was an inheritance from my family.

Yet for nearly six years now, with four more to follow, perhaps until I die, your government has summarily cut me, and countless others, off from that very vital and precious life-giving force called *human interaction.*

Perhaps your government has told *you* why it took the criminal decision to deny and rob me and my colleagues of all social, political, and human intercourse with our fellow beings, making it a crime even to speak to a group of children.

I was given no reason whatsoever.

And did any of you ask your government why I am prohibited from attending my daughter's birthday party? Or why I must wait outside a hall when my own son is being handed a trophy or a badge? Or why I have to ask your Chief Magistrate for permission to attend the funeral of a loved one or a friend or a great leader?

Have any of you ever been prohibited from weeping at a graveside?

Well, I have been.

Have any of you white people experienced the horror of raids by the secret police? Do you know how humiliating it is to hear that loud and vicious banging at the door, and watch helplessly as armed police search the house, pulling blankets off the sleeping children? Searching, scratching and stamping, until the whole damn house is filled with hatred and anger.

Have any Afrikaner mothers or wives ever sat up wide-eyed on their beds, afraid and bewildered with tears flowing uncontrollably as the husband is bundled into a police vehicle?

Well, my wife has.

And has any white ten-year-old boy ever run barefoot into the night to the waiting police car and, with his fragile fists, banged against the door, crying and screaming as his father is taken away to some cold and dark cell, perhaps never to return again?

My little son has done just that. And it is the same child that rushes to switch off the television set when your South African flag and your anthem appear at the end of the programs.

I am not telling you these things out of self-pity. Nor do I want to be unbanned. These things are being said so that you, unlike the German nation, cannot tomorrow say, *But we did not know.* For you there must be no excuse. History will be the judge.

I don't think that you can answer these questions unless you are a

Helen Joseph, a *Braam Fischer,* or a *Beyers Naude.* Or any of those white men and women who have stood up to be counted, and are dead or suffering as a result of their consciences. Also, I don't think you have the capacity for such remorse as would move me to say, "Forgive them, for they know not what they do. . . ."

You know what you do.

And what is being done in your name.

Yes, day by day, bitterness and anger overwhelm me, robbing me of clear thoughts, transforming me to a near vegetable. I have been so demeaned that I can no longer truly fulfill myself as a poet or a person.

And today my children, affected by this terrible change in me, reflect the bitterness I carry within my heart. I don't know why, though I have tried very hard, I cannot hate you. But my children watch me closely: asking when I laugh, crying when I am sad. Asking me, forever asking me why it is that I endure so much pain and humiliation. Or why the setting sun no longer moves me. Or why I have rejected Christianity.

They will find the answers.

And no doubt this letter will hurt and offend your government, especially your secret police. If I know you, as I know your rulers, these words will spur you to vengeance and violence against me. Against my family. It has happened before. But I do not care.

I am prepared to die.

DON MATTERA: Donald Francisco Mattera is a journalist and poet who is currently restricted under his second five-year banning order.* He worked with the Johannesburg daily newspaper, the *Star,* but has been prevented from writing for publication since he was barred administratively in October 1973; his present banning order is due to expire on October 31, 1983.

Don Mattera is unable to work as a writer, to publish his writings in South Africa, or to send them abroad to be published. He works as a subeditor on the Johannesburg paper where he was once a rising young reporter. His mail is interfered with. The police confiscated his unfinished autobiography. As a banned person, he cannot be quoted

* Don Mattera's second banning order was lifted early, in May 1982.

in South Africa. He joins a long list of black writers and journalists whose work cannot be read in their own country.

Born in 1935 in Johannesburg's Western Native Township, Mattera spent his early childhood in various orphanages. He participated in the great bus boycotts of the fifties, then joined the African National Congress and later the breakaway Pan-African Congress. He was a supporter of the Black Consciousness movement in South Africa at the time of his first banning in late 1973.

Some of his poems have been published in *Index on Censorship*. For example:

No Time Blackman . . .

Stand Blackman
and put that cap
back on your beaten head
Look him in the eye
cold and blue
Like devil's fire
and tell him enough
three centuries is more than you can take, enough
. . .
Don't bargain with oppression
There isn't time man
just no more time
for the Blackman to fool around. . . . .

JORGE MARIO SOZA EGANA

SIX POEMS

We Had Only Our Love

I want to walk with you without fear
It doesn't matter that the square we walk in
no longer exists.
I want to board any train for the south
and get off at the last station
to see the birth of the rain.
I want to lie down with you under the blue sky
of that beach where we discovered the world.
The cherry trees had just begun to blossom
when they broke down the door.
We had only our love to defend us.

Beyond

The sun hangs in the broken windows
Beyond your eyes
nothing more sky and earth,
the dust that whirls with the wind,
the night filled with boots.

Each Day

Each day is a pinhole
where the sun falls in pieces.

Beyond the barbed wire
only desert and sky.

I think of my dead companions.

My soul fills
with sand and wind.

The Word Love

Someone moves during the curfew
the wind distributes prohibited songs.

I see you there
with a crayon in your hand.

The eye of the machine gun
watches you in vain.

Among the names of the disappeared
you always write the word love.

I Have Nothing More

Maybe I should offer you a pile of swords
or the ear of a torturer.
But I have nothing more
than this fist full of old words
and some kisses full of scars.

In Any Part of the World

You always talked of bells and trains,
of the little stations forgotten beneath the rain.
Suddenly you wanted to light up the world
or run off with a young poet to I don't know where.

Sometimes I think of you
and I send you messages with the stars.

In any part of the world you might be
choose a favourable night and contemplate the sky:
You will hear in your heart
the same song we sang together in the square.

—Translated by Florrie S. Chacon

JORGE MARIO SOZA EGANA: A journalist, poet, and short story writer, Jorge Mario Soza Egana, aged fifty-seven, was sentenced in August 1980 to four years' internal exile in Freirina, a town of two thousand inhabitants in the semidesert region of northern Chile. He has been there ever since November 1980. He is unable to find work and has had to build himself a small shack to live in.

Jorge Soza was arrested at home in Santiago on May 20, 1980, and charged, with three other people, under the Law of Internal State Security and Decree Law No. 77, which prohibits "Marxist" organizations. He was specifically accused of being editor of *Unidad Antifascista,* a clandestine opposition publication, and of belonging—with the other three—to a Communist party cell specializing in propaganda.

Before the coup in 1973, he had been editor of *El Siglo,* one of many newspapers closed by the military junta. Immediately after his arrest, Jorge Soza is reported to have been held in a secret detention center used by the CNI, Chile's secret police, and to have been tortured with electric shock.

Jorge Soza's poems have appeared in several anthologies of works by Chilean writers. He is married and has two teenage daughters.

During the congress, it was learned that Jorge Soza was granted a "right of option" to complete his sentence in external exile. He has gone with his family to France.

VASYL STUS

THREE POEMS

Hide Within

Hide within the copper mountain,
Conceal the arrogant blue.
A shadow trumpets above me,
And a shadow fills in every step.
Hide within the horizon's oboes
And whisper: I am still alive.
A thunder of resurrection on the mountain
Is being announced for me.
Smash your fists against despair,
hiding within the copper mountain.

The Sun Seemed Never

The sun seemed never to have shone here
Till suddenly came a spray:
Lilacs gleamed in bloom, bronze-bodied pines
Gushed at the crowns, sipping in the day,
And the shrieks ran into the humid valley
Where frogs sat dreaming.

Time stands still here.
The oak tests its age against eternity,
Hornbeams writhe in contortion,
Mountain ashes dive into the depths,
Observing with a swallow's eye
The timeless world and their own timeless age.

Live here awhile and you will think
Ukraine is still a home for nightingales
And a wood nymph may flit through the glade,
Her hands extended to a squirrel,
And a flute may sing across the foothills
And the wood nymph's human lover will appear.

How Good It Is

How good it is that I've no fear of dying
Nor ask myself how ponderous my toil
Nor bow to cunning magistrates, decrying
Presentiments of unfamiliar soil,
That I have lived and loved, yet never burdening
My soul with hatred, curses or regret.
My people! It is to you I am returning.
In death I somehow find my fate.
I turn my pained but goodly face to living
And in filial prostration I begin.
I meet your eyes in fair thanksgiving
And join my kindred earth as closest kin.

—Translated by Marko Carynnyk

VASYL STUS: Vasyl Stus, a leading Ukrainian poet and human rights activist, aged forty-five, is presently serving a fifteen-year sentence of imprisonment and exile for his activities as a member of the Helsinki Monitoring Group; he was convicted of "anti-Soviet agitation and propaganda" in 1980.

In 1965 Vasyl Stus lost his job as a literary researcher after he had spoken out against the arrest of intellectuals protesting what they saw as the Russification of Ukrainian culture. He was unemployed until he was arrested in 1972. During this period of imprisonment and exile he joined the Ukrainian Helsinki Monitoring Group. This group is one of several set up unofficially in different Soviet republics to monitor the Soviet Government's compliance with the human rights provisions of the Helsinki Final Act of 1975. When his sentence was completed in 1975, Vasyl Stus tried to become an active member of the Kiev group of Helsinki monitors. He was rearrested in May 1980 during a nationwide crackdown on Soviet dissenters, along with thirty-two other members of the monitoring group.

As a "recidivist," Vasyl Stus is now undergoing the harshest regime of corrective labor in the corrective labor colony in the Perm complex. He suffers from a stomach ulcer contracted during his previous term of imprisonment.

He is married and has a son aged about eighteen.

His work as a poet has been recognized by invitations to lecture at American universities and by honorary membership in the English section of International PEN.

YANG CH'ING-CH'U

from ENEMIES

IT WAS getting dark. The clock struck six, seven, eight, and still Feng-ch'un was nowhere to be found. Po-fu hadn't returned either. Po-mu went to the *pao-cheng*'s place three times, begging him to bail out Po-fu. The *pao-cheng* just kept putting him off until on the third visit Po-mu gave him some money. It was only then that he finally agreed to do it.

When Po-fu came back, his face was ashen and he limped along like a man with one leg shorter than the other. As he strode into the hallway, a mouthful of blood spurted from his mouth. Po-mu hurried to support him, tears gushing down as if from a burst dam. "Oh, no!" she cried. "He has internal injuries!"

Po-fu leaned against the wall and gasped. There was a swell of rage in his disconsolation. "I'll kill him! I'll kill him!" He grabbed a hoe by his side and was about to hobble off. Po-mu caught hold of him, but he flung her hand away. Like a bull going berserk, he limped across the fields heading for the Hsieh place. Po-mu became frantic. She hurriedly sent for Father. "Your brother has gone to the Hsiehs! Hurry up and catch up with him. And make sure nothing happens to him!"

I followed Father. He called out as he gave chase. Without even turning his head, Po-fu half hobbled, half ran on one leg into the Hsieh compound. The main living room was lit by oil lamps, and milling with people. Hoe in hand, Po-fu stood in the yard and yelled, "Hsieh Erh-lang, get out here. I'm out to kill you today. You've brought ruin to our family and left us in disgrace. Come on out! Get the hell out here if you are a man!" With that Po-fu spit out a lot of something.

"Let's go home, Brother. You're hurt. We'll settle it later," Father urged him in a low voice.

Po-fu kept his gaze fixed on the movements inside the living room as though he hadn't heard anything. The people inside stood immobilized as though cast in a spell. Po-fu yelled again. Slowly an old man with a long flowing beard emerged; it was Han-shan Po-kung of the Wang family. He was learned and highly regarded, a person Po-fu had always showed great respect for. "They have all gone to look for Ehr-lang," said Han-shan Po-kung. "He was working in the sugarcane fields behind the temple in the afternoon and hasn't been back since. Maybe the two of them ran off together. What worries me most is that they might have . . . The important thing now is to find them. We can't afford to make things worse. No good will come out of it, only grief—it's bad for both families. Let's try to bear with it."

"The way things are, how can I face people without shame from now on?"

"The important thing is to find them. Let's worry about other things later."

Po-fu numbly let Han-shan Po-kung and Father drag him back home. It was eleven o'clock at night. The searchers all came back to our house. The wells in the village had all been probed with a bamboo pole. The woods in the hills had all been gone over with flashlights, and someone had been put to work groping around underwater in the ditches and the pond next to Huang-ts'o Village. Still no one was to be found.

Po-mu's tears had run dry. With that look of desolation, her face appeared severely shrunken. Taking two flashlights she dragged Mother and Shu-shu out again.

"Feng-ch'un—come back. . . ." The sound came from the woods in the back hills like thin strains from far, far away, so mournful, so helpless, so full of despair, as if a spirit were calling for its soul from the very depths of the earth. "Come back—Feng-ch'un. . . ." The cry gradually turned to the sugarcane field behind the temple.

"Erh-lang—come back. . . ."

"Erh-lang. . . ." From the dike on the east side of the Hsiehs, near the end of the village, cries could also be heard. They wavered as though coming from the groves of ancient tombs. Rising from the east side and falling to the west, the calls echoed. The cries from both places gradually drew together, mingled into one, then gradually receded toward the wilds. "Erh-lang—Feng-ch'un—come back. . . ." It was impossible to tell if the voices were ours or the Hsiehs'. Both families were calling together.

Five policemen groped through the dark and burst into our house.

Three guarded the front and rear doors while two came in to make the arrest. Po-fu told them no one had been found yet. Unconvinced, they turned on their flashlights and searched everywhere—under the bed, in the closet, the kitchen, the cattle shed, the haystacks.

"Feng—ch'un—Erh—lang—come on back. . . ." Both families called together. One couldn't tell whether the voices were ours or the Hsiehs'.

Not one of us went to bed. Instead, we waited in distress, as if Feng-ch'un would return only during the depths of the night, when everyone was dead asleep.

—Translated by Jeanne Kelly and Joseph S. M. Lau

YANG CH'ING-CH'U: Yang Ch'ing-ch'u is forty-three years old. He started writing stories while still at high school. His family was poor: in his teens, he worked during the day and studied at evening school. His stories are social observations of Taiwan society—they describe the difficult life of people in the poorer classes.

Yang Ch'ing-ch'u worked in an oil refinery in Kaohsiung, was a candidate for the legislative Yuan in the 1978 elections, and was a member of the *Formosa* magazine editorial committee and director of their Kaohsiung office. He wrote on labor issues and addressed seminars organized by the magazine on this subject.

He was arrested along with many other editors and associates of the *Formosa* staff when a demonstration on Human Rights Day (December 10) 1979 ended in violent confrontation with the police. The arrested journalists were charged and convicted of "inciting a group of persons to commit or threaten violence." At his trial, Yang denied inciting the demonstrators, and his sentence was later reduced on appeal to four years and two months.

Of his own work, he has said, "I want to make people respect society's unfortunates." He has published twelve books. Some of his short stories have been translated into English: *Selected Short Stories of Yang Ch'ing Ch'u* and *Enemies*. He has gone on record as saying that he portrays many lower-middle-class people in his fiction "because I feel that I must speak for these people and record their unnoticed lives, thoughts, actions and emotions. Their outlook on life, on the cosmos, on religion, and their conduct in the world are the results of the conditions of their lives, and are worth more than those of the intellectuals, whose reality comes from books."

CONGRESS PARTICIPANTS

Ian Adams (Canada)

Vassily Aksenov (U.S.S.R., now living in U.S.A.)

Yehuda Amichai (Israel)

Britt Arenander (Sweden)

Manlio Argueta (El Salvador, now living in Costa Rica)

Margaret Atwood (Canada)

Pierre Berton (Canada)

Mongo Beti (Cameroon, now living in France)

Earle Birney (Canada)

Marie-Claire Blais (Canada)

Josef Brodsky (U.S.S.R., now living in U.S.A.)

Hans Christoph Buch (Federal Republic of Germany)

Vincent Buckley (Australia)

June Callwood (Canada)

Hans Magnus Enzensberger (Federal Republic of Germany)

Timothy Findley (Canada)

Carolyn Forché (U.S.A.)

John Fraser (Canada)

Eduardo Galeano (Uruguay, now living in Spain)

Allen Ginsberg (U.S.A.)

Natalya Gorbanevskaya (U.S.S.R., now living in France)

Nadine Gordimer (South Africa)

Bertrand de la Grange (Canada)

Jiří Gruša (Czechoslovakia)

Michael Hamburger (U.K.)

Thomas Hammarberg (Sweden)

Richard Howard (U.S.A.)

Naim Kattan (Canada)

Thomas Kinsella (Ireland)

Joy Kogawa (Canada)

Yotaro Konaka (Japan)

Michèle Lalonde (Canada)

Patrick Lane (Canada)

Irving Layton (Canada)

Jack Ludwig (Canada)

Sergio Marras (Chile)

Angelika Mechtel (Federal Republic of Germany)

Gaston Miron (Canada)

Chuong Tang Nguyen (Vietnam, now living in Canada)

Zegoua Nokan (Ivory Coast)

Michael Ondaatje (Canada)

Ernest Pépin (Martinique)

Richard Reoch (Canada)

Rick Salutin (Canada)

Loreina Santos Silva (U.S.A.)

Michael Scammell (U.K.)

Alan Sillitoe (U.K.)

Josef Škvorecký (Czechoslovakia, now living in Canada)

Susan Sontag (U.S.A.)

Wole Soyinka (Nigeria)

Mümtaz Soysal (Turkey)

Grigory Svirsky (U.S.S.R., now living in Canada)

Romesh Thapar (India)

Jacobo Timerman (Argentina, now living in Israel)

Julius Tomin (Czechoslovakia, now living in the U.K.)

Zdena Tomin (Czechoslovakia, now living in the U.K.)

Fawaz Turki (Palestine, now living in the U.S.A.)

Luisa Valenzuela (Argentina, now living in Mexico)

Michel Van Schendel (Canada)

Vassilis Vassilikos (Greece)

Daniel Viglietti (Uruguay, now living in France)

Arved Viirlaid (Estonia, now living in Canada)

Per Wästberg (Sweden)

Phyllis Webb (Canada)

Leon Whiteson (Zimbabwe, now living in Canada)

Rudy Wiebe (Canada)

Eduardo Yentzen (Chile)

Robert Zend (Hungary, now living in Canada)

Daniel Mdluli Zwelonke (South Africa, now living in Canada)

TORONTO ARTS GROUP FOR
HUMAN RIGHTS

President: Rosemary Sullivan, Congress Coordinator
Vice-President: Donald Bruce
Secretary: Lorne Macdonald
Treasurer: Audrey Campbell
Directors: Genevieve Cowgill
                   Mark Levene
                   Daniel Schwartz
                   Josef Škvorecký, Honorary Chairperson of
                      the Congress
                   Ira Vine
                   Arthur Young

STAFF

Congress Administrator: Connie Guberman
Congress Secretary: Robin Holmes Laperrière
Publicist: Bob McArthur

CONGRESS VOLUNTEERS

Nancy Adamson, Mary Allodi, Uzma Ansari, Donna
Baker, William Barker, Anna Berkeley, Robert Billings,
Elizabeth Blomme, Brian Boake, Christopher Britton, Iris
Bruce, Cecelia Burke, Mike Carroll, Marko Carynnyk,
Damon Chevrier, Sue Collard, Bob Coo, Diana Cooper-
Clark, Laura Corbeil, Gail Corbett, Monika Croyden,
Ann-Marie Dempsey, Louise Dennys, Alan Dorward,
Catherine Drake, Eve Drobot, Mark Epprecht, Donna
Fairholm, Alex Fallis, Moira Farr, Karen Flanagan-
McCarthy, Jerry Fox, Sandy Fox, Michael Galler, Juan

Carlos Garcia, Suzanne Garland, Susan Glickman, Sue Golding, Ila Goody, Shelley Gordon, Allan Greenbaum, Anne Hart, Danny Harvey, Martin Heavisides, Paul Hennig, Valerae Howes, John Iacono, Mary Kandiuk, Patricia Keeney-Smith, Mark Krebbs, Bob Lang, Gilles LeClair, Ellen Levine, Kurt Lush, David MacFarlane, Bob MacMillan, Elliot Malamet, Sandra Mark, Ann Michaels, Ann Mandel, Gladys Mayers, Dawn McDonald, Karin Michael, Paul Morrison, Sada Niang, Naim Nomez, Grainne O'Donnell, Ann Rigney, Valerie Ross, William Rueter, Paul Santamaura, Paul Saunders, Beth Savan, Jay Scott, Karen Shook, Karla Skoutajan, Catherine Smith, Frances Smith, Sylvia Söderlind, Evan Stewart, Eileen Thalenberg, Mariana Valverde, Jocelyn Ward, Claire Watson, Rebecca Watts, Catherine Yolles

SPECIAL ACKNOWLEDGMENTS

Works by the following artists were offered for sale at the International Writers' Congress and proceeds were donated to Amnesty International:

Walter Bachinski, Ronald Bloore, Claude Breeze, Dennis Burton, Graham Coughtry, Greg Curnoe, Kosso Eloul, Paterson Ewen, K. M. Graham, Art Green, Gershon Iskowitz, Rita Letendre, John MacGregor, Hugh Mackenzie, Robert Markle, Louis de Niverville, Charles Pachter, Gordon Rayner, William Ronald, Michael Snow, Harold Town, Tony Urquhart, Tim Whiten, Joyce Wieland

The following artists took part in *Imprisoned Voices,* a theatrical event based on the works of silenced writers:

Christopher Britton (Director), Douglas Campbell, Don Francks, Barbara Gordon, Martha Henry, Tony Lancette, Jim Plaxton, Erika Ritter, Winston Sutton, R. H. Thomson

The following musicians performed at benefit concerts during the congress:

Maya Bannerman Band, Heather Bishop, The Cee Dees, Heather Chetwyn, Dario Domingues, Klo, Odetta, Tom Paxton, Marcelo Puente, Ian Tamblyn, Daniel Viglietti

ACKNOWLEDGMENTS

J. S. Anthony and Company Limited, Australia Council, British Council, The Samuel and Saidye Bronfman Family Foundation, Canada Council, City of Toronto, Douglas Cohen, Theo Dimson, Executive Secretarial Services: Pat Rogers, Goethe Institute, Goodhost Charitable Foundation: Elaine Slater, The Walter and Duncan Gordon Foundation, Harbourfront Corporation, Government of Israel, Barbara Jackman, Harry Laforme, Linda Lane, McLean Foundation, Mark Michasiw, Municipality of Metropolitan Toronto, Ontario Arts Council, Ontario Institute for Studies in Education, Ontario Ministry of Culture and Recreation: Wintario, Peat Marwick Mitchell and Company, Perly's Maps Ltd., Gouvernement du Québec, Frederika Rotter, Secretary of State: Cultural Initiatives, Secretary of State: Multicultural Program, The Writers' Development Trust, Colleen Sullivan, Government of Sweden, The University of Toronto: Office of the President, Erindale College, Innis College, Trinity College, University College

INDEX